Linux Device Driver Development Cookbook

Develop custom drivers for your embedded Linux applications

Rodolfo Giometti

BIRMINGHAM - MUMBAI

Linux Device Driver Development Cookbook

Copyright © 2019 Packt Publishing

Commissioning Editor: Karan Sadawana
Acquisition Editor: Meeta Rajani
Content Development Editor: Ronn Kurien
Technical Editor: Pratik Shet
Copy Editor: Safis Editing
Project Coordinator: Jagdish Prabhu
Proofreader: Safis Editing
Indexer: Rekha Nair
Graphics: Alishon Mendonsa
Production Coordinator: Jisha Chirayil

First published: May 2019

Production reference: 1300519

Published by Packt Publishing Ltd.
Livery Place
35 Livery Street
Birmingham
B3 2PB, UK.

ISBN 978-1-83855-880-2

www.packtpub.com

`mapt.io`

Mapt is an online digital library that gives you full access to over 5,000 books and videos, as well as industry leading tools to help you plan your personal development and advance your career. For more information, please visit our website.

Why subscribe?

- Spend less time learning and more time coding with practical eBooks and Videos from over 4,000 industry professionals

- Improve your learning with Skill Plans built especially for you

- Get a free eBook or video every month

- Mapt is fully searchable

- Copy and paste, print, and bookmark content

Packt.com

Did you know that Packt offers eBook versions of every book published, with PDF and ePub files available? You can upgrade to the eBook version at `www.packt.com` and as a print book customer, you are entitled to a discount on the eBook copy. Get in touch with us at `customercare@packtpub.com` for more details.

At `www.packt.com`, you can also read a collection of free technical articles, sign up for a range of free newsletters, and receive exclusive discounts and offers on Packt books and eBooks.

Contributors

About the author

Rodolfo Giometti is an engineer, IT specialist, GNU/Linux expert and software libre evangelist. He is the author of the books *BeagleBone Essentials*, *BeagleBone Home Automation Blueprints* and *GNU/Linux Rapid Embedded Programming* by Packt Publishing and maintainer of the LinuxPPS projects. He still actively contributes to the Linux source code with several patches and new device drivers for industrial applications devices.

During his 20+ years of experience, he has worked on the x86, ARM, MIPS, and PowerPC-based platforms.

Now, he is the co-chief at HCE Engineering S.r.l., where he designs new hardware and software systems for the quick prototyping in industry environment, control automation, and remote monitoring.

I would like to thank my wife, Valentina, and my children, Romina and Raffaele, for their patience during the writing of this book. Thanks to Packt's guys: Meeta, who gave me the opportunity; and Ronn, who helped me in finishing this book. Many thanks to Antonio and Cristian for their efforts in reviewing this book.
Finally, I would thank my parents for giving me my first computer when I was a child, which allowed me to do what I do today.

About the reviewers

Cristian Marussi earned his bachelor's degree in Computer Science at the University of Udine (Italy), and spent almost 15 years working with embedded Linux. Cristian has been lucky enough to journey all the way through the software stack, from the userspace down to the lands of the kernel and firmware, while spanning a wide set of different products, from network appliances to consumer mobile devices. He has a keen interest in OS and system software development and internals. He has worked for companies such as Eurotech SPA, VDS Rail, and Samsung Cambridge Solution Center; he is currently a kernel developer in the OSS department at ARM Ltd. in Cambridge (UK).

Antonio Tringali is an electronic engineer working as a freelancer. He specializes in automation and remote system control. Most of his work in recent years is concentrated on automated parking systems, security access control, renewable energy data processing, and 3D printers. He likes to work from the silicon up, equally at ease with an oscilloscope as he is with a compiler.

Antonio had the pleasure of getting to know Rodolfo years ago, when writing for the same leading Italian Linux magazine. In 2015, he reviewed another of Rodolfo's books, *BeagleBone Essentials*. Now, he is eagerly awaiting the next book to come from this prolific author's keyboard.

Packt is searching for authors like you

If you're interested in becoming an author for Packt, please visit `authors.packtpub.com` and apply today. We have worked with thousands of developers and tech professionals, just like you, to help them share their insight with the global tech community. You can make a general application, apply for a specific hot topic that we are recruiting an author for, or submit your own idea.

Table of Contents

Preface

Kernel device driver development is one of the most important parts of a complex operating system, which is what Linux is. Device drivers are very important for developers that use a computer as a monitoring or administrative machine in real environments such as industry, domestic, or medical applications. In fact, even if Linux is now widely supported everywhere, new peripherals are created every day, and these devices need drivers to be efficiently used on a GNU/Linux machine.

This book will present the implementation of a complete character driver (usually called a *char driver*) by presenting all the necessary techniques to exchange data between the kernel and userspace, to implement process synchronization with the peripheral's interrupts, to get access to I/O memory mapped to (internal or external) devices, and to efficiently manage the time within the kernel.

All code presented in this book is compatible with Linux 4.18+ releases (that is, as far as the latest 5.x kernels). The code can be tested on the Marvell ESPRESSObin, which has an onboard ARM 64-bit CPU, but any other similar GNU/Linux embedded device can be used. In this manner, the readers can verify whether what they have read has been correctly understood.

Who this book is for

If you want to learn about how to implement a complete character driver on a Linux machine, or to find out how several kernel mechanisms work (such as workqueues, completions, and kernel timers, among others) in order to better understand how a generic driver works, then this book is for you.

If you need to know how to write a custom kernel module and how to pass parameters to it, or how to read and better manage kernel messages, or even how to add custom code to the kernel sources, then this book has been written with you in mind.

If you need to better understand a device tree, how to modify it, or even how to write a new device tree in order to meet your requirements and learn how to manage your new device driver, then you will also benefit from this book.

What this book covers

Chapter 1, *Installing the Development System*, presents how to install a complete development system based on Ubuntu 18.04.1 LTS, along with a complete testing system based on the Marvell ESPRESSObin board. The chapter will also present how to use the serial console and how to recompile the kernel from scratch, and will teach you some tricks for performing cross-compilations and software emulations.

Chapter 2, *A Peek Inside the Kernel*, discusses how to create a custom kernel module, and how to read and manage kernel messages. Both of these skills are very useful for helping the developer to understand what is happening inside the kernel.

Chapter 3, *Working with Char Drivers*, examines how to implement a really simple char driver, and how to exchange data between it and the userspace. The chapter ends by proposing some examples in order to underline the *Everything is a file* abstraction against a device driver.

Chapter 4, *Using the Device Tree*, presents the device tree. The reader will learn how to read and understand it, how to write a custom device tree and then how to compile it in order to get a binary form that can be passed to the kernel. The chapter ends with a section about downloading firmware (within a peripheral) and how to configure the CPU's pins by using a Pin MUX tool. Examples are provided using the Armada 3720, i.Mx 7Dual, and SAMA5D3 CPUs.

Chapter 5, *Managing Interrupts and Concurrency*, looks at how to manage interrupts and concurrency within the Linux kernel. It shows how to install an interrupt handler, how to defer a job to a later time, and how to manage kernel timers. At the end of the chapter, the reader will learn how to wait for an event (such as waiting for some data to be read) and how to protect their data against race conditions.

Chapter 6, *Miscellaneous Kernel Internals*, discusses how to dynamically allocate memory inside the kernel, and how to use several helper functions that are useful for several everyday programming actions (such as strings manipulations, lists, and hash tables manipulations). The chapter will also introduce how to do I/O memory access, and how to safely spend time within the kernel in order to create well-defined busy loop delays.

Chapter 7, *Advanced Char Driver Operations*, presents all the advanced operations that are available on character drivers: `ioctl()`, `mmap()`, `lseek()`, the `poll()`/`select()` system calls implementation, and asynchronous I/O via the `SIGIO` signal.

`Appendix A`, *Additional Information: Working with Char Drivers*, This contains additional information on chapter 3.

`Appendix B`, *Additional Information: Using the Device Tree*, This contains additional information on chapter 4.

`Appendix C`, *Additional Information: Managing Interrupts and Concurrency*, This contains additional information on chapter 5.

`Appendix D`, *Additional Information: Miscellaneous Kernel Internals*, This contains additional information on chapter 6.

`Appendix E`, *Additional Information: Advanced Char Driver Operations*, This contains additional information on chapter 7.

To get the most out of this book

- You should have a little knowledge of a non-graphical text editor such as `vi`, `emacs`, or `nano`. You can't connect an LCD display, a keyboard, and a mouse directly to the embedded kit to carry out little modifications to text files, so you should have a working knowledge of these tools to do such modifications remotely.
- You should know how to manage an Ubuntu system, or at least a generic GNU/Linux-based one. My host PC is running on Ubuntu 18.04.1 LTS, but you can use also a newer Ubuntu LTS release, or a Debian-based system with a few modifications. You can also use another GNU/Linux distribution, but this will require a little effort from you, mainly with regard to the installation of cross-compile tools, libraries dependencies, and package management.
  Foreign systems, such as Windows, macOS, and others, are not covered by this book due the fact that you should not use low-tech systems to develop code for a high-tech system!
- Working knowledge of the C programming language, how a C compiler works, and how to manage a makefile are all mandatory requirements.

Download the example code files

You can download the example code files for this book from your account at `www.packt.com`. If you purchased this book elsewhere, you can visit `www.packt.com/support` and register to have the files emailed directly to you.

You can download the code files by following these steps:

1. Log in or register at `www.packt.com`.
2. Select the **SUPPORT** tab.
3. Click on **Code Downloads & Errata**.
4. Enter the name of the book in the **Search** box and follow the onscreen instructions.

Once the file is downloaded, please make sure that you unzip or extract the folder using the latest version of:

- WinRAR/7-Zip for Windows
- Zipeg/iZip/UnRarX for Mac
- 7-Zip/PeaZip for Linux

The code bundle for the book is hosted on GitHub at `https://github.com/giometti/linux_device_driver_development_cookbook`. In case there's an update to the code, it will be updated on the existing GitHub repository.

The code bundle for the book is also hosted on GitHub at `https://github.com/PacktPublishing/Linux-Device-Driver-Development-Cookbook`. In case there's an update to the code, it will be updated on the existing GitHub repository.

We also have other code bundles from our rich catalog of books and videos available at `https://github.com/PacktPublishing/`. Check them out!

Download the color images

We also provide a PDF file that has color images of the screenshots/diagrams used in this book. You can download it here: `https://www.packtpub.com/sites/default/files/downloads/9781838558802_ColorImages.pdf`.

Conventions used

There are a number of text conventions used throughout this book.

Code words in text folder names, filenames, file extensions, pathnames, dummy URLs and user input are shown as follows: "To get the preceding kernel messages, we can use both the `dmesg` and `tail -f /var/log/kern.log` commands."

A block of code is set as follows:

```
#include <stdio.h>

int main(int argc, char *argv[])
{
    printf("Hello World!\n");

    return 0;
}
```

You should note that most code in this book has 4-space indentation, while the example code you can find in the files provided with this book on the GitHub or Packt sites uses 8-space indentation. So, the preceding code will look as follows:

```
#include <stdio.h>

int main(int argc, char *argv[])
{
        printf("Hello World!\n");

        return 0;
}
```

Obviously, they are perfectly equivalent in practice!

Any command-line input or output on the embedded kit used in this book is presented as follows:

```
# make CFLAGS="-Wall -O2" helloworld
cc -Wall -O2 helloworld.c -o helloworld
```

Commands are in bold, while their output is in normal text. You should also notice that the prompt string has been removed due to space constraints; in fact, on your Terminal, the complete prompt should look like the following:

```
root@espressobin:~# make CFLAGS="-Wall -O2" helloworld
cc -Wall -O2 helloworld.c -o helloworld
```

Note also that due to space constraints in the book, you may encounter very long command lines as follows:

```
$ make CFLAGS="-Wall -O2" \
        CC=aarch64-linux-gnu-gcc \
            chrdev_test
aarch64-linux-gnu-gcc -Wall -O2 chrdev_test.c -o chrdev_test
```

Otherwise, I have had to break the command line. However, in some special cases, you can find broken output lines (especially on kernel messages) as follows:

```
[ 526.318674] mem_alloc:mem_alloc_init: kmalloc(..., GFP_KERNEL)
=ffff80007982f
000
[ 526.325210] mem_alloc:mem_alloc_init: kmalloc(..., GFP_ATOMIC)
=ffff80007982f
000
```

Unluckily, these lines cannot easily be reproduced in a printed book, but you should consider them as a single line.

Any command-line input or output given on my host computer as a non-privileged user is written as follows:

```
$ tail -f /var/log/kern.log
```

When I need to give a command as a privileged user (root) on my host computer, the command-line input or output is then written as follows:

```
# insmod mem_alloc.ko
```

You should note that all privileged commands can be executed by a normal user, too, by using the `sudo` command in the following format:

```
$ sudo <command>
```

So, the preceding command can be executed by a normal user as follows:

```
$ sudo /insmod mem_alloc.ko
```

Kernel and logging messages

On several GNU/Linux distribution, kernel messages have this usual form:

```
[ 3.421397] mvneta d0030000.ethernet eth0: Using random mac address
3e:a1:6b:
f5:c3:2f
```

This is a quite a long line for this book, so that's why we drop the characters from the start of each line up to the point where the real information begins. So, in the preceding example, the lines output will be reported as follow:

```
mvneta d0030000.ethernet eth0: Using random mac address 3e:a1:6b:f5:c3:2f
```

However, as already said, if the line is still too long, it will be broken anyway.

Long outputs, or repeated or less important lines in the Terminal, are dropped by replacing them with three dots, . . ., as follows:

```
output begin
output line 1
output line 2
...
output line 10
output end
```

When the three dots are at the end of a line, it means that the output continues, but I decided cut it for space reasons.

File modifications

When you should modify a text file, I'm going to use the *unified context diff* format since this is a very efficient and compact way to represent a text modification. This format can be obtained by using the `diff` command with the `-u` option argument, or by using the `git diff` command within a `git` repository.

As a simple example, let's consider the following text in `file1.old`:

```
This is first line
This is the second line
This is the third line
...
...
This is the last line
```

Suppose we have to modify the third line, as highlighted in the following snippet:

```
This is first line
This is the second line
This is the new third line modified by me
...
...
This is the last line
```

You can easily understand that reporting the whole file each time for a simple modification is unnecessary and space-consuming; however, by using the *unified context diff* format, the preceding modification can be written as follows:

```
$ diff -u file1.old file1.new
--- file1.old 2019-05-18 14:49:04.354377460 +0100
+++ file1.new 2019-05-18 14:51:57.450373836 +0100
@@ -1,6 +1,6 @@
 This is first line
```

```
   This is the second line
  -This is the third line
  +This is the new third line modified by me
   . . .
   . . .
   This is the last line
```

Now, the modification is very clear and written in a compact form! It starts with a two-line header, where the original file is preceded by --- and the new file is preceded by +++. Then, it follows one or more change hunks that contain the line differences in the file. The preceding example has just one hunk where the unchanged lines are preceded by a space character, while the lines to be added are preceded by a + character and the lines to be removed are preceded by a - character.

Nonetheless, for space reasons, most patches reproduced in this book have reduced indentation in order to fit the width of printed pages; however, they are still perfectly readable. For the full patch, you should refer to the provided files on GitHub or the Packt site.

Serial and network connections

In this book, I'm mainly going to use two different kinds of connections to interact with the embedded kit: the serial console, and an SSH terminal and Ethernet connection.

The serial console, implemented over a USB connection, is mainly used to manage the system from the command line. It's largely used for monitoring the system, and especially for taking control of kernel messages.

An SSH terminal is quite similar to the serial console, even if is not exactly the same (for example, kernel messages do not automatically appear on a Terminal), but it can be used in the same manner as a serial console to give commands and edit files from the command line.

In the chapters, I'm going to use a Terminal on the serial console or over an SSH connection to give the most of the commands and configuration settings needed to implement all the prototypes explained in this book.

To get access to the serial console from your host PC, you can use the minicon command, as follows:

```
$ minicom -o -D /dev/ttyUSB0
```

However, in Chapter 1 , *Installing the Development System*, these aspects are explained and you should not worry about them. Note also that on some systems, you may need root privileges to get access to the /dev/ttyUSB0 device. In this case, you can fix this issue or by using the sudo command or, better, by properly adding your system's user to the right group by using the following command:

```
$ sudo adduser $LOGNAME dialout
```

Then log out and log back in again, and you should be able to access the serial devices without any problem.

To get access to the SSH Terminal, you can use Ethernet connection. It is used mainly to download files from the host PC or the internet and can be established by connecting an Ethernet cable to the embedded kit's Ethernet port, and then configuring the port accordingly to the reader's LAN settings (see all the instructions in Chapter 1 , *Installing the Development System*).

Other conventions

Bold: Indicates a new term, an important word, or words that you see onscreen. For example, words in menus or dialog boxes appear in the text like this. Here is an example: "Select **System info** from the **Administration** panel."

Warnings or important notes appear like this.

Tips and tricks appear like this.

Sections

In this book, you will find several headings that appear frequently (*Getting ready, How to do it..., How it works..., There's more...,* and *See also*).

To give clear instructions on how to complete a recipe, use these sections as follows:

Getting ready

This section tells you what to expect in the recipe and describes how to set up any software or any preliminary settings required for the recipe.

How to do it...

This section contains the steps required to follow the recipe.

How it works...

This section usually consists of a detailed explanation of what happened in the previous section.

There's more...

This section consists of additional information about the recipe in order to make you more knowledgeable about the recipe.

See also

This section provides helpful links to other useful information for the recipe.

Get in touch

Feedback from our readers is always welcome.

General feedback: If you have questions about any aspect of this book, mention the book title in the subject of your message and email us at `customercare@packtpub.com`.

Errata: Although we have taken every care to ensure the accuracy of our content, mistakes do happen. If you have found a mistake in this book, we would be grateful if you would report this to us. Please visit `www.packt.com/submit-errata`, selecting your book, clicking on the Errata Submission Form link, and entering the details.

Piracy: If you come across any illegal copies of our works in any form on the Internet, we would be grateful if you would provide us with the location address or website name. Please contact us at `copyright@packt.com` with a link to the material.

If you are interested in becoming an author: If there is a topic that you have expertise in and you are interested in either writing or contributing to a book, please visit `authors.packtpub.com`.

Reviews

Please leave a review. Once you have read and used this book, why not leave a review on the site that you purchased it from? Potential readers can then see and use your unbiased opinion to make purchase decisions, we at Packt can understand what you think about our products, and our authors can see your feedback on their book. Thank you!

For more information about Packt, please visit `packt.com`.

1
Installing the Development System

In this chapter, we will present and set up our working platform. In fact, even if we write and then test our own device drivers on our working PC, it is recommended to use a second device to test the code. This is because we're going to work in the kernel space where even a little bug can cause severe malfunctioning! Also, using a platform where several kinds of peripherals are available allows us to test a large variety of devices that are not always available on a PC. Of course, you are free to use your own system to write and test your drivers but, in this case, you should take care of the modifications needed to fit your board specifications.

In this book, I'm going to use the **Marvell ESPRESSObin** system, which is a powerful **Advanced RISC Machines** (**ARM**) 64-bit machine with a lot of interesting features. In the following figure, you can see the ESPRESSObin alongside a credit card and can gain an idea about the real dimensions of the board:

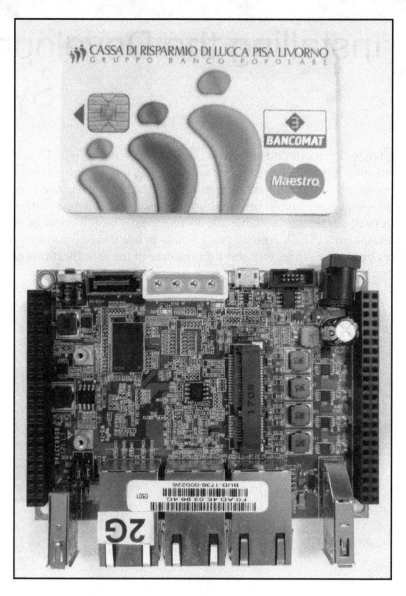

My board is the v5 release of ESPRESSObin while the latest version at the time of writing (announced on September 2018) is v7, so the reader should be able to get this new release by the time this book is published. The new ESPRESSObin v7 will feature 1GB DDR4 and 2GB DDR4 configurations (while v5 has DDR3 RAM chips), and a new 1.2GHz chipset will replace the currently sold configurations, which sports 800MHz and 1GHz CPU frequency limits. Even by taking a quick look at the new board layout, we see that a single SATA connector has taken the place of the existing two-pieces combination of SATA power and interface, the LED layout is now rearranged in a row, and an on-board eMMC is now in place. Moreover, this new revision will ship with an optional 802.11ac + Bluetooth 4.2 mini PCIe Wi-Fi card, which is sold separately.

 Lastly, you will now have the option to order your v7 ESPRESSObin with a complete enclosure. This product has FCC and CE certifications to help to enable mass deployment. Further information regarding the revision v7 (and v5) can be found at `http://wiki.espressobin.net/tiki-index.php?page=Quick+User+Guide`.

In order to test our new drivers, we will cover the following recipes in this first chapter:

- Setting up the host machine
- Working with the serial console
- Configuring and building the kernel
- Setting up the target machine
- Doing native compiling on foreign hardware

Technical requirements

Following are some interesting URLs where we can get useful technical information regarding the board:

- The home page: http://espressobin.net/
- The documentation wiki: http://wiki.espressobin.net/tiki-index.php
- Forums: http://espressobin.net/forums/

Taking a look at the technical specifications at http://espressobin.net/tech-spec/, we get the following information where we can see what the ESPRESSObin v5 can offer in terms of computational power, storage, networking, and expandability:

System on chip (SoC)	Marvell Armada 3700LP (88F3720) dual core ARM Cortex A53 processor up to 1.2GHz
System memory	1 GB DDR3 or optional 2GB DDR3
Storage	1x SATA interface 1x micro SD card slot with footprint for an optional 4GB EMMC
Network connectivity	1x Topaz Networking Switch 2x GbE Ethernet LAN 1x Ethernet WAN 1x MiniPCIe slot for wireless/BLE peripherals
USB	1x USB 3.0 1x USB 2.0 1x micro USB port
Expansion	2x 46-pin GPIO headers for accessories and shields with I2C, GPIOs, PWM, UART, SPI, MMC, and so on.
Misc	Reset button and JTAG interface
Power supply	12V DC jack or 5V via micro USB port
Power consumption	Less than 1W thermal dissipation at 1 GHz

In particular, the following screenshot shows the top view of the Marvell ESPRESSObin v5 (from now on, please take into account that I'm not going to explicitly add "v5" anymore):

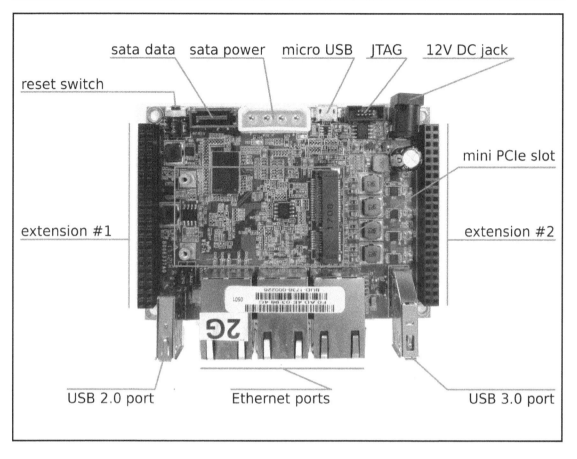

In the preceding screenshot, we can see the following components:

- The power connector (12V DC jack)
- The reset switch
- The micro USB device port (serial console)
- The Ethernet ports
- The USB host ports

The next screenshot shows the bottom view of the board where the microSD slot is located; this is where we should plug in the microSD we're going to create later on in this chapter:

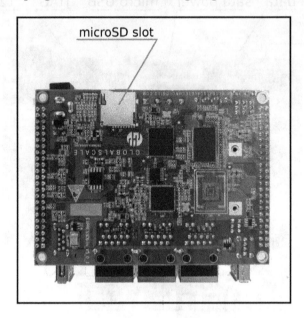

In this book, we'll see how we can manage (and reinstall) a complete Debian distribution, something that will allow us to have a wide set of ready-to-run software packages, as in a normal PC (in fact, the Debian ARM64 version is equivalent to the Debian x86 version). Afterward, we will develop our device drivers for the board, and then, when possible, we will test them with real devices connected to the ESPRESSObin itself. A little tutorial about how to set up the host system is also present in this chapter, and you can use it to set up a GNU/Linux-based working machine or a dedicated virtual one.

The code and other files used in this chapter can be downloaded from GitHub at `https://github.com/giometti/linux_device_driver_development_cookbook/tree/master/chapter_01`.

Setting up the host machine

As every good device driver developer knows, a host machine is absolutely necessary. Even if the embedded devices are getting more powerful nowadays (and the ESPRESSObin is one of these), there are some resource-consuming tasks where a host machine can help. That's why, in this section, we're going to show how to set up our host machine.

The host machine we decide to use could be a normal PC or a virtualized one—they are equivalent—but the important thing is that it must run a GNU/Linux-based OS.

Getting ready

In this book, I will use an Ubuntu 18.04 LTS based system but you can decide to try to replicate some settings and installation commands that we will use during the course of this book into another major Linux distribution, with little effort for a Debian derivative, or in a bit more of a complicated manner in the case of non-Debian derivative distributions.

I'm not going to show how to install a fresh Ubuntu system on a PC nor on a virtualized machine since it's a really easy task for a real programmer; however, as the last step of this chapter (the *Doing native compiling on foreign hardware* recipe), I will introduce, with detailed steps about how to install it, an interesting cross-platform environment that proved useful to compile foreign target code on the host machine as we were on the target. This procedure is very useful when we need several different OSes running on your development PC.

So, at this point, the reader should have their own PC running (natively or virtualized) a fresh installed Ubuntu 18.04 LTS OS.

The main usage of a host PC is to edit and then cross-compile our new device drivers and to manage our target device via the serial console, to create its root filesystem, and so on.

In order to do it properly, we need some basic tools; some of them are general while others depend on the specific platform onto which we are going to write our drivers.

General tools are surely an editor, a version control system, and a compiler and its related components, while specific platform tools are essentially the cross-compiler and its related components (on some platforms we may need additional tools but our mileage may vary and, in any case, each manufacturer will give us all of the needed requirements for a comfortable compilation environment).

About the editor: I'm not going to spend any words on it because the reader can use whatever they want (regarding myself, for example, I'm still programming with vi editor) but regarding others tools, I'll have to be more specific.

How to do it...

Now that our GNU/Linux distribution is up and running on our host PC we can start to install some programs we're going to use in this book:

1. First of all, let's install the basic compiling tools:

```
$ sudo apt install gcc make pkg-config \
         bison flex ncurses-dev libssl-dev \
         qemu-user-static debootstrap
```

 As you know already, the sudo command is used to execute a command as a privileged user. It should be already present in your system, otherwise you can install it by using the apt install sudo command as the root user.

2. Next, we have to test the compiling tools. We should be able to compile a C program. As a simple test, let's use the following standard *Hello World* code stored in the helloworld.c file:

```
#include <stdio.h>

int main(int argc, char *argv[])
{
    printf("Hello World!\n");

    return 0;
}
```

 Remember that code can be downloaded from our GitHub repository.

3. Now, we should be able to compile it by using the following command:

```
$ make CFLAGS="-Wall -O2" helloworld
cc -Wall -O2 helloworld.c -o helloworld
```

In the preceding command, we used both the compiler and the make tool, which is required to compile every Linux driver in a comfortable and reliable manner.

You can get more information regarding `make` by taking a look at `https://www.gnu.org/software/make/`, and for `gcc`, you can go to `https://www.gnu.org/software/gcc/`.

4. Finally, we can test it on the host PC, as follows:

```
$ ./helloworld
Hello World!
```

5. The next step is to install the cross-compiler. Since we're going to work with an ARM64 system, we need a cross-compiler and its related tools. To install them, we simply use the following command:

```
$ sudo apt install gcc-7-aarch64-linux-gnu
```

Note that we can also use an external toolchain as reported in the ESPRESSObin wiki at `http://wiki.espressobin.net/tiki-index.php?page=Build+From+Source+-+Toolchain`; however, the Ubuntu toolchain works perfectly!

6. When the installation is complete, test our new cross-compiler by using the preceding *Hello World* program, as follows:

```
$ sudo ln -s /usr/bin/aarch64-linux-gnu-gcc-7 /usr/bin/aarch64-
linux-gnu-gcc
$ make CC=aarch64-linux-gnu-gcc CFLAGS="-Wall -O2" helloworld
aarch64-linux-gnu-gcc-7 -Wall -O2 helloworld.c -o helloworld
```

Note that I've removed the previously compiled `helloworld` program in order to be able to correctly compile this new version. To do so, I used the `mv helloworld helloworld.x86_64` command due to the fact I'll need the x86 version again.

Also, note that since Ubuntu doesn't automatically create the standard cross-compiler name, `aarch64-linux-gnu-gcc`, we have to do it manually by using the preceding `ln` command before executing `make`.

7. OK, now we can verify that newly created version of the `helloworld` program for ARM64 by using the following `file` command. This will point out which platform the program is compiled for:

```
$ file helloworld
helloworld: ELF 64-bit LSB shared object, ARM aarch64, version 1
(SYSV), dynamically linked, interpreter /lib/ld-linux-aarch64.so.1,
for GNU/Linux 3.7.0,
BuildID[sha1]=c0d6e9ab89057e8f9101f51ad517a253e5fc4f10, not
stripped
```

If we again use the `file` command on the previously renamed version, `helloworld.x86_64`, we get the following:

```
$ file helloworld.x86_64
helloworld.x86_64: ELF 64-bit LSB shared object, x86-64, version 1
(SYSV), dynamically linked, interpreter /lib64/ld-linux-
x86-64.so.2, for GNU/Linux 3.2.0,
BuildID[sha1]=cf932fab45d36f89c30889df98ed382f6f648203, not
stripped
```

8. To test whether this new release is really for the ARM64 platform, we can use **QEMU**, which is an open source and generic machine emulator and virtualizer that is able to execute foreign code on the running platform. To install it, we can use `apt` command as in the preceding code, specifying the `qemu-user-static` package:

```
$ sudo apt install qemu-user-static
```

9. Then, we can execute our ARM64 program:

```
$ qemu-aarch64-static -L /usr/aarch64-linux-gnu/ ./helloworld
Hello World!
```

 To get further information about QEMU, a good staring point is its home page at `https://www.qemu.org/`.

10. The next step is to install the version control system. We must install the version control system used for the Linux project, that is, `git`. To install it, we can use the following command in a similar manner as before:

```
$ sudo apt install git
```

If everything works well, we should be able to execute it as follows:

```
$ git --help
usage: git [--version] [--help] [-C <path>] [-c <name>=<value>]
           [--exec-path[=<path>]] [--html-path] [--man-path]
           [--info-path] [-p | --paginate | --no-pager]
           [--no-replace-objects] [--bare] [--git-dir=<path>]
           [--work-tree=<path>] [--namespace=<name>]
           <command> [<args>]

These are common Git commands used in various situations:

start a working area (see also: git help tutorial)
   clone Clone a repository into a new directory
   init Create an empty Git repository or reinitialise an existing
one
...
```

 In this book, I'm going to explain every `git` command used but for complete knowledge of this powerful tool, I suggest you start reading `https://git-scm.com/`.

See also

- For further information regarding Debian's packages management, you can surf the internet, but a good starting point is at `https://wiki.debian.org/Apt`, while regarding the compiling tools (`gcc`, `make`, and other GNU software), the best documentation is at `https://www.gnu.org/software/`.
- Then, the best place for better documentation about `git` is at `https://git-scm.com/book/en/v2`, where the wonderful book *Pro Git* is available online!

Working with the serial console

As already stated (and as any real programmer of embedded devices knows), the serial console is a must-have during the device drivers development stages! So, let's see how we can get access to our ESPRESSObin through its serial console.

Getting ready

As shown in the screenshot in the *Technical requirements* section, a micro USB connector is available and it's directly connected with ESPRESSObin's serial console. So, using a proper USB cable, we can connect it to our host PC.

If all connections are OK, we can execute any serial Terminal emulator to see data from the serial console. Regarding this tool, I have to state that, as editor program, we can use whatever we prefer. However, I'm going to show how to install two of the more used Terminal emulation programs—minicom and screen.

 Note that this tool is not strictly required and its usage depends on the platform you're going to work on; however, in my humble opinion, this is the most powerful development and debugging tool ever! So, you definitely need it.

To install minicom, use the following command:

```
$ sudo apt install minicom
```

Now, to install the Terminal emulator named screen, we just have to replace minicom string with the screen packet name, as shown in the following:

```
$ sudo apt install screen
```

Both of them need a serial port to work on and the invocation command is quite similar. For brevity, I'm going to report their usage to get connected with the ESPRESSObin only; however, for further information about them, you should refer to their man pages (use man minicom and man screen to show them).

How to do it...

To test the serial connection with our target system we can do the following steps:

1. First of all, we have to locate the right serial port. Since the ESPRESSObin uses an USB emulated serial port (at 115,200 baud rate), usually our target port is named ttyUSB0 (but your mileage may vary, so let's verify it before continuing) so the minicom command we have to use to get connected with the ESPRESSObin serial console is the following:

```
$ minicom -o -D /dev/ttyUSB0
```

To correctly get access to the serial console, we may need proper privileges. In fact, we may try to execute the preceding `minicom` command, and we don't get an output! This is because the `minicom` command silently exits if we don't have enough privileges to get access to the port. We can verify our access to privileges by simply using another command on it, as shown here:

```
$ cat /dev/ttyUSB0
cat: /dev/ttyUSB0: Permission denied
```

In this case, the `cat` command perfectly tells us what's wrong so we can fix this issue using `sudo` or, even better, by properly adding our system's user to the right group as shown here:

```
$ ls -l /dev/ttyUSB0
crw-rw---- 1 root dialout 188, 0 Jan 12 23:06 /dev
/ttyUSB0
$ sudo adduser $LOGNAME dialout
```

Then, we log out and log in again, and we can access the serial devices without any problem.

2. The equivalent command by using `screen` is reported as follows:

   $ screen /dev/ttyUSB0 115200

   Note that, on `minicom`, I didn't specify the serial communication options (baud rate, parity, and so on) while, for `screen`, I've added the baud rate on the command line; this is because my default `minicom` configuration automatically uses correct communication options while `screen` uses 9,600 baud as a default baud rate. Please refer to the program man pages for further information about how to do this setting in order to fit your needs.

3. If everything works well, after executing your Terminal emulator on the right serial port, turn on our ESPRESSObin (simply by plugging in the power). We should see the following output on our Terminal:

   ```
   NOTICE: Booting Trusted Firmware
   NOTICE: BL1: v1.3(release):armada-17.06.2:a37c108
   NOTICE: BL1: Built : 14:31:03, Jul 5 2NOTICE: BL2:
   v1.3(release):armada-17.06.2:a37c108
   NOTICE: BL2: Built : 14:31:04, Jul 5 201NOTICE: BL31:
   v1.3(release):armada-17.06.2:a37c108
   NOTICE: BL31:

   U-Boot 2017.03-armada-17.06.3-ga33ecb8 (Jul 05 2017 - 14:30:47
   +0800)
   ```

```
Model: Marvell Armada 3720 Community Board ESPRESSOBin
       CPU @ 1000 [MHz]
       L2 @ 800 [MHz]
       TClock @ 200 [MHz]
       DDR @ 800 [MHz]
DRAM: 2 GiB
U-Boot DComphy-0: USB3 5 Gbps
Comphy-1: PEX0 2.5 Gbps
Comphy-2: SATA0 6 Gbps
SATA link 0 timeout.
AHCI 0001.0300 32 slots 1 ports 6 Gbps 0x1 impl SATA mode
flags: ncq led only pmp fbss pio slum part sxs
PCIE-0: Link down
MMC: sdhci@d0000: 0
SF: Detected w25q32dw with page size 256 Bytes, erase size 4 KiB,
total 4 MiB
Net: eth0: neta@30000 [PRIME]
Hit any key to stop autoboot: 2
```

See also

- For more information about how to get connected with the ESPRESSObin serial port, you can take a look at its wiki section about serial connections at `http://wiki.espressobin.net/tiki-index.php?page=Serial+connection+-+Linux`.

Configuring and building the kernel

Now, it's time to download the kernel sources and then configure and build them. This step is needed for several reasons: the first one is that we need a kernel for our ESPRESSObin in order to boot an OS, and the second one is that we need a configured kernel sources tree to compile our drivers into.

Getting ready

Since our ESPRESSObin is now supported into vanilla kernel since the 4.11 release, we can get Linux sources by using the following `git` command:

```
$ git clone
git://git.kernel.org/pub/scm/linux/kernel/git/torvalds/linux.git
```

 This command will take a lot of time to finish so I would suggest you take a break by drinking your favorite cup of coffee (as real programmers should do).

When finished, we can enter into the `linux` directory to see the Linux sources:

```
$ cd linux/
$ ls
arch CREDITS firmware ipc lib mm scripts usr
block crypto fs Kbuild LICENSES net security virt
certs Documentation include Kconfig MAINTAINERS README sound
COPYING drivers init kernel Makefile samples tools
```

These sources are related to the latest kernel release that could be unstable, so to be sure that we're using a stable kernel release (or a *long-term release*), let's extract release 4.18, which is the current stable release at time of writing this chapter, as follows:

```
$ git checkout -b v4.18 v4.18
```

How to do it...

Before starting the compilation, we have to configure the kernel and our compiling environment.

1. The last task is quite easy and it consists of executing the following environment variables assignments:

```
$ export ARCH=arm64
$ export CROSS_COMPILE=aarch64-linux-gnu-
```

2. Then, we can select the ESPRESSObin standard kernel configuration by simply using the following command:

```
$ make defconfig
```

Depending on the kernel release you're using, the default configuration file may be also called `mvebu_defconfig` or either `mvebu_v5_defconfig` or `mvebu_v7_defconfig`. So, please take a look into the `linux/arch/arm64/configs/` directory in order to see which file is present that best suits your needs.

In my system, I have the following:

```
$ ls linux/arch/arm64/configs/
defconfig
```

3. If we wish to modify this default configuration, we can execute the `make menuconfig` command, which will show us a pretty menu where we can enter our modifications in order to fit our needs. The following screenshot shows how the kernel configuration menu appears on the Terminal:

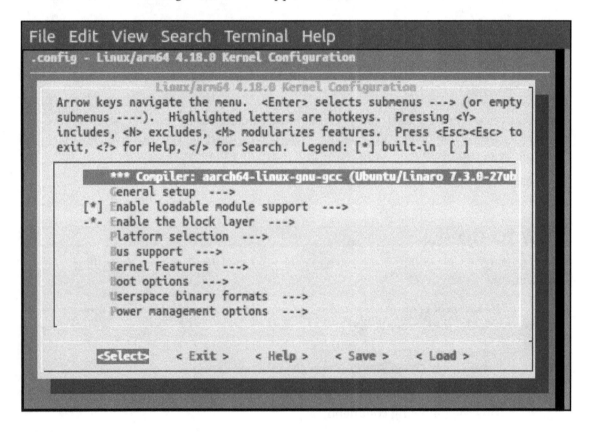

4. Before continuing, we must be sure that the **Distributed Switch Architecture** (**DSA**) is enabled into the kernel, otherwise we're not able to use the Ethernet ports at all! This is because the ESPRESSObin has a complex (and really powerful) internal network switch that must be managed by using this special support.

For further information regarding the DSA, you can start reading the `linux/Documentation/networking/dsa/dsa.txt` file, located in the kernel sources we're currently working on.

5. To enable DSA support, just navigate into the kernel menu at **Networking support.** Go to **Networking options** and, at the end, enable the entry **Distributed Switch Architecture** support. After that, we have to go back to the menu's top level and then select these entries: **Device Drivers** | **Network device support** | **Distributed Switch Architecture drivers** and then enable **Marvell 88E6xxx Ethernet switch fabric support**, which is the ESPRESSObin's on-board switch chip.

Remember that, to enable a kernel feature as a module or a built-in, you need to highlight the desired feature and then press the spacebar until the character inside the <> characters changes to * (which means built-in, that is, <*>) or to **M** (which means module, that is, <**M**>).

Note that, to enable DSA as a built-in instead of as a module, we have to disable **802.1d Ethernet Bridging** support (that is, the entry just above).

6. Well, after all kernel settings are in place, we can start the kernel compilation by using the following `make` command:

```
$ make Image dtbs modules
```

Again, as the downloading command, this command will need a lot of time to finish, so let me suggest you take another break. However, in order to speed up the compilation process, you may try using the -j option argument in order to tell make to use several simultaneous process to compile the code. For example, on my machine, having eight CPU threads, I use the following command:

```
$ make -j8 Image dtbs modules
```

So, let's try using the following lscpu command to get how many CPUs your system has:

```
lscpu | grep '^CPU(s):'
CPU(s):  8
```

Alternatively, on Ubuntu/Debian, there's also the pre-installed nproc utility, so the following command also does the trick:

```
$ make -j$(nproc)
```

When finished, we should have the kernel image into the arch/arm64/boot/Image file and the device tree binary into the arch/arm64/boot/dts/marvell/armada-3720-espressobin.dtb file, which are ready to be transferred into the microSD we're going to build in the next recipe, *Setting up the target machine*.

See also

- For further information regarding available ESPRESSObin's kernel releases and how to get them and compile and install them, just take a look at ESPRESSObin's wiki pages at http://wiki.espressobin.net/tiki-index.php?page= Build+From+Source+-+Kernel.

Setting up the target machine

Now, it's time to install whatever we needed on our target system; since the ESPRESSObin is sold with just the bootloader, we have to do some work in order to get a fully functional system with a proper OS.

In this book, I'm going to use a Debian OS for the ESPRESSObin but you may use other OSes as reported at http://wiki.espressobin.net/tiki-index.php?page=Software+HowTo. On this site, you can get more detailed information about how to properly set up your ESPRESSObin to fit your needs.

Getting ready

Even if the ESPRESSObin can boot from different media, we're going to use a microSD since it's the most easy and useful way to set up the system. For different media, please refer to the ESPRESSObin's wiki pages—see `http://wiki.espressobin.net/tiki-index.php?page=Boot+from+removable+storage+-+Ubuntu` for some examples.

How to do it...

To set up the microSD, we have to use our host PC, so plug it in and then locate the corresponding device.

1. If we're using an SD/microSD slot, as soon as we plug the media in, we'll get something like this in the kernel messages:

```
mmc0: cannot verify signal voltage switch
mmc0: new ultra high speed SDR50 SDHC card at address aaaa
mmcblk0: mmc0:aaaa SL08G 7.40 GiB
 mmcblk0: p1
```

To get kernel messages on the Terminal, we can use the `dmesg` command.

However, if we're going to use a microSD to USB adapter kernel, messages will look like the following:

```
usb 1-6: new high-speed USB device number 5 using xhci_hcd
usb 1-6: New USB device found, idVendor=05e3, idProduct=0736
usb 1-6: New USB device strings: Mfr=3, Product=4, SerialNumber=2
usb 1-6: Product: USB Storage
usb 1-6: Manufacturer: Generic
usb 1-6: SerialNumber: 000000000272
usb-storage 1-6:1.0: USB Mass Storage device detected
scsi host4: usb-storage 1-6:1.0
usbcore: registered new interface driver usb-storage
usbcore: registered new interface driver uas
scsi 4:0:0:0: Direct-Access Generic STORAGE DEVICE 0272 PQ: 0 ANSI: 0
sd 4:0:0:0: Attached scsi generic sg3 type 0
sd 4:0:0:0: [sdc] 15523840 512-byte logical blocks: (7.95 GB/7.40 GiB)
sd 4:0:0:0: [sdc] Write Protect is off
sd 4:0:0:0: [sdc] Mode Sense: 0b 00 00 08
```

```
sd 4:0:0:0: [sdc] No Caching mode page found
sd 4:0:0:0: [sdc] Assuming drive cache: write through
 sdc: sdc1
sd 4:0:0:0: [sdc] Attached SCSI removable disk
```

2. Another easy way to locate the media is by using the `lsblk` command, as follows:

```
$ lsblk
NAME MAJ:MIN RM SIZE RO TYPE MOUNTPOINT
loop0 7:0 0 5M 1 loop /snap/gedit/66
loop1 7:1 0 4.9M 1 loop /snap/canonical-livepatch/50
...
sdb 8:16 0 931.5G 0 disk
└─sdb1 8:17 0 931.5G 0 part /run/schroot/mount/ubuntu-xenial-
amd64-f72c490
sr0 11:0 1 1024M 0 rom
mmcblk0 179:0 0 7.4G 0 disk
└─mmcblk0p1
        179:1 0 7.4G 0 part /media/giometti/5C60-6750
```

3. It's now obvious that our microSD card is here listed as /dev/mmcblk0 but it is not empty. Since we want to clear everything from it, we have to clear it first by using the following command:

```
$ sudo dd if=/dev/zero of=/dev/mmcblk0 bs=1M count=100
```

4. You may need to unmount the device before proceeding with the clearing in order to work safely on the media device, so let's unmount all of the device's partitions by using the umount command on all of them as I will do in the following with the only defined partition on my microSD:

```
$ sudo umount /dev/mmcblk0p1
```

You have to just repeat this command for each defined partition on your microSD.

5. Now, we will create a new partition, /dev/mmcblk0p1, on the empty SD card with the next command:

```
$ (echo n; echo p; echo 1; echo ''; echo ''; echo w) | sudo fdisk
/dev/mmcblk0
```

If everything works well, our microSD media should appear formatted, as in the following:

```
$ sudo fdisk -l /dev/mmcblk0
Disk /dev/mmcblk0: 7.4 GiB, 7948206080 bytes, 15523840 sectors
Units: sectors of 1 * 512 = 512 bytes
Sector size (logical/physical): 512 bytes / 512 bytes
I/O size (minimum/optimal): 512 bytes / 512 bytes
Disklabel type: dos
Disk identifier: 0x34f32673

Device Boot Start End Sectors Size Id Type
/dev/mmcblk0p1 2048 15523839 15521792 7.4G 83 Linux
```

6. Then, we have to format it as EXT4 with the following command:

```
$ sudo mkfs.ext4 -O ^metadata_csum,^64bit -L root /dev/mmcblk0p1
```

Note that this command line works for the `e2fsprogs` version >=1.43 only! If you're using an older release, you should use the following command:
```
$ sudo mkfs.ext4 -L root /dev/mmcblk0p1
```

7. Next, mount this partition on your local Linux machine:

```
$ sudo mount /dev/mmcblk0p1 /mnt/
```

Note that, on some OSes (and especially on Ubuntu), as soon as we unplug and then we plug in the media device again, it is mounted automatically into `/media/$USER/root` where `$USER` is an environment variable holding your username. For instance, on my machine, I have the following:
```
$ ls -ld /media/$USER/root
drwxr-xr-x 3 root root 4096 Jan 10 14:28
/media/giometti/root/
```

Adding Debian files

I decided to use Debian as the target OS since it's my favorite distribution for development (and, when possible, for production) systems:

1. To install it, we use QEMU software again, using the following command:

    ```
    $ sudo qemu-debootstrap \
        --arch=arm64 \
        --include="sudo,file,openssh-server" \
        --exclude="debfoster" \
        stretch ./debian-stretch-arm64 http://deb.debian.org/debian
    ```

You could see warnings about keyring here; they are harmless and they can be safely ignored:
```
W: Cannot check Release signature;
```

I suppose this is another coffee-break command.

2. Once finished, we should find, in `debian-stretch-arm64`, a clean Debian root filesystem for the ESPRESSObin but, before transferring it into the microSD, we should fix the `hostname` file contents as shown here:

    ```
    $ sudo bash -c 'echo espressobin | cat > ./debian-stretch-
    arm64/etc/hostname'
    ```

3. Then, we have to add the serial device `ttyMV0` to the `/etc/securetty` file in order to be able to log in as the root user through the serial device, `/dev/ttyMV0`. Use the following command:

    ```
    $ sudo bash -c 'echo -e "\n# Marvell serial ports\nttyMV0" | \
                cat >> ./debian-stretch-arm64/etc/securetty'
    ```

Use `man securetty` for further information about the root login through a serial connection.

4. And, as a last step, we have to set up a root password:

```
$ sudo chroot debian-stretch-arm64/ passwd
Enter new UNIX password:
Retype new UNIX password:
passwd: password updated successfully
```

Here, I used the `root` string as password for the root user (it is up to you to choose yours).

In order to have further information regarding this usage of the `chroot` command, you can use the `man chroot` command or continue reading till the end of this chapter where I'm going to explain a bit better how it works.

Now, we can safely copy all files into our microSD using the following command:

```
$ sudo cp -a debian-stretch-arm64/* /media/$USER/root/
```

Here is what the microSD content should look like:

```
$ ls /media/$USER/root/
bin   dev   home  lost+found  mnt  proc  run   srv  tmp  var
boot  etc   lib   media            opt   root  sbin  sys  usr
```

Adding the kernel

After OS files, we need also kernel images to get a running kernel and, in the previous section, we got the kernel image into the `arch/arm64/boot/Image` file and the device tree binary into the `arch/arm64/boot/dts/marvell/armada-3720-espressobin.dtb` file, which are ready to be transferred into our freshly created microSD:

1. Let's copy them into the `/boot` directory as done here:

```
$ sudo cp arch/arm64/boot/Image \
        arch/arm64/boot/dts/marvell/armada-3720-espressobin.dtb \
        /media/$USER/root/boot/
```

If the `/boot` directory was not present in the microSD and the preceding command returned an error, you can recover by using the following command and rerun the preceding `cp` command:
```
$ sudo mkdir /media/$USER/root/boot
```

Then, the `/boot` directory should look like this:

```
$ ls /media/$USER/root/boot/
armada-3720-espressobin.dtb   Image
```

2. The preceding files are sufficient to boot the system; however, to also install kernel modules and headers files, which are useful for compiling new software, we can use the next commands after all Debian files have been installed into the microSD (to avoid overwriting with Debian files):

```
$ sudo -E make modules_install INSTALL_MOD_PATH=/media/$USER/root/
$ sudo -E make headers_install
INSTALL_HDR_PATH=/media/$USER/root/usr/
```

Well, now we are finally ready to tie it all up and run our new Debian system, so let's unmount the microSD and plug it into the ESPRESSObin.

Setting up the booting variables

After powering up, we should get the bootloader's messages from the serial console and then we should see a timeout running to 0 before doing the autoboot:

1. Quickly stop the countdown by hitting the *Enter* key on the keyboard to get the bootloader's prompt, as follows:

```
Model: Marvell Armada 3720 Community Board ESPRESSOBin
        CPU @ 1000 [MHz]
        L2 @ 800 [MHz]
        TClock @ 200 [MHz]
        DDR @ 800 [MHz]
DRAM: 2 GiB
U-Boot DComphy-0: USB3 5 Gbps
Comphy-1: PEX0 2.5 Gbps
Comphy-2: SATA0 6 Gbps
SATA link 0 timeout.
AHCI 0001.0300 32 slots 1 ports 6 Gbps 0x1 impl SATA mode
flags: ncq led only pmp fbss pio slum part sxs
PCIE-0: Link down
MMC: sdhci@d0000: 0
SF: Detected w25q32dw with page size 256 Bytes, erase size 4 KiB,
total 4 MiB
Net: eth0: neta@30000 [PRIME]
Hit any key to stop autoboot: 0
Marvell>>
```

The ESPRESSObin's bootloader is U-Boot, which has its home page at
`https://www.denx.de/wiki/U-Boot`.

2. Now, let's check again that the microSD card has the necessary files using the `ext4ls` command, as follows:

```
Marvell>> ext4ls mmc 0:1 boot
<DIR> 4096 .
<DIR> 4096 ..
       18489856 Image
          8359 armada-3720-espressobin.dtb
```

OK, everything is in place, so there are only a few variables required to boot from the microSD card.

3. We can display the currently defined variables at any point by using the `echo` command and optionally reconfigure them by using `setenv` command. First, check and set proper image and device tree paths and names:

```
Marvell>> echo $image_name
Image
Marvell>> setenv image_name boot/Image
Marvell>> echo $fdt_name
armada-3720-espressobin.dtb
Marvell>> setenv fdt_name boot/armada-3720-espressobin.dtb
```

Note that, filenames were correct but the path names were not; that's why I used the `setenv` command to correctly redefine them.

4. Next, define the `bootcmd` variable, which we will use to boot from the microSD card:

```
Marvell>> setenv bootcmd 'mmc dev 0; \
            ext4load mmc 0:1 $kernel_addr $image_name; \
            ext4load mmc 0:1 $fdt_addr $fdt_name; \
            setenv bootargs $console root=/dev/mmcblk0p1 rw
rootwait; \
            booti $kernel_addr - $fdt_addr'
```

We must be careful to set the preceding root path to point to where we have extracted the Debian filesystem (the first partition in our case).

5. Save the set variables at any time using the `saveenv` command.
6. Finally, we boot up the ESPRESSObin by simply typing the `reset` command and, if everything works well, we should see the system start and running and, at the end, we should get system login prompt, as follows:

```
Debian GNU/Linux 9 espressobin ttyMV0

giometti-VirtualBox login:
```

7. Now, log in as root with the `root` password that was previously set up:

```
Debian GNU/Linux 9 espressobin ttyMV0

espressobin login: root
Password:
Linux espressobin 4.18.0 #2 SMP PREEMPT Sun Jan 13 13:05:03 CET
2019 aarch64

The programs included with the Debian GNU/Linux system are free
software;
the exact distribution terms for each program are described in the
individual files in /usr/share/doc/*/copyright.

Debian GNU/Linux comes with ABSOLUTELY NO WARRANTY, to the extent
permitted by applicable law.
root@espressobin:~#
```

Setting up the networking

OK, now our ESPRESSObin is ready to execute our code and our drivers! However, before ending this section, let's take a look at the networking configuration since it can be further useful to log in to the board using an SSH connection or just to copy files from/to the board quickly (even if we can remove the microSD and then copy our files from the host PC directly):

1. Taking a look at available network interfaces on the ESPRESSObin, we see the following:

```
# ip link
1: lo: <LOOPBACK,UP,LOWER_UP> mtu 65536 qdisc noqueue state UNKNOWN
mode DEFAULT
 group default qlen 1000
    link/loopback 00:00:00:00:00:00 brd 00:00:00:00:00:00
2: eth0: <BROADCAST,MULTICAST> mtu 1500 qdisc noop state DOWN mode
DEFAULT group
 default qlen 532
    link/ether 3a:ac:9b:44:90:e9 brd ff:ff:ff:ff:ff:ff
3: wan@eth0: <BROADCAST,MULTICAST,M-DOWN> mtu 1500 qdisc noop state
DOWN mode DE
FAULT group default qlen 1000
    link/ether 3a:ac:9b:44:90:e9 brd ff:ff:ff:ff:ff:ff
4: lan0@eth0: <BROADCAST,MULTICAST,M-DOWN> mtu 1500 qdisc noop
state DOWN mode D
EFAULT group default qlen 1000
    link/ether 3a:ac:9b:44:90:e9 brd ff:ff:ff:ff:ff:ff
5: lan1@eth0: <BROADCAST,MULTICAST,M-DOWN> mtu 1500 qdisc noop
state DOWN mode D
EFAULT group default qlen 1000
    link/ether 3a:ac:9b:44:90:e9 brd ff:ff:ff:ff:ff:ff
```

The `eth0` interface is the one that connects the CPU with the Ethernet switch while the `wan`, `lan0`, and `lan1` interfaces are the ones where we can physically connect our Ethernet cables (note that the system calls them `wan@eth0`, `lan0@eth0`, and `lan1@eth1` just to underline the fact they are slaves of `eth0`). Following is a photograph of the ESPRESSObin, where we can see each Ethernet port with its label:

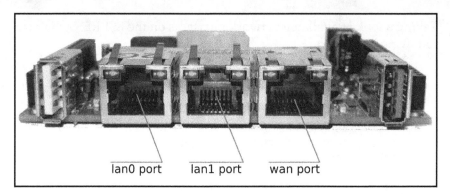

2. Despite their names, all ports are equivalent so connect the Ethernet cable into one port (I'm going to use `wan`) and then enable it after `eth0`, as follows:

```
# ip link set eth0 up
mvneta d0030000.ethernet eth0: configuring for fixed/rgmii-id link
mode
mvneta d0030000.ethernet eth0: Link is Up - 1Gbps/Full - flow
control off
# ip link set wan up
mv88e6085 d0032004.mdio-mii:01 wan: configuring for phy/ link mode
mv88e6085 d0032004.mdio-mii:01 wan: Link is Up - 100Mbps/Full -
flow control rx/tx
```

Note that, in the preceding output, there are also kernel messages that show what you should see if everything is working well.

3. Now, we can manually set an IP address or we can ask our DHCP server whatever we need to surf the internet with the `dhclient` command:

```
# dhclient wan
```

Here is my network configuration:

```
# ip addr show wan
3: wan@eth0: <BROADCAST,MULTICAST,UP,LOWER_UP> mtu 1500 qdisc
noqueue state UP g
roup default qlen 1000
    link/ether 9e:9f:6b:5c:cf:fc brd ff:ff:ff:ff:ff:ff
    inet 192.168.0.100/24 brd 192.168.0.255 scope global wan
        valid_lft forever preferred_lft forever
```

4. Now, we're ready to install new software or to try to establish an SSH connection to the ESPRESSObin; to do so, let's verify that we have the following SSH server's configuration in the /etc/ssh/sshd_config file:

```
# grep 'PermitRootLogin yes' /etc/ssh/sshd_config
PermitRootLogin yes
```

5. If we get no output, we cannot log in as root into our ESPRESSObin, so we must change the PermitRootLogin setting to yes and then restart the daemon:

```
# /etc/init.d/ssh restart

Restarting ssh (via systemctl): ssh.service.
```

6. Now, on the host PC, we can try the login via SSH, as follows:

```
$ ssh root@192.168.0.100
root@192.168.0.100's password:
Linux espressobin 4.18.0 #2 SMP PREEMPT Sun Jan 13 13:05:03 CET
2019 aarch64

The programs included with the Debian GNU/Linux system are free
software;
the exact distribution terms for each program are described in the
individual files in /usr/share/doc/*/copyright.

Debian GNU/Linux comes with ABSOLUTELY NO WARRANTY, to the extent
permitted by applicable law.
Last login: Thu Nov 3 17:16:59 2016
-bash: warning: setlocale: LC_ALL: cannot change locale
(en_GB.UTF-8)
```

See also

- To get more information regarding how to set up the ESPRESSObin even on different OSes, you can take a look at `http://wiki.espressobin.net/tiki-index.php?page=Software+HowTo`.
- For further information regarding `qemu-debootstrap`, a good starting point is at `https://wiki.ubuntu.com/ARM/RootfsFromScratch/QemuDebootstrap`. To manage Ethernet devices and for further information about networking on a Debian OS, you can take a look at the following: `https://wiki.debian.org/NetworkConfiguration`.

Doing native compiling on foreign hardware

Before ending this chapter, I'd like to introduce an interesting cross-platform system that's useful when we need several different OSes running on your development PC. This step is very useful when we need a complete OS to compile a device driver or an application but we do not have a target device to compile onto. We can use our host PC to compile code for a foreign hardware across different OS and OS release.

Getting ready

During my career, I worked with tons of different platforms and having one virtual machine for all of them is very complex and really system consuming (especially if we decide to run several of them at the same time!). That's why it can be interesting to have a lightweight system that can execute foreign code on your PC. Of course, this method cannot be used to test a device driver (we need real hardware for that), but we can use it to run a native compiler and/or native userspace code really quickly just in case our embedded platform is not working. Let's see what I'm talking about.

In the *Setting up the target machine* recipe, regarding the Debian OS installation, we used the `chroot` command to set up the root's password. This command worked thanks to QEMU; in fact, in the `debian-stretch-arm64` directory, we have an ARM64 root filesystem, which can be executed on an x86_64 platform by using QEMU only. It's then clear that, in this manner, we should be able to execute whatever command we'd like and, of course, we will be able to execute the Bash shell as in the next recipe.

How to do it...

Now it's time to see how `chroot` works:

1. Execute an ARM64 `bash` command by using our x86_64 host, as follows:

```
$ sudo chroot debian-stretch-arm64/ bash
bash: warning: setlocale: LC_ALL: cannot change locale
(en_GB.UTF-8)
root@giometti-VirtualBox:/#
```

2. Then, we can use each ARM64 command as we did on the ESPRESSObin; for example, to list files into the current directory; we can use the following:

```
# ls /
bin   dev  home media  opt   root  sbin  sys  usr
boot  etc  lib  mnt    proc  run   srv   tmp  var
# cat /etc/hostname
espressobin
```

However, there are some traps; for instance, we completely miss the `/proc` and `/sys` directories and programs, which rely on them and will fail for sure:

```
# ls /{proc,sys}
/proc:

/sys:
# ps
Error: /proc must be mounted
  To mount /proc at boot you need an /etc/fstab line like:
      proc /proc proc defaults
  In the meantime, run "mount proc /proc -t proc"
```

To resolve these problems, we can manually mount these missing directories before executing `chroot`, but this is quite annoying due to the fact that they are so many, so we can try using the `schroot` utility, which, in turn, can do all of these steps for us. Let's see how.

 For detailed information regarding `schroot`, you can see its man pages with `man schroot`.

Installing and configuring schroot

This task is quite trivial in Ubuntu:

1. First of all, we install the program in the usual way:

   ```
   $ sudo apt install schroot
   ```

2. Then, we have to configure it in order to correctly enter into our ARM64 system. To do so, let's copy the root filesystem created before into a dedicated directory (where we can also add any other distributions we wish to emulate with schroot):

   ```
   $ sudo mkdir /srv/chroot/
   $ sudo cp -a debian-stretch-arm64/ /srv/chroot/
   ```

3. Then, we must create a proper configuration for our new system by adding a new file into the schroot configuration directory, as follows:

   ```
   $ sudo bash -c 'cat > /etc/schroot/chroot.d/debian-stretch-arm64
   <<__EOF__
   [debian-stretch-arm64]
   description=Debian Stretch (arm64)
   directory=/srv/chroot/debian-stretch-arm64
   users=giometti
   #groups=sbuild
   #root-groups=root
   #aliases=unstable,default
   type=directory
   profile=desktop
   personality=linux
   preserve-environment=true
   __EOF__'
   ```

Note that the directory parameter is set to the path holding our ARM64 system and users is set to giometti, which is my username (this is a comma-separated list of users that are allowed access to the chroot environment—see man schroot.conf).

Looking at the preceding settings, we see that the `profile` parameter is set to `desktop`; this means that it will be taking into account all files in the `/etc/schroot/desktop/` directory. In particular, the `fstab` file holds all mount points we'd like to be mounted into our system. So, we should verify that it holds at least the following lines:

```
# <filesystem>  <mount point>  <type>  <options>  <dump>  <pass>
/proc           /proc          none    rw,bind    0       0
/sys            /sys           none    rw,bind    0       0
/dev            /dev           none    rw,bind    0       0
/dev/pts        /dev/pts       none    rw,bind    0       0
/home           /home          none    rw,bind    0       0
/tmp            /tmp           none    rw,bind    0       0
/opt            /opt           none    rw,bind    0       0
/srv            /srv           none    rw,bind    0       0
tmpfs           /dev/shm       tmpfs   defaults   0       0
```

4. Now, we have to restart the `schroot` service, as follows:

```
$ sudo systemctl restart schroot
```

Note that you can also restart using the old-fashioned way:
```
$ sudo /etc/init.d/schroot restart
```

5. Now we can list all available environments by asking them to `schroot`, as follows:

```
$ schroot -l
chroot:debian-stretch-arm64
```

6. OK, everything is in place and we can enter into the emulated ARM64 system:

```
$ schroot -c debian-stretch-arm64
bash: warning: setlocale: LC_ALL: cannot change locale
(en_GB.UTF-8)
```

Since we haven't installed any locale support, the preceding warning is quite obvious and it should be safely ignored.

7. Now, to verify we're really executing ARM64 code, let's try some commands. For example, we can ask for some system information with the `uname` command:

```
$ uname -a
Linux giometti-VirtualBox 4.15.0-43-generic #46-Ubuntu SMP Thu Dec
6 14:45:28 UTC 2018 aarch64 GNU/Linux
```

As we can see, the system says that its platform is `aarch64`, which is ARM64. Then, we can try to execute our `helloworld` program that was cross-compiled before; since, after `chroot`, the current directory is not changed (and our home directory is still the same), we can simply go back where we did the compilation and then execute the program as usual:

```
$ cd ~/Projects/ldddc/github/chapter_1/
$ file helloworld
helloworld: ELF 64-bit LSB shared object, ARM aarch64, version 1
(SYSV), dynamically linked, interpreter /lib/ld-linux-aarch64.so.1,
for GNU/Linux 3.7.0,
BuildID[sha1]=c0d6e9ab89057e8f9101f51ad517a253e5fc4f10, not
stripped
$ ./helloworld
Hello World!
```

The program still executes as when we were on an ARM64 system. Great!

Configuring the emulated OS

What we just saw about `schroot` is nothing if we do not configure our new system to do native compilation, and to do so, we can use every Debian tool we use on our host PC:

1. To install a complete compiling environment, we can issue the following command once inside the `schroot` environment:

```
$ sudo apt install gcc make \
        bison flex ncurses-dev libssl-dev
```

Note that `sudo` will ask your usual password, that is, the password you currently use to log in to your host PC.

You might not get a password request from sudo with the following error message:

sudo: no tty present and no askpass program specified

You can try executing the preceding sudo command again, adding to it the -s option argument.

It could be possible that the apt command will notify you that some packages cannot be authenticated. Just ignore this warning and continue installation, answering yes by pressing the Y key.

If everything works well, we should now be able to execute every compiling command we used before. For instance, we can try to recompile the helloworld program again but natively (we should remove the current executable in order; make will try to recompile it again):

```
$ rm helloworld
$ make CFLAGS="-Wall -O2" helloworld
cc -Wall -O2 helloworld.c -o helloworld
$ file helloworld
helloworld: ELF 64-bit LSB shared object, ARM aarch64, version 1
(SYSV), dynamically linked, interpreter /lib/ld-linux-aarch64.so.1,
for GNU/Linux 3.7.0,
BuildID[sha1]=1393450a08fb9eea22babfb9296ce848bb806c21, not
stripped
$ ./helloworld
Hello World!
```

Note that networking support is fully functional so we're now working on an emulated ARM64 environment on our hosts PC as we were on the ESPRESSObin.

See also

- On the internet, there are several examples regarding schroot usage and a good starting point is https://wiki.debian.org/Schroot.

2
A Peek Inside the Kernel

Simple operating systems (such as MS-DOS) always execute in a single CPU mode, but Unix-like operating systems use dual modes to effectively implement timesharing and resource allocation and protection. At any time in Linux, the CPU is either operating in a trusted **kernel mode** (where we can do everything we wish) or in a restricted **user mode** (where some operations are not allowed). All user processes execute in user mode, whereas the core kernel itself and most device drivers (except ones implemented in user space) run in kernel mode so that they have unrestricted access to the entire processor instruction set and to the full memory and I/O space.

When a user mode process needs to get access to peripherals, it cannot do it by itself, but it has to channel requests through device drivers or other kernel mode code via **system calls**, which play a major role in controlling process activities and managing data exchange. In this chapter, we will not see system calls yet (they will be introduced in Chapter 3, *Working with Char Drivers*), but we will start programming into the kernel by directly adding new code into its sources or by using kernel modules, which is another, more versatile, manner to add code to the kernel.

Once we get started writing kernel code, we must not forget that, while in user mode, every resource allocation (the CPU, RAM, and so on) is automatically managed by the kernel (which can properly release them when a process dies), in kernel mode, we are allowed to monopolize the processor until either we voluntarily relinquish the CPU or an interrupt or exception occurs; moreover, every requested resource (as the RAM, for instance) is lost if not properly released. That's why it's really important to correctly manage the CPU usage and to free whatever resource we request!

Now, it's time to do a first jump into the kernel, so in this chapter, we will cover the following recipes:

- Adding custom code to the sources
- Using kernel messages
- Working with kernel modules
- Using module parameters

Technical requirements

During this chapter, we need kernel sources we already downloaded in the *Configuring and building the kernel* recipe in Chapter 1, *Installing the Development System,* and, of course, we also need our cross-compiler installed, as seen in the *Setting up the host machine* recipe in Chapter 1, *Installing the Development System.* The code and other files used in this chapter can be downloaded from GitHub at https://github.com/giometti/linux_device_driver_development_cookbook/tree/master/chapter_02.

Adding custom code to the sources

As a first step, let's see how we can add some simple code to our kernel sources. In this recipe, we'll simply add silly code just to demonstrate how easy it is, but further into this book, we're going to add even more complex code.

Getting ready

Since we need to add our code to the Linux sources, let's go into the directory where all sources are located. On my system, I use the Projects/ldddc/linux/ path located in my home directory. Here is what the kernel sources look like:

```
$ cd Projects/ldddc/linux/
$ ls
arch            Documentation  Kbuild      mm                scripts   virt
block           drivers        Kconfig     modules.builtin   security  vmlinux
built-in.a      firmware       kernel      modules.order     sound
vmlinux.o
certs           fs             lib         Module.symvers    stNXtP40
COPYING         include        LICENSES    net System.map
CREDITS         init           MAINTAINERS README tools
crypto          ipc            Makefile    samples usr
```

Now, we need to set the environment variables, ARCH and CROSS_COMPILE, as follows in order to be able to cross-compile code for the ESPRESSObin:

```
$ export ARCH=arm64
$ export CROSS_COMPILE=aarch64-linux-gnu-
```

So, if we try to execute a make command as follows, the system should start compiling the kernel as usual:

```
$ make Image dtbs modules
  CALL scripts/checksyscalls.sh
...
```

Note that you may avoid exporting preceding variables by just specifying them on the following command line:
```
$ make ARCH=arm64 CROSS_COMPILE=aarch64-linux-gnu- \
  Image dtbs modules
```

At this point, kernel sources and the compiling environment are ready.

How to do it...

Let's see how to do it by following these steps:

1. Since this book talks about device drivers, let's start by adding our code under the drivers directory of the Linux sources, and specifically in drivers/misc, where miscellaneous drivers lie. We should place a file named dummy-code.c in drivers/misc with the following contents:

```
/*
 * Dummy code
 */

#include <linux/module.h>

static int __init dummy_code_init(void)
{
    printk(KERN_INFO "dummy-code loaded\n");
    return 0;
}

static void __exit dummy_code_exit(void)
{
    printk(KERN_INFO "dummy-code unloaded\n");
}
```

```
module_init(dummy_code_init);
module_exit(dummy_code_exit);

MODULE_LICENSE("GPL");
MODULE_AUTHOR("Rodolfo Giometti");
MODULE_DESCRIPTION("Dummy code");
```

2. Our new file, `drivers/misc/dummy-code.c`, will have no effect if we don't properly insert it into the kernel configuration and building system. In order to do so, we have to modify the `drivers/misc/Kconfig` and `drivers/misc/Makefile` files as follows. The former file must be changed, as follows:

```
--- a/drivers/misc/Kconfig
+++ b/drivers/misc/Kconfig
@@ -527,4 +527,10 @@ source "drivers/misc/echo/Kconfig"
 source "drivers/misc/cxl/Kconfig"
 source "drivers/misc/ocxl/Kconfig"
 source "drivers/misc/cardreader/Kconfig"
+
+config DUMMY_CODE
+        tristate "Dummy code"
+        default n
+        ---help---
+          This module is just for demonstration purposes.
 endmenu
```

The modifications for the latter are as follows:

```
--- a/drivers/misc/Makefile
+++ b/drivers/misc/Makefile
@@ -58,3 +58,4 @@ obj-$(CONFIG_ASPEED_LPC_SNOOP) += aspeed-lpc-snoop.o
 obj-$(CONFIG_PCI_ENDPOINT_TEST) += pci_endpoint_test.o
 obj-$(CONFIG_OCXL) += ocxl/
 obj-$(CONFIG_MISC_RTSX) += cardreader/
+obj-$(CONFIG_DUMMY_CODE) += dummy-code.o
```

 Note that you can easily add the preceding code and whatever is needed to compile it by just using the `patch` command, as follows, in your main directory of Linux sources:

```
$ patch -p1 < add_custom_code.patch
```

3. Well, if we now use the `make menuconfig` command and we navigate through **Device Drivers** to the bottom of the **Misc devices** menu entries, we should get something as shown in the following screenshot:

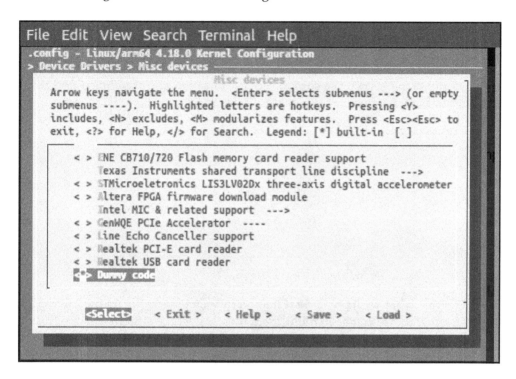

In the preceding screenshot, I've already selected the **Dummy code** entry so that we can see what the final settings should look like.

Note that the **Dummy code** entry must be selected as built-in (the `*` character) and not as module (the `M` character).

Note also that, if we do not execute the `make menuconfig` command and we execute directly the `make Image` command to compile the kernel, then the building system will ask us what to do with the `DUMMY_CODE` setting, as shown in the following. Obviously, we have to answer **yes** by using the `y` character:

```
$ make Image
scripts/kconfig/conf --syncconfig Kconfig
*
* Restart config...
*
*
```

```
* Misc devices
*
Analog Devices Digital Potentiometers (AD525X_DPOT)
[N/m/y/?] n
...
Dummy code (DUMMY_CODE) [N/m/y/?] (NEW) y
```

4. If everything is correctly in place, then we execute the make Image command to recompile the kernel. We should see that our new file is compiled and then added to the kernel Image file, as follows:

```
$ make Image
scripts/kconfig/conf --syncconfig Kconfig
...
  CC drivers/misc/dummy-code.o
  AR drivers/misc/built-in.a
  AR drivers/built-in.a
...
  LD vmlinux
  SORTEX vmlinux
  SYSMAP System.map
  OBJCOPY arch/arm64/boot/Image
```

5. OK, now what we have to do is just replace the Image file on the microSD with the one that has just been rebuilt and then restart the system (see the *How to add the kernel* recipe in Chapter 1, *Installing the Development System*).

How it works...

Now, it's time to see how all of the previous steps work. In future sections, we're going to explain better what this code really does. However, at the moment, we should just notice the following.

In *step 1*, notice the calls to module_init() and module_exit(), kernel-provided C macros, which are used to tell the kernel that, during the boot or shutdown of the system, it must call the functions we provided, named dummy_code_init() and dummy_code_exit(), which, in turn, just print some information messages.

Later on in this chapter, we're going to see in detail what printk() does and what the KERN_INFO macro means but, for now, we should take into account only that they are used to print a message during the boot (or shutdown). For instance, the preceding code instructs the kernel to print out the message **dummy-code loaded** at some time during the boot stage.

In *step 2*, in the `Makefile`, we are simply telling the kernel that if `CONFIG_DUMMY_CODE` has been enabled (that is `CONFIG_DUMMY_CODE=y`), then `dummy-code.c` must be compiled and inserted into the kernel binary (linked), while with the `Kconfig` file, we just add our new module into the kernel configuration system.

In *step 3*, we enable the compilation of our code by using the `make menuconfig` command.

In *step 4*, finally, we recompiled the kernel in order to add our code within it.

In *step 5*, during the boot, we should see the following kernel message:

```
...
loop: module loaded
dummy-code loaded
ahci-mvebu d00e0000.sata: AHCI 0001.0300 32 slots 1 ports 6 Gbps
...
```

See also

- For more information regarding how kernel configuration and its building systems work, we can take a look into the kernel documentation file within kernel sources in the following file: `linux/Documentation/kbuild/kconfig-macro-language.txt`.

Using kernel messages

As already stated, the serial console is very helpful if we need to set up a system from scratch, but it's also very useful if we wish to see kernel messages as soon as they are generated. In order to generate kernel messages, we can use several functions and, in this recipe, we will take a look at them and how to display messages on the serial console or over an SSH connection.

Getting ready

Our ESPRESSObin is the system that generates kernel messages, so we need a connection to it. Through the serial console, these messages are automatically displayed as soon as they arrive, but if we are using an SSH connection, we can still display them by reading specific files, as with the following command:

```
# tail -f /var/log/kern.log
```

However, the serial console deserves a special note: in fact, in our example, the kernel messages will be automatically displayed on the serial console, if, and only if, the leftmost number, among the ones found inside the `/proc/sys/kernel/printk` file, happens to be greater than seven, as shown in the following:

```
# cat /proc/sys/kernel/printk
10      4       1       7
```

These magic numbers have a well-defined meaning; in particular, the first one represents the error message level that the kernel must show on the serial console. These levels are defined in the `linux/include/linux/kern_levels.h` file, as follows:

```
#define KERN_EMERG KERN_SOH "0"     /* system is unusable */
#define KERN_ALERT KERN_SOH "1"     /* action must be taken immediately */
#define KERN_CRIT KERN_SOH "2"      /* critical conditions */
#define KERN_ERR KERN_SOH "3"       /* error conditions */
#define KERN_WARNING KERN_SOH "4"   /* warning conditions */
#define KERN_NOTICE KERN_SOH "5"    /* normal but significant condition */
#define KERN_INFO KERN_SOH "6"      /* informational */
#define KERN_DEBUG KERN_SOH "7"     /* debug-level messages */
```

For example, if the contents of the preceding file were 4, as reported in the following, only messages having the `KERN_EMERG`, `KERN_ALERT`, `KERN_CRIT`, and `KERN_ERR` levels will be automatically displayed on the serial console:

```
# cat /proc/sys/kernel/printk
4       4       1       7
```

In order to allow all messages, a subset of them, or none to be displayed, we have to modify the leftmost number of the `/proc/sys/kernel/printk` file by using the `echo` command, as in the following example in which we act in such a way to completely disable the printing of all kernel messages. This is because no message can have a priority level greater than 0:

```
# echo 0 > /proc/sys/kernel/printk
```

Kernel message priorities start from 0 (the highest) and go up to 7 (the lowest)!

Now that we know how to display kernel messages, we can try to perform some modifications to our kernel code in order to do some experimentation with kernel messages.

How to do it...

In the previous example, we saw that we can use the `printk()` function to generate kernel messages, but there are other functions that we can use in place of `printk()` in order to have more efficient messages and compact and readable code:

1. Use the following macros (as defined in the `include/linux/printk.h` file), which are listed in the following:

```
#define pr_emerg(fmt, ...) \
        printk(KERN_EMERG pr_fmt(fmt), ##__VA_ARGS__)
#define pr_alert(fmt, ...) \
        printk(KERN_ALERT pr_fmt(fmt), ##__VA_ARGS__)
#define pr_crit(fmt, ...) \
        printk(KERN_CRIT pr_fmt(fmt), ##__VA_ARGS__)
#define pr_err(fmt, ...) \
        printk(KERN_ERR pr_fmt(fmt), ##__VA_ARGS__)
#define pr_warning(fmt, ...) \
        printk(KERN_WARNING pr_fmt(fmt), ##__VA_ARGS__)
#define pr_warn pr_warning
#define pr_notice(fmt, ...) \
        printk(KERN_NOTICE pr_fmt(fmt), ##__VA_ARGS__)
#define pr_info(fmt, ...) \
        printk(KERN_INFO pr_fmt(fmt), ##__VA_ARGS__)
```

2. Now, to generate a kernel message, we can do the following: looking at these definitions, we can rewrite our `dummy_code_init()` and `dummy_code_exit()` functions from the previous example into the `dummy-code.c` file, as follows:

```
static int __init dummy_code_init(void)
{
        pr_info("dummy-code loaded\n");
        return 0;
}

static void __exit dummy_code_exit(void)
{
        pr_info("dummy-code unloaded\n");
}
```

How it works...

If we look carefully at the preceding printing functions (`pr_info()` and similar functions), we notice that they also depend on the `pr_fmt(fmt)` parameter, which can be used to add other useful information into our message. For instance, the following definition alters all messages generated by `pr_info()` by adding the current module and calling function names:

```
#define pr_fmt(fmt) "%s:%s: " fmt, KBUILD_MODNAME, __func__
```

 Note that the `pr_fmt()` macro definition must appear at the start of the file, even before the includes, to have any effect.

If we add this line to our `dummy-code.c`, as shown in the following code block, the kernel messages will change as described:

```
/*
 * Dummy code
 */

#define pr_fmt(fmt) "%s:%s: " fmt, KBUILD_MODNAME, __func__
#include <linux/module.h>
```

In fact, when the `pr_info()` function is executed the output message, telling us that the module has been inserted turns in the following form, where we can see the module name and the calling function name followed by the loading message:

```
dummy_code:dummy_code_init: dummy-code loaded
```

There is another set of printing functions but, before starting to talk about them, we need some information that is located in Chapter 3, *Using the Device Tree*, so, for the moment, we'll continue using these functions only.

There's more...

here are many kernel activities, many of them really complex, and frequently, a kernel developer has to work with several messages and not all of them interesting; so, we need to find some ways to filter out interesting messages.

Filtering kernel messages

Suppose we wish to know which serial ports have been detected during boot. We know we can use the `tail` command, but by using it, we can see only the latest messages; on the other hand, we could use the `cat` command to recall all kernel messages since boot, but that's a lot of information! Alternatively, we can use these steps to filter the kernel messages:

1. Here, we use the `grep` command as follows to filter out lines within the `uart` (or UART) string:

```
# cat /var/log/kern.log | grep -i uart
Feb 7 19:33:14 espressobin kernel: [ 0.000000] earlycon:
ar3700_uart0 at MMIO 0x00000000d0012000 (options '')
Feb 7 19:33:14 espressobin kernel: [ 0.000000] bootconsole
[ar3700_uart0] enabled
Feb 7 19:33:14 espressobin kernel: [ 0.000000] Kernel command line:
console=ttyMV0,115200 earlycon=ar3700_uart,0xd0012000 loglevel=0
debug root=/dev/mmcblk0p1 rw rootwait net.ifnames=0 biosdevname=0
Feb 7 19:33:14 espressobin kernel: [ 0.289914] Serial: AMBA PL011
UART driver
Feb 7 19:33:14 espressobin kernel: [ 0.296443] mvebu-uart
d0012000.serial: could not find pctldev for node /soc/internal-
regs@d0000000/pinctrl@13800/uart1-pins, deferring probe
...
```

The preceding output can also be obtained by using the `dmesg` command as follows, which is a tool designed for this purpose:

```
# dmesg | grep -i uart
[ 0.000000] earlycon: ar3700_uart0 at MMIO 0x00000000d0012000
(options '')
[ 0.000000] bootconsole [ar3700_uart0] enabled
[ 0.000000] Kernel command line: console=ttyMV0,115200
earlycon=ar3700_uart,0
xd0012000 loglevel=0 debug root=/dev/mmcblk0p1 rw rootwait
net.ifnames=0 biosdev
name=0
[ 0.289914] Serial: AMBA PL011 UART driver
[ 0.296443] mvebu-uart d0012000.serial: could not find pctldev for
node /soc/
internal-regs@d0000000/pinctrl@13800/uart1-pins, deferring probe
...
```

Note that, while `cat` displays everything in the log file, even very old messages from previous OS executions, `dmesg` displays current OS execution messages only. This is because `dmesg` takes kernel messages directly from the current running system via its ring buffer (that is, the buffer where all messages are stored).

2. On the other hand, if we want to gather information regarding early boot activities, we can still use the `dmesg` command with the `head` command in order to display the first 10 lines of `dmesg` output only:

```
# dmesg | head -10
[ 0.000000] Booting Linux on physical CPU 0x0000000000 [0x410fd034]
[ 0.000000] Linux version 4.18.0-dirty (giometti@giometti-
VirtualBox) (gcc ve
rsion 7.3.0 (Ubuntu/Linaro 7.3.0-27ubuntu1~18.04)) #5 SMP PREEMPT
Sun Jan 27 13:
33:24 CET 2019
[ 0.000000] Machine model: Globalscale Marvell ESPRESSOBin Board
[ 0.000000] earlycon: ar3700_uart0 at MMIO 0x00000000d0012000
(options '')
[ 0.000000] bootconsole [ar3700_uart0] enabled
[ 0.000000] efi: Getting EFI parameters from FDT:
[ 0.000000] efi: UEFI not found.
[ 0.000000] cma: Reserved 32 MiB at 0x000000007e000000
[ 0.000000] NUMA: No NUMA configuration found
[ 0.000000] NUMA: Faking a node at [mem
0x0000000000000000-0x000000007fffffff]
```

3. On the other hand, if we are interested in the last 10 lines, we can use the `tail` command. In fact, we already saw that, to monitor kernel activities, we can use it as shown in the following:

```
# tail -f /var/log/kern.log
```

So, to see the last 10 lines, we can do the following:

```
# dmesg | tail -10
```

4. The same can be done with `dmesg`, too, by adding the `-w` option argument, as shown in the following example:

```
# dmesg -w
```

5. The `dmesg` command can also filter out kernel messages according to their level by using the `-l` (or `--level`) option argument, as follows:

```
# dmesg -l 3
[ 1.687783] advk-pcie d0070000.pcie: link never came up
[ 3.153849] advk-pcie d0070000.pcie: Posted PIO Response Status:
CA, 0xe00 @ 0x0
[ 3.688578] Unable to create integrity sysfs dir: -19
```

The preceding command shows kernel messages having the KERN_ERR level, while the following is the command to show messages having the KERN_WARNING level instead:

```
# dmesg -l 4
[ 3.164121] EINJ: ACPI disabled.
[ 3.197263] cacheinfo: Unable to detect cache hierarchy for CPU 0
[ 4.572660] xenon-sdhci d00d0000.sdhci: Timing issue might occur in
DDR mode
[ 5.316949] systemd-sysv-ge: 10 output lines suppressed due to
ratelimiting
```

6. We can also combine levels in order to have both KERN_ERR and KERN_WARNING:

```
# dmesg -l 3,4
[ 1.687783] advk-pcie d0070000.pcie: link never came up
[ 3.153849] advk-pcie d0070000.pcie: Posted PIO Response Status:
CA, 0xe00 @ 0x0
[ 3.164121] EINJ: ACPI disabled.
[ 3.197263] cacheinfo: Unable to detect cache hierarchy for CPU 0
[ 3.688578] Unable to create integrity sysfs dir: -19
[ 4.572660] xenon-sdhci d00d0000.sdhci: Timing issue might occur in
DDR mode
[ 5.316949] systemd-sysv-ge: 10 output lines suppressed due to
ratelimiting
```

7. In the end, in the event of a lot of noisy messages, we can ask the system to clean the kernel ring buffer (where all kernel messages are stored) by using the following command:

```
# dmesg -C
```

Now, if we use `dmesg` again, we will see newly generated kernel messages only.

See also

- For more information regarding kernel messages management, a good starting point is the `dmesg` man pages, which we can display by executing the `man dmesg` command.

Working with kernel modules

Knowing how to add custom code to the kernel is useful but, when we have to write a new driver, it can be more useful writing our code as a **kernel module**. In fact, by using a module, we can easily modify kernel code and then test it without rebooting the system every time! We simply have to remove and then reinsert the module (after the necessary modifications) in order to test the new version of our code.

In this recipe, we'll take a look at how kernel modules can get compiled even on a directory outside the kernel tree.

Getting ready

To turn our `dummy-code.c` file into a kernel module, we only have to change our kernel settings, allowing the compilation of our example module (by replacing the `*` character with `M` in the kernel configuration menu). However, under some circumstances, it could be more useful having our driver released into a dedicated archive completely separated from kernel sources. Even in this case, no changes are to be done to the existing code, and we will be able to compile `dummy-code.c` inside the kernel source tree, or even outside it!

To build up our first kernel module as external code, we can safely take the preceding `dummy-code.c` file and then put it into a dedicated directory with the following `Makefile`:

```
ifndef KERNEL_DIR
$(error KERNEL_DIR must be set in the command line)
endif
PWD := $(shell pwd)
ARCH ?= arm64
CROSS_COMPILE ?= aarch64-linux-gnu-

# This specifies the kernel module to be compiled
obj-m += dummy-code.o

# The default action
```

```
all: modules

# The main tasks
modules clean:
    make -C $(KERNEL_DIR) \
            ARCH=$(ARCH) \
            CROSS_COMPILE=$(CROSS_COMPILE) \
            SUBDIRS=$(PWD) $@
```

Looking at the preceding code, we see that the KERNEL_DIR variable must be supplied on the command line pointing to the path to ESPRESSObin's previously compiled kernel sources, while the ARCH and CROSS_COMPILE variables are not mandatory since Makefile specifies them (however, supplying them on the command line will take precedence).

Also, we should verify that the insmod and rmmod commands are available in our ESPRESSObin, as follows:

```
# insmod -h
Usage:
        insmod [options] filename [args]
Options:
        -V, --version show version
        -h, --help show this help
```

If they are not present, then they can be installed by adding the kmod package with the usual apt install kmod command.

How to do it...

Let's see how to do it by following these steps:

1. After placing the dummy-code.c and Makefile files in our current working directory on the host PC, it should look like the following when using the ls command, as follows:

   ```
   $ ls
   dummy-code.c  Makefile
   ```

2. Then, we can compile our module by using the following command:

   ```
   $ make KERNEL_DIR=../../../linux/
   make -C ../../../linux/ \
    ARCH=arm64 \
    CROSS_COMPILE=aarch64-linux-gnu- \
    SUBDIRS=/home/giometti/Projects/lddc/github/chapter_2/module
   ```

```
modules
make[1]: Entering directory '/home/giometti/Projects/ldddc/linux'
 CC [M]
/home/giometti/Projects/ldddc/github/chapter_2/module/dummy-code.o
 Building modules, stage 2.
 MODPOST 1 modules
 CC /home/giometti/Projects/ldddc/github/chapter_2/module/dummy-
code.mod.o
 LD [M]
/home/giometti/Projects/ldddc/github/chapter_2/module/dummy-code.ko
make[1]: Leaving directory '/home/giometti/Projects/ldddc/linux'
```

As we can see, now we have several files in the current working directory, and one of them is named `dummy-code.ko`; this is our kernel module ready to be transferred to the ESPRESSObin!

3. Once the module has been moved into the target system (for example, by using the `scp` command), we can load it by using the `insmod` utility, as follows:

   # insmod dummy-code.ko

4. Now, by using the `lsmod` command, we can ask the system to display all loaded modules. On my ESPRESSObin, I only have the `dummy-code.ko` module, so my output is as shown:

   ```
   # lsmod
   Module          Size   Used by
   dummy_code      16384  0
   ```

Note that the `.ko` postfix has been removed by the kernel module name, as the – character is replaced by _.

5. Then, we can remove our module from the kernel by using the `rmmod` command, as follows:

   # rmmod dummy_code

In case you get the following error, please verify you're running the correct `Image` file we got in Chapter 1, *Installing the Development System*
```
rmmod: ERROR: ../libkmod/libkmod.c:514
lookup_builtin_file() could not open builtin file
'/lib/modules/4.18.0-dirty/modules.builtin.bin'
```

How it works...

The `insmod` command just takes our module and inserts it into the kernel; after that, it executes the `module_init()` function.

During module insertion, if we're over an SSH connection, we'll see nothing on the Terminal and we have to use `dmesg` to see kernel messages (or `tail` on the `/var/log/kern.log` file, as discussed previously); otherwise, on the serial console, after inserting the module, we should see something like the following:

```
dummy_code: loading out-of-tree module taints kernel.
dummy_code:dummy_code_init: dummy-code loaded
```

 Note that the message, **loading out-of-tree module taints kernel,** is just a warning and can be safely ignored for our purposes. See `https://www.kernel.org/doc/html/v4.15/admin-guide/tainted-kernels.html` for further information about tainted kernels.

The `rmmod` command does the inverse steps of `insmod`, that is, it executes the `module_exit()` function and then removes the module from the kernel.

See also

- For more information regarding the **modutils**, their man pages are a good starting point (the commands are: `man insmod`, `man rmmod`, and `man modinfo`); also, we can take a look at the `modprobe` command by reading its man pages (`man modprobe`).

Using module parameters

During kernel module development, it can be very useful having some way to dynamically set some variables during module insertion and not only at compile time. In Linux, this can be done by using the kernel module's parameters, which allow arguments to be passed to a module by specifying them on the command line of the `insmod` command.

Getting ready

In order to show an example, let's consider a situation where we have a new module information file, `module_par.c` (this file is also in our GitHub repository).

How to do it...

Let's see how to do it by following these steps:

1. First, let's define our module parameters, as follows:

```
static int var = 0x3f;
module_param(var, int, S_IRUSR | S_IWUSR);
MODULE_PARM_DESC(var, "an integer value");

static char *str = "default string";
module_param(str, charp, S_IRUSR | S_IWUSR);
MODULE_PARM_DESC(str, "a string value");

#define ARR_SIZE 8
static int arr[ARR_SIZE];
static int arr_count;
module_param_array(arr, int, &arr_count, S_IRUSR | S_IWUSR);
MODULE_PARM_DESC(arr, "an array of " __stringify(ARR_SIZE) "
values");
```

2. Then, we can use the following `init` and `exit` functions:

```
static int __init module_par_init(void)
{
    int i;

    pr_info("loaded\n");
    pr_info("var = 0x%02x\n", var);
    pr_info("str = \"%s\"\n", str);
    pr_info("arr = ");
    for (i = 0; i < ARR_SIZE; i++)
        pr_cont("%d ", arr[i]);
    pr_cont("\n");

    return 0;
}

static void __exit module_par_exit(void)
{
    pr_info("unloaded\n");
```

```
}

module_init(module_par_init);
module_exit(module_par_exit);
```

3. Finally, at the end, we can add module description macros as usual:

```
MODULE_LICENSE("GPL");
MODULE_AUTHOR("Rodolfo Giometti");
MODULE_DESCRIPTION("Module with parameters");
MODULE_VERSION("0.1");
```

How it works...

Once compiled as before, a new file, `module_par.ko`, should be ready to be loaded into our ESPRESSObin. However, before doing it, let's use the `modinfo` utility on it, as follows:

```
# modinfo module_par.ko
filename:     /root/module_par.ko
version:      0.1
description:  Module with parameters
author:       Rodolfo Giometti
license:      GPL
srcversion:   21315B65C307ABE9769814F
depends:
name:         module_par
vermagic:     4.18.0 SMP preempt mod_unload aarch64
parm:         var:an integer value (int)
parm:         str:a string value (charp)
parm:         arr:an array of 8 values (array of int)
```

 The `modinfo` command is also included in the `kmod` package as `insmod`.

As we can see in the last three lines (all prefixed by the `parm:` string), we have a list of module's parameters defined in the code by the `module_param()` and `module_param_array()` macros and described with `MODULE_PARM_DESC()`.

Now, if we simply insert the module as before, we get default values, as shown in the following code block:

```
# insmod module_par.ko
[ 6021.345064] module_par:module_par_init: loaded
```

```
[ 6021.347028] module_par:module_par_init: var = 0x3f
[ 6021.351810] module_par:module_par_init: str = "default string"
[ 6021.357904] module_par:module_par_init: arr = 0 0 0 0 0 0 0 0
```

But if we use the next command line, we force new values:

```
# insmod module_par.ko var=0x01 str=\"new value\" arr='1,2,3'
[ 6074.175964] module_par:module_par_init: loaded
[ 6074.177915] module_par:module_par_init: var = 0x01
[ 6074.184932] module_par:module_par_init: str = "new value"
[ 6074.189765] module_par:module_par_init: arr = 1 2 3 0 0 0 0 0
```

Don't forget to remove the `module_par` module by using the `rmmod` `module_par` command before trying to reload it with new values!

As a final note, let me suggest taking a closer look at the following module parameter definition:

```
static int var = 0x3f;
module_param(var, int, S_IRUSR | S_IWUSR);
MODULE_PARM_DESC(var, "an integer value");
```

First, we have the declaration of the variable that represents the parameter, then we have the real module parameter definition (where we specify the type and the file access permissions), and then we have the description.

The `modinfo` command is able to display all of the preceding information, except the file access permissions, which refer to the file related to this parameter within the sysfs filesystem! In fact, if we take a look at the `/sys/module/module_par/parameters/` directory, we get the following:

```
# ls -l /sys/module/module_par/parameters/
total 0
-rw------- 1 root root 4096 Feb 1 12:46 arr
-rw------- 1 root root 4096 Feb 1 12:46 str
-rw------- 1 root root 4096 Feb 1 12:46 var
```

Now, it should be clear what parameters `S_IRUSR` and `S_IWUSR` means; they allow the module user (that is, the root user) to write into these files and then read from them the corresponding parameters.

Defines `S_IRUSR` and related function are defined in the following file: `linux/include/uapi/linux/stat.h`.

See also

- Regarding kernel modules in general and about how to export kernel symbols, you can take a look at *The Linux Kernel Module Programming Guide,* available online at `https://www.tldp.org/LDP/lkmpg/2.6/html/index.html`.

3
Working with Char Drivers

A device driver is special code (running in kernel space) that interfaces a physical device to the system and exports it to the user space processes using a well-defined API, that is, by implementing some **system calls** on a **special file**. This is due to the fact that, in a Unix-like OS, **everything is a file** and physical devices are represented as special files (usually placed in the /dev directory), each one connected to a particular device (so, for instance, the keyboard can be a file named /dev/input0, a serial port can be a file named /dev/ttyS1, and a real-time clock can be /dev/rtc2).

We can expect that network devices belong to a particular set of devices not respecting this rule because we have no /dev/eth0 file for the eth0 interface. This is true, since network devices are the only devices class that doesn't respect this rule because network-related applications don't care about individual network interfaces; they work at a higher level by referring sockets instead. That's why Linux doesn't provide direct access to network devices, as for other devices classes.

Looking at the next diagram, we see that the kernel space is used to abstract hardware to user space, so that every process uses the same interface to get access to peripherals, and this interface is composed by a set of system calls:

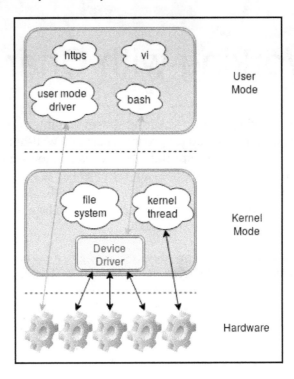

The diagram also shows that it is possible to get access to peripherals not only by using device drivers but also by using another interface such as **sysfs** or by implementing a user space driver.

Since our peripherals are just (special) files, our drivers should implement the system calls we need to manipulate these files and especially the ones useful to exchange data. For example, we need `open()` and `close()` system calls to start and stop the communication with the peripheral and `read()` and `write()` system calls to exchange data with it.

The main difference between a normal C function and a system call is just the fact that the latter is mainly executed into the kernel, while a function executes into the user space only. For example, `printf()` is a function, while `write()` is a system call. The latter (except for the prologue and epilogue part of a C function) executes in the kernel space, while the former executes predominantly in the user space even if, at the and, it calls `write()` to actually write its data to the output stream (this is because all input/output data flows must pass through the kernel anyway).

For more information check this book
out: `https://prod.packtpub.com/hardware-and-creative/gnulinux-rapid-embedded-pr ogramming`

Well, this chapter will show us how to implement at least the `open()`, `close()`, `read()`, and `write()` system calls in order to introduce device drivers programming and the first steps into char drivers development.

Now it's time to write our first device driver! In this chapter, we will start with a very simple character (or char) driver in order to cover the following recipes:

- Creating the simplest char driver
- Exchanging data with a char driver
- Using the "Everything Is a File" abstraction

Technical requirements

Throughout this chapter, we'll need whatever we used in `Chapter 1`, *Installing the Development System*, and `Chapter 2`, *A Peek Inside the Kernel*, so please refer to them for cross-compilation, kernel modules loading and management, and so on.

For more information on this chapter please read the *Appendix*.

The code and other files used in this chapter can be downloaded from GitHub at `https:// github.com/giometti/linux_device_driver_development_cookbook/tree/master/ chapter_03`.

Creating the simplest char driver

In the Linux kernel, three major device types exist—char device, block device, and net device. And of course, we have three major device driver types; that is, char, block, and net drivers. In this chapter, we're taking a look at a char (or character) device, which is a kind of peripheral that can be accessed as a stream of bytes, such as a serial port, audio device, and so on. However, in this recipe, we're going to present a really basic char driver, which simply registers itself and does nothing more than this. Even if it may seem useless, we will discover that this step really introduces plenty of new concepts!

Actually, it could be possible to exchange data between peripherals and user space without a char, block, or net driver but by simply using some mechanism offered by the **sysfs**, but this is a special case and it is generally used only for very simple devices that have to exchange simple data types.

Getting ready

To realize our first char driver, we need the module presented in the previous chapter. This is because using kernel modules is the simplest method we have to inject code into kernel space. Of course, we can decide to compile our driver as built in to the kernel but, in this manner, we have to fully recompile the kernel and reboot our system each time we have to modify the code (it's a possibility but definitely not the best!).

Just a note before carrying on: to provide a clearer explanation regarding how a char driver works and to present a really simple example, I decided to use the legacy way to register a char driver into the kernel. There's nothing to be concerned about, since this mode of operation is perfectly legal and still supported and, in any case, in the *Using a device tree to describe a character driver* recipe, in Chapter 4, *Using the Device Tree*, I'm going to present the currently advised way of registering char drivers.

How to do it...

Let's look into the `chrdev_legacy.c` file from GitHub sources. We have our very first driver, so let's start and examine it in detail:

1. First of all, let's take a look at the beginning of the file:

```
#define pr_fmt(fmt) "%s:%s: " fmt, KBUILD_MODNAME, __func__
#include <linux/kernel.h>
#include <linux/module.h>
#include <linux/fs.h>

/* Device major umber */
static int major;
```

2. At the end of `chrdev_legacy.c`, check the following code where the module's `init()` function is defined as below:

```
static int __init chrdev_init(void)
{
```

```
    int ret;

    ret = register_chrdev(0, "chrdev", &chrdev_fops);
    if (ret < 0) {
        pr_err("unable to register char device! Error %d\n", ret);
        return ret;
    }
    major = ret;
    pr_info("got major %d\n", major);

    return 0;
}
```

And the module's `exit()` function looks like the following:

```
static void __exit chrdev_exit(void)
{
    unregister_chrdev(major, "chrdev");
}


module_init(chrdev_init);
module_exit(chrdev_exit);
```

3. If the `major` number is the driver reference into the kernel from the user space, the **file operations** structure (referenced by `chrdev_fops`) represents the only allowed system calls that we can execute on our driver, and they are defined as follows:

```
static struct file_operations chrdev_fops = {
    .owner    = THIS_MODULE,
    .read     = chrdev_read,
    .write    = chrdev_write,
    .open     = chrdev_open,
    .release  = chrdev_release
};
```

4. Methods are then basically implemented as follows. Here are the `read()` and `write()` methods:

```
static ssize_t chrdev_read(struct file *filp,
                            char __user *buf, size_t count,
                            loff_t *ppos)
{
    pr_info("return EOF\n");

    return 0;
}
```

```
static ssize_t chrdev_write(struct file *filp,
                            const char __user *buf, size_t count,
                            loff_t *ppos)
{
    pr_info("got %ld bytes\n", count);

    return count;
}
```

While here are the `open()` and `release()` (aka the `close()`) methods:

```
static int chrdev_open(struct inode *inode, struct file *filp)
{
    pr_info("chrdev opened\n");

    return 0;
}

static int chrdev_release(struct inode *inode, struct file *filp)
{
    pr_info("chrdev released\n");

    return 0;
}
```

5. To compile the code, we can do it the usual way on the host machine, as follows:

```
$ make KERNEL_DIR=../../../linux/
make -C ../../../linux/ \
            ARCH=arm64 \
            CROSS_COMPILE=aarch64-linux-gnu- \
SUBDIRS=/home/giometti/Projects/ldddc/github/chapter_3/chrdev_legac
y modules
make[1]: Entering directory '/home/giometti/Projects/ldddc/linux'
  CC [M]
/home/giometti/Projects/ldddc/github/chapter_3/chrdev_legacy/chrdev
_legacy.o
  Building modules, stage 2.
  MODPOST 1 modules
  CC
/home/giometti/Projects/ldddc/github/chapter_3/chrdev_legacy/chrdev
_legacy.mod.o
  LD [M]
/home/giometti/Projects/ldddc/github/chapter_3/chrdev_legacy/chrdev
_legacy.ko
make[1]: Leaving directory '/home/giometti/Projects/ldddc/linux'
```

6. Then, to test our driver, we can load it in our target system (again we can use the `scp` command to load the module file into the ESPRESSObin):

```
# insmod chrdev_legacy.ko
chrdev_legacy: loading out-of-tree module taints kernel.
chrdev_legacy:chrdev_init: got major 239
```

OK. The driver has been loaded and our major number is 239.

7. As a final note, let me suggest you take a look into the `/proc/devices` file on the ESPRESSObin. This special file is generated on the fly when someone reads it and it holds all character (and block) drivers registered into the system; that's why we should find something as follows if we filter it with the `grep` command:

```
# grep chrdev /proc/devices
239 chrdev
```

Of course, your major number can be a different number! There's nothing strange about that; just rewrite the next commands according to the number you get.

8. To effectively execute some system calls on our driver, we can use the program stored in the `chrdev_test.c` file (still from GitHub sources); the beginning of its `main()` function looks like the following:

```c
int main(int argc, char *argv[])
{
    int fd;
    char buf[] = "DUMMY DATA";
    int n, c;
    int ret;

    if (argc < 2) {
        fprintf(stderr, "usage: %s <dev>\n", argv[0]);
        exit(EXIT_FAILURE);
    }

    ret = open(argv[1], O_RDWR);
    if (ret < 0) {
        perror("open");
        exit(EXIT_FAILURE);
    }
    printf("file %s opened\n", argv[1]);
    fd = ret;
```

9. First of all, we need to open the file device and then get a file descriptor; this can be done by using the `open()` system call.

10. Then, the `main()` function continues, as follow by writing data in the device:

```
for (c = 0; c < sizeof(buf); c += n) {
    ret = write(fd, buf + c, sizeof(buf) - c);
    if (ret < 0) {
        perror("write");
        exit(EXIT_FAILURE);
    }
    n = ret;

    printf("wrote %d bytes into file %s\n", n, argv[1]);
    dump("data written are: ", buf + c, n);
}
```

And the by reading just written data from it:

```
for (c = 0; c < sizeof(buf); c += n) {
    ret = read(fd, buf, sizeof(buf));
    if (ret == 0) {
        printf("read EOF\n");
        break;
    } else if (ret < 0) {
        perror("read");
        exit(EXIT_FAILURE);
    }
    n = ret;

    printf("read %d bytes from file %s\n", n, argv[1]);
    dump("data read are: ", buf, n);
}
```

After the device opens, our program performs `write()` followed by a `read()` system call.

We should notice that I call `read()` and `write()` system calls inside a `for()` loop; the reason behind this implementation will be clearer in the following recipe, *Exchanging data with a char driver,* where we're going to see how these system calls actually work.

11. Finally, `main()` can close the file device and then exit:

```
close(fd);

return 0;
}
```

In this manner, we can test the system calls we implemented earlier.

How it works...

In *step 1*, As you can see, it's very similar to the kernel module we presented in the previous chapter, even if there are some new `include` files. However, the most important new entry is the `major` variable and, in order to understand what it is useful for, we should directly go to the end of the file, where we find the real char driver registration.

In step 2, Again, we have the `module_init()` and `module_exit()` functions and macros such as `MODULE_LICENSE()` (see `Chapter 2`, *A Peek Inside the Kernel*, the Working with kernel modules recipe); however, what is really important here is what the `chrdev_init()` and `chrdev_exit()` functions effectively do. In fact, `chrdev_init()` calls the `register_chrdev()` function, which, in turn, is the one that registers a new char driver into the system, labeling it as `chrdev` and using the provided `chrdev_fops` as file operations, while storing the return value into the major variable.

We should take into account this fact because, in case no errors were returned, `major` is the main reference of our new driver in the system! In fact, the kernel distinguishes one char driver from another by just using its **major number** (that's why we save it and then we use it in the `chrdev_exit()` function as a parameter of `unregister_chrdev()`).

In *step 3*, Each field then points to a well-defined function, which, in turn, implements the system call body. The only non-function field here is `owner`, which is just used to point to the module's owner and it's not related to the driver but to the kernel modules management system only.

In *step 4*, Through the means of the preceding code our char driver implements four system calls by using four methods: `open()`, `close()` (called as `release()`), `read()`, and `write()`, which are a very minimal (and simple) system calls set we can define into a char driver.

Note that, at this time, all methods simply do nothing! When we issue a `read()` system call on our driver, the `chrdev_read()` method is properly called inside our driver in kernel space (see the next section in order to understand how to exchange data with the user space).

> I use both **function** and **method** names interchangeably because all of these functions can be seen as methods in object programming, where the same function names specialize into different steps according to the object they are applied to.
> With drivers it is the same: for example, they all have a `read()` method, but this method's behavior changes according to the object (or peripheral) it is applied to.

In *step 6*, Again, the `loading out-of-tree module taints kernel` message is just a warning and can be safely ignored; please note, however, that the module filename is `chrdev_legacy.ko` while the driver's name is just `chrdev`.

There's more...

We can verify how our new driver works, so let's compile the program stored in the `chrdev_test.c` file we saw earlier. To do so, we can use the next command on the ESPRESSObin:

```
# make CFLAGS="-Wall -O2" chrdev_test
cc -Wall -O2 chrdev_test.c -o chrdev_test
```

> If not yet installed, both the `make` and `gcc` commands can be easily installed into your ESPRESSObin, just using the usual `apt` command `apt install make gcc` (after the ESPRESSObin has been connected to the internet!).

Now we can try it by executing it:

```
# ./chrdev_test
usage: ./chrdev_test <dev>
```

Yes! Which is the filename we have to use? We always said that our devices are files in a Unix OS, but which file? Well, to generate this file—that is, the file which represents our driver—we must use the `mknod` command, as follows:

```
# mknod chrdev c 239 0
```

For further information regarding the `mknod` command, you can take a look at its man pages by using the command line `man mknod`.

 Usually `mknod` created files are located in the `/dev` directory; however, they can be created wherever we wish and this is just an example to show how the mechanism works.

The preceding command creates a file named `chrdev` in the current directory, which is a special file of the type **character** (or **unbuffered**), having as a major number `239` (which is, of course, the major number of our driver as seen in *step 1*) and as a minor number `0`.

 At this time, we still haven't introduced minor numbers however, you should consider them as just a simple extra parameter that the kernel simply passes to the driver without changing it. It's the driver itself that knows how to manage the minor number.

In fact, if we examine it by using the `ls` command, we see the following:

```
# ls -l chrdev
crw-r--r-- 1 root root 239, 0 Feb 7 14:30 chrdev
```

Here, the initial character, `c`, points out that this `chrdev` file is not a usual file (which is represented by a – character) but it's a character device file instead.

OK. Now that we have our file *connected* to our driver, let's try our testing program on it.

We get the following output on the Terminal:

```
# ./chrdev_test chrdev
file chrdev opened
wrote 11 bytes into file chrdev
data written are: 44 55 4d 4d 59 20 44 41 54 41 00
read EOF
```

However, on the serial console (or via `dmesg`), we get the following:

```
chrdev_legacy:chrdev_open: chrdev opened
chrdev_legacy:chrdev_write: got 11 bytes
chrdev_legacy:chrdev_read: return EOF
chrdev_legacy:chrdev_release: chrdev released
```

This is exactly what we expected! As stated in *step 4* here we can verify that all system calls `open()`, `close()` (called as `release()`), `read()`, and `write()`, we defined in the driver, are effectively executed by the call of the corresponding method.

 Note that, if you execute the `chrdev_test` program directly on the serial console, all of the preceding messages will overlap each other and you may not easily recognize them! So, let me suggest you use a SSH connection to execute the test.

See also

- For further information regarding how to register character devices by using legacy functions, a good starting point are some old (but still existing) pages of *The Linux Kernel Module Programming Guide* at `https://www.tldp.org/LDP/lkmpg/2.6/html/x569.html`

Exchanging data with a char driver

In this recipe we'll see how to read and write data to and from a driver according to `read()` and `write()` system calls behaviors.

Getting ready

To modify our first char driver in order to allow it to exchange data between user space we can still work on the module used in the previous recipe.

How to do it...

In order to exchange data with our new driver, we need to modify the `read()` and `write()` methods according to what we said earlier, and we have to add a data buffer where exchanged data can be stored:

1. So, let's modify our file, `chrdev_legacy.c`, as follows, in order to include the `linux/uaccess.h` file and to define our internal buffer:

```
#define pr_fmt(fmt) "%s:%s: " fmt, KBUILD_MODNAME, __func__
#include <linux/kernel.h>
#include <linux/module.h>
```

```
#include <linux/fs.h>
#include <linux/uaccess.h>

/* Device major umber */
static int major;

/* Device data */
#define BUF_LEN 300
static char chrdev_buf[BUF_LEN];
```

2. Then, the `chrdev_read()` method should be modified, as follows:

```
static ssize_t chrdev_read(struct file *filp,
                char __user *buf, size_t count, loff_t *ppos)
{
    int ret;

    pr_info("should read %ld bytes (*ppos=%lld)\n",
                                    count, *ppos);

    /* Check for end-of-buffer */
    if (*ppos + count >= BUF_LEN)
        count = BUF_LEN - *ppos;

    /* Return data to the user space */
    ret = copy_to_user(buf, chrdev_buf + *ppos, count);
    if (ret < 0)
        return -EFAULT;

    *ppos += count;
    pr_info("return %ld bytes (*ppos=%lld)\n", count, *ppos);

    return count;
}
```

All of the preceding modifications and the next ones in this section can be easily applied by using the `modify_read_write_to_chrdev_legacy.patch` patch file from GitHub sources, issuing the following command line in the same directory where the `chrdev_legacy.c` file is located:
`$ patch -p3 < modify_read_write_to_chrdev_legacy.patch`

3. We can repeat this for the `chrdev_write()` method:

```
static ssize_t chrdev_write(struct file *filp,
                const char __user *buf, size_t count, loff_t *ppos)
```

```
    {
        int ret;

        pr_info("should write %ld bytes (*ppos=%lld)\n", count, *ppos);

        /* Check for end-of-buffer */
        if (*ppos + count >= BUF_LEN)
            count = BUF_LEN - *ppos;

        /* Get data from the user space */
        ret = copy_from_user(chrdev_buf + *ppos, buf, count);
        if (ret < 0)
            return -EFAULT;

        *ppos += count;
        pr_info("got %ld bytes (*ppos=%lld)\n", count, *ppos);

        return count;
    }
```

How it works...

In *step 2*, with the preceding modifications to our `chrdev_read()` method, now we will copy the supplied data from the user space by using the `copy_to_user()` function in the driver's internal buffer while moving the `ppos` pointer accordingly and then returning how much data has been read (or error).

Note that `copy_from/to_user()` functions return zero on success or non-zero to indicate the number of bytes that weren't transferred, so, here, we should account for this situation (even if rare) and properly update `count`, subtracting the number of bytes not transferred (if any), in order to correctly update `ppos` and return a correct count value to user space. However, to keep the example as simple as possible, we simply prefer return an error condition.

Note also that, in case `*ppos + count` points beyond the buffer end, `count` is recomputed accordingly and the function will return a value representing the number of transferred bytes, which is smaller than the original `count` value provided in input (which represented the size of the provided destination user buffer and so the maximum length of data allowed for transfer).

In *step 3*, we can consider the same note as before regarding the `copy_to_user()` return value. However, additionally on `copy_from_user()`, if some data could not be copied, this function will pad the copied data to the requested size using zero bytes.

As we can see, this function is very similar to the preceding one, even if it implements the opposite data flow.

There's more...

After the modifications are in place and the new driver version has been recompiled and correctly loaded into ESPRESSObin's kernel, we can again execute our testing program, chrdev_test. We should get the following output:

```
# ./chrdev_test chrdev
file chrdev opened
wrote 11 bytes into file chrdev
data written are: 44 55 4d 4d 59 20 44 41 54 41 00
read 11 bytes from file chrdev
data read are: 00 00 00 00 00 00 00 00 00 00 00
```

From the serial console, we should see something as similar to the following:

```
chrdev_legacy:chrdev_open: chrdev opened
chrdev_legacy:chrdev_write: should write 11 bytes (*ppos=0)
chrdev_legacy:chrdev_write: got 11 bytes (*ppos=11)
chrdev_legacy:chrdev_read: should read 11 bytes (*ppos=11)
chrdev_legacy:chrdev_read: return 11 bytes (*ppos=22)
chrdev_legacy:chrdev_release: chrdev released
```

OK. We got exactly what we expected! In fact, from kernel messages, we can see the calling of chrdev_open() and then what happens when chrdev_write() and chrdev_read() are called: 11 bytes are transferred and the ppos pointer is moved as we expected. Then, chrdev_release() is called and the file definitely closed.

Now a question: what happens if we call the preceding command again?

Well, we should expect exactly the same output; in fact, each time the file is opened, ppos is re-positioned at the file beginning (that is, to 0) and we continue reading and writing at the same positions.

The following is the output of this second execution:

```
# ./chrdev_test chrdev
file chrdev opened
wrote 11 bytes into file chrdev
data written are: 44 55 4d 4d 59 20 44 41 54 41 00
read 11 bytes from file chrdev
data read are: 00 00 00 00 00 00 00 00 00 00 00
```

Additionally, the following are the related kernel messages:

```
chrdev_legacy:chrdev_open: chrdev opened
chrdev_legacy:chrdev_write: should write 11 bytes (*ppos=0)
chrdev_legacy:chrdev_write: got 11 bytes (*ppos=11)
chrdev_legacy:chrdev_read: should read 11 bytes (*ppos=11)
chrdev_legacy:chrdev_read: return 11 bytes (*ppos=22)
chrdev_legacy:chrdev_release: chrdev released
```

If we wish to read the data just written data, we can modify the `chrdev_test` program in such a way it will close and then reopen the file after calling `write()`:

```
...
        printf("wrote %d bytes into file %s\n", n, argv[1]);
        dump("data written are: ", buf, n);
    }

    close(fd);

    ret = open(argv[1], O_RDWR);
    if (ret < 0) {
        perror("open");
        exit(EXIT_FAILURE);
    }
    printf("file %s reopened\n", argv[1]);
    fd = ret;

    for (c = 0; c < sizeof(buf); c += n) {
        ret = read(fd, buf, sizeof(buf));
...
```

Note that all of these modifications are stored in the `modify_close_open_to_chrdev_test.patch` patch file from GitHub sources and it can be applied by using the following command where the `chrdev_test.c` file is located:

`$ patch -p2 < modify_close_open_to_chrdev_test.patch`

Now, if we try to execute `chrdev_test` again, we should get the following output:

```
# ./chrdev_test chrdev
file chrdev opened
wrote 11 bytes into file chrdev
data written are: 44 55 4d 4d 59 20 44 41 54 41 00
file chrdev reopened
read 11 bytes from file chrdev
data read are: 44 55 4d 4d 59 20 44 41 54 41 00
```

Perfect! Now, we read exactly what we wrote and, from the kernel space, we get the following messages:

```
chrdev_legacy:chrdev_open: chrdev opened
chrdev_legacy:chrdev_write: should write 11 bytes (*ppos=0)
chrdev_legacy:chrdev_write: got 11 bytes (*ppos=11)
chrdev_legacy:chrdev_release: chrdev released
chrdev_legacy:chrdev_open: chrdev opened
chrdev_legacy:chrdev_read: should read 11 bytes (*ppos=0)
chrdev_legacy:chrdev_read: return 11 bytes (*ppos=11)
chrdev_legacy:chrdev_release: chrdev released
```

Now, we can see perfectly what happens to `ppos`, and how the `chrdev_read()` and `chrdev_write()` methods work in order to exchange data with the user space.

See also

- For further information regarding `read()` and `write()` system calls, the reader can start reading the related man pages, which can be obtained with the usual commands: `man 2 read` and `man 2 write`.

> Note that, this time, we have to specify section 2 of the man pages (system-calls); otherwise, we will get information straight from section 1 (executable programs).

- Alternatively, regarding the `copy_from_user()` and `copy_to_user()` functions, the reader can take a look at *The Linux Kernel API* at `https://www.kernel.org/doc/htmldocs/kernel-api/API---copy-from-user.html` and `https://www.kernel.org/doc/htmldocs/kernel-api/API---copy-to-user.html`.

Using the "Everything Is a File" abstraction

When we introduced device drivers we said that they lay under the Unix file abstraction; that is, in a Unix-like OS, everything is a file. Now, it's time to verify it, so let's see what happens if we try to execute some file-related utility programs against our new driver.

Thanks to our latest modifications to the `chrdev_legacy.c` file, our driver simulates a file 300 bytes long (see the `chrdev_buf[BUF_LEN]` buffer where `BUF_LEN` is set to `300`), where we're able to execute `read()` and `write()` system calls on it, just as we do on a *normal* file.

However, we may still have some doubts, so let's consider standard `cat` or `dd` commands, as we know they are utilities useful to manipulate files content. For example, in the man pages of the `cat` command, we can read the following definition:

```
NAME
        cat - concatenate files and print on the standard output

SYNOPSIS
        cat [OPTION]... [FILE]...

DESCRIPTION
        Concatenate FILE(s) to standard output.
```

And, for `dd`, we have the following definition:

```
NAME
        dd - convert and copy a file

SYNOPSIS
        dd [OPERAND]...
        dd OPTION

DESCRIPTION
        Copy a file, converting and formatting according to the operands.
```

We don't see any reference to device drivers, only to files, so if our driver works like a file, we should be able to use these commands on it!

Getting ready

To check how the "Everything Is a File" abstraction we can still use our new character driver which can be managed as it was a regular file. So let's be sure that the driver is correctly loaded in the kernel and move to the next section.

How to do it...

Let's see how to do it by following these steps:

1. First of all, we can try to clear the driver's buffer by writing into it all 0 characters with the following command:

```
# dd if=/dev/zero bs=100 count=3 of=chrdev
3+0 records in
3+0 records out
300 bytes copied, 0.0524863 s, 5.7 kB/s
```

2. Now, we can read just written data by using the cat command, as follows:

```
# cat chrdev | tr '\000' '0'
0000000000000000000000000000000000000000000000000000000000000000000000000000
0000000000000000000000000000000000000000000000000000000000000000000000000000
0000000000000000000000000000000000000000000000000000000000000000000000000000
0000000000000000000000000000000000000000000000000000000000000000000000000000
00000000000000000000000000000000000
```

Perfect! As we can see, we erased the driver's internal buffer, as expected.

The reader should notice that we use the tr command in order to translate data bytes 0 to the printable character 0; otherwise, we'll see garbage (or most probably nothing).
See the tr man page with man tr for further information about its usage.

3. Now, we can try to move a normal file data into our char device; for instance, if we consider the /etc/passwd file, we should see something as follows:

```
# ls -lh /etc/passwd
-rw-r--r-- 1 root root 1.3K Jan 10 14:16 /etc/passwd
```

This file is larger than 300 bytes but we can still try to move it into our char driver with the next command line:

```
# cat /etc/passwd > chrdev
cat: write error: No space left on device
```

We get an error message, as expected, due to the fact our file cannot hold more than 300 bytes. However, the really interesting things to see are in the kernel:

```
chrdev_legacy:chrdev_open: chrdev opened
chrdev_legacy:chrdev_write: should write 1285 bytes (*ppos=0)
chrdev_legacy:chrdev_write: got 300 bytes (*ppos=300)
chrdev_legacy:chrdev_write: should write 985 bytes (*ppos=300)
```

```
chrdev_legacy:chrdev_write: got 0 bytes (*ppos=300)
chrdev_legacy:chrdev_release: chrdev released
```

4. Even if we get an error, from the preceding kernel messages, we see that some data has been actually written in our char driver, so we can try to find a specific line in it with the next command line using the `grep` command:

```
# grep root chrdev
root:x:0:0:root:/root:/bin/bash
```

For further information about `grep`, just see its man page with `man grep`.

Since the line referring to the root user is one of the first lines in `/etc/passwd`, it has definitely been copied into the char driver, and then we get it as expected. For completeness, below are reported the relative kernel messages where we can see all system calls that `grep` does on our driver:

```
chrdev_legacy:chrdev_open: chrdev opened
chrdev_legacy:chrdev_read: should read 32768 bytes (*ppos=0)
chrdev_legacy:chrdev_read: return 300 bytes (*ppos=300)
chrdev_legacy:chrdev_read: should read 32768 bytes (*ppos=300)
chrdev_legacy:chrdev_read: return 0 bytes (*ppos=300)
chrdev_legacy:chrdev_release: chrdev released
```

How it works...

With the preceding `dd` command, we generate three blocks that are 100 bytes long and that we pass to the `write()` system calls; in fact, if we take a look at kernel messages, we explicitly see what happens:

```
chrdev_legacy:chrdev_open: chrdev opened
chrdev_legacy:chrdev_write: should write 100 bytes (*ppos=0)
chrdev_legacy:chrdev_write: got 100 bytes (*ppos=100)
chrdev_legacy:chrdev_write: should write 100 bytes (*ppos=100)
chrdev_legacy:chrdev_write: got 100 bytes (*ppos=200)
chrdev_legacy:chrdev_write: should write 100 bytes (*ppos=200)
chrdev_legacy:chrdev_write: got 100 bytes (*ppos=300)
chrdev_legacy:chrdev_release: chrdev released
```

At first calling, after `open()`, ppos is set to 0, and then it's moved to 100 after the data has been written. Then, on the next calls, ppos is increased by 100 bytes until it reaches 300.

In *step 2*, it's really interesting to see what happened in the kernel space when we issue the `cat` command, so let's see the kernel messages related to it:

```
chrdev_legacy:chrdev_open: chrdev opened
chrdev_legacy:chrdev_read: should read 131072 bytes (*ppos=0)
chrdev_legacy:chrdev_read: return 300 bytes (*ppos=300)
chrdev_legacy:chrdev_read: should read 131072 bytes (*ppos=300)
chrdev_legacy:chrdev_read: return 0 bytes (*ppos=300)
chrdev_legacy:chrdev_release: chrdev released
```

As we can see, `cat` asks for 131,072 bytes but, since our buffer is shorter, only 300 bytes are returned; then, `cat` executes again `read()` asking for 131,072 bytes but now `ppos` points to the end of file, so 0 is returned just to signal the end-of-file condition.

When we try to write too much data into our device file, we obviously get an error message, but the really interesting things to see are in the kernel:

```
chrdev_legacy:chrdev_open: chrdev opened
chrdev_legacy:chrdev_write: should write 1285 bytes (*ppos=0)
chrdev_legacy:chrdev_write: got 300 bytes (*ppos=300)
chrdev_legacy:chrdev_write: should write 985 bytes (*ppos=300)
chrdev_legacy:chrdev_write: got 0 bytes (*ppos=300)
chrdev_legacy:chrdev_release: chrdev released
```

First, the `write()` call asks to write 1,285 bytes (which is the real size of `/etc/passwd`) but only 300 bytes are actually written (due to the limited buffer size). Then, the second `write()` call asks to write 985 bytes (*1,285-300* bytes) but now `ppos` points to 300, which means that the buffer is full and then 0 (bytes written) is returned, which has been interpreted as a **No space left on device** error condition by the write command.

In *step 4*, the kernel messages relative to the preceding `grep` command are reported as follows:

```
chrdev_legacy:chrdev_open: chrdev opened
chrdev_legacy:chrdev_read: should read 32768 bytes (*ppos=0)
chrdev_legacy:chrdev_read: return 300 bytes (*ppos=300)
chrdev_legacy:chrdev_read: should read 32768 bytes (*ppos=300)
chrdev_legacy:chrdev_read: return 0 bytes (*ppos=300)
chrdev_legacy:chrdev_release: chrdev released
```

We can easily see that the `grep` command first opens our device file by using the `open()` system call, then it keeps reading data with `read()` until our driver returns end-of-file (which is addressed by 0), and finally it executes the `close()` system call to release our driver.

Using the Device Tree

4

Modern computers are really complex systems composed of complex peripherals, which have tons of different configuration settings; that's why having all possible variants of device driver configurations in a dedicated file can solve a lot of problems. Having a logical description about how a system is structured (that is how they are interconnected to each other and not just their list) can allow system developers to focus their attention on device driver mechanisms without the boring job of managing all possible user settings.

Moreover, knowing how every peripheral is connected to the system (for example, which bus a peripheral is dependent on) allows the implementation of a really smart peripheral management system. Such a system can correctly activate (or deactivate), in the right order, all the subsystems needed, by a specific device, to work.

Let's review an example: think about a USB key, which activates several devices when plugged into your PC. The system knows that the USB port is connected to a specific USB controller, which is mapped at a specific address into the system's memory, and so on.

For all these reasons (and others), Linux developers adopted **the device tree,** which is, simply speaking, a data structure to describe hardware. Rather than hard-coding every kernel setting into the code, it can be described in a well-defined data structure which is passed to the kernel during booting by the bootloader. This is also where all device drivers (and other kernel entities) can fetch their configuration data.

The main difference between the device tree and the kernel configuration file (the `.config` file in the upper directory of Linux sources) is that while such files tell us which components of the kernel are enabled and which are not, the device tree holds their configurations. So, if we wish to add a driver from the kernel's sources to our system, we have to specify it in the `.config` file. On the other hand, if we wish to specify the driver's settings (memory addresses, special settings, and so on), we have to specify them in the device tree.

In this chapter, we'll see how to write a device tree and how we can get useful information for our driver from it.

This chapter consists of the following recipes:

- Using the device tree compiler and utilities
- Getting application-specific data from a device tree
- Using a device tree to describe a character driver
- Downloading the firmware
- Configuring a CPU's pin for specific peripherals

Technical requirements

You can find more information on this chapter in the *Appendix*.

The code and other files used in this chapter can be downloaded from GitHub at `https://github.com/giometti/linux_device_driver_development_cookbook/tree/master/chapter_04`.

Using the device tree compiler and utilities

We need proper tools to convert our code into a binary format that Linux can understand. Specifically, we need a way to convert a **device tree source** (**DTS**) file into its binary form: **device tree binary** (**DTB**).

In this recipe, we'll discover how to install the **device tree compiler** (`dtc`) on our system and how we can use it to generate the binary for any device tree.

Getting ready

To convert a DTS file into a DTB one we have to use the **device tree compiler** (named `dtc`) and a set of proper tools we can use to inspect or manipulate DTB files (**device tree utilities**).

Every recent Linux release has its own copy of the `dtc` program in the `linux/scripts/dtc` directory, which is used during kernel compilation. However, we don't need to install Linux sources to have a working release of `dtc` and its utilities on Ubuntu; in fact, we can get them all by using the usual install command as below:

```
$ sudo apt install device-tree-compiler
```

After installation, we can execute the `dtc` compiler as follows in order to display its release:

```
$ dtc -v
Version: DTC 1.4.5
```

How to do it...

Now we are ready to convert our first DTS file into its equivalent DTB binary form using the following step.

1. We can do this by using the `dtc` compiler with the following command line:

    ```
    $ dtc -o simple_platform.dtb simple_platform.dts
    ```

     `simple_platform.dts` can be retrieved from GitHub sources; however the reader can use his/her own DTS file to test `dtc`.

    Now our DTB file should be available in the current directory:

    ```
    $ file simple_platform.dtb
    simple_platform.dtb: Device Tree Blob version 17, size=1602, boot
    CPU=0, string block size=270, DT structure block size=1276
    ```

How it works...

Converting a DTS file into a DTB one is similar to how a normal compiler works, but something should be said about the reverse operation.

If we take a look at `simple_platform-reverted.dts`, we notice that it looks very similar to the original `simple_platform.dts` file (apart from phandles, labels, and numbers in hexadecimal form); in fact, we have the following differences regarding clock settings:

```
$ diff -u simple_platform.dts simple_platform-reverted.dts | tail -29
-        clks: clock@f00 {
+        clock@f00 {
            compatible = "fsl,mpc5121-clock";
            reg = <0xf00 0x100>;
-            #clock-cells = <1>;
-            clocks = <&osc>;
+            #clock-cells = <0x1>;
+            clocks = <0x1>;
            clock-names = "osc";
```

```
+            phandle = <0x3>;
        };
```

And we have the following differences regarding the serial controller settings:

```
-        serial0: serial@11100 {
+        serial@11100 {
            compatible = "fsl,mpc5125-psc-uart", "fsl,mpc5125-psc";
            reg = <0x11100 0x100>;
-            interrupt-parent = <&ipic>;
-            interrupts = <40 0x8>;
-            fsl,rx-fifo-size = <16>;
-            fsl,tx-fifo-size = <16>;
-            clocks = <&clks 47>, <&clks 34>;
+            interrupt-parent = <0x2>;
+            interrupts = <0x28 0x8>;
+            fsl,rx-fifo-size = <0x10>;
+            fsl,tx-fifo-size = <0x10>;
+            clocks = <0x3 0x2f 0x3 0x22>;
            clock-names = "ipg", "mclk";
        };
    };
```

From the preceding output, we can see that the `serial0` and `clks` labels have disappeared since they are not needed in a DTB file; phandles are also now explicitly reported and, with corresponding symbolic names such as `ipic` and `clks`, have been replaced accordingly, and all numbers have been converted to their hexadecimal form.

There's more...

The device tree is a really complex piece of software and it's a powerful way to describe a system, which is why we need to talk a bit more about it. We should also take a look at device tree utilities due to the fact it is very useful for a kernel developer to manage a device tree binary form.

Reverting a binary device tree into its source

The `dtc` program can revert the compilation process, allowing the developer to retrieve a source file from a binary using a command line such as the following:

```
$ dtc -o simple_platform-reverted.dts simple_platform.dtb
```

This can be very useful when we need to inspect a DTB file.

See also

- For further information about the dtc compiler, the reader can take a look at the device tree user manual at https://git.kernel.org/pub/scm/utils/dtc/dtc.git/tree/Documentation/manual.txt.
- Regarding device tree utilities, a good starting point is their respective man pages (man fdtput, man fdtget and so on).

Getting application-specific data from a device tree

Now we know how to read a device tree file and how to manage it in userspace. In this recipe, we will see how we can extract the configuration settings it holds within the kernel.

Getting ready

To do our job, we can use all the data stored in the DTB to boot our ESPRESSObin and then use the ESPRESSObin as a system test.

As we know, ESPRESSObin's DTS file is stored in kernel sources at linux/arch/arm64/boot/dts/marvell/armada-3720-espressobin.dts or it can be extracted from the running kernel by executing the dtc command as presented in the following code:

```
# dtc -I fs -o espressobin-reverted.dts /proc/device-tree/
```

Now let's take this file apart since we can use it to verify that the data that we just read is correct.

How to do it...

To show how we can read data from the running device tree, we can use a kernel module (like the one reported in file `get_dt_data.c`) from GitHub sources.

1. In the file, we have an empty module `exit()` function, due to the fact we don't allocate anything in the module's `init()` function; in fact, it just shows us how we can parse a device tree. The `get_dt_data_init()` function takes an optional input parameter: a device tree path stored into the `path` variable defined in the following snippet:

```
#define PATH_DEFAULT "/"
static char *path = PATH_DEFAULT;
module_param(path, charp, S_IRUSR | S_IWUSR);
MODULE_PARM_DESC(path, "a device tree pathname " \
                       "(default is \"" PATH_DEFAULT "\")");
```

2. Then, as the first step, the `get_dt_data_init()` function uses the `of_find_node_by_path()` function to get a pointer to the desired node to inspect:

```
static int __init get_dt_data_init(void)
{
    struct device_node *node, *child;
    struct property *prop;

    pr_info("path = \"%s\"\n", path);

    /* Find node by its pathname */
    node = of_find_node_by_path(path);
    if (!node) {
        pr_err("failed to find device-tree node \"%s\"\n",
path);
        return -ENODEV;
    }
    pr_info("device-tree node found!\n");
```

3. Next, it calls the `print_main_prop()` function, which just prints the node's main properties as shown in the following:

```
static void print_main_prop(struct device_node *node)
{
    pr_info("+ node = %s\n", node->full_name);
    print_property_u32(node, "#address-cells");
    print_property_u32(node, "#size-cells");
    print_property_u32(node, "reg");
```

```
    print_property_string(node, "name");
    print_property_string(node, "compatible");
    print_property_string(node, "status");
}
```

Each printing function is reported as the following:

```
static void print_property_u32(struct device_node *node, const char
*name)
{
    u32 val32;
    if (of_property_read_u32(node, name, &val32) == 0)
        pr_info(" \%s = %d\n", name, val32);
}

static void print_property_string(struct device_node *node, const
char *name)
{
    const char *str;
    if (of_property_read_string(node, name, &str) == 0)
        pr_info(" \%s = %s\n", name, str);
}
```

4. For the last two steps, the `get_dt_data_init()` function uses
   the `for_each_property_of_node()` macro to display all of the node's
   property, and the `for_each_child_of_node()` macro to iterate all the node's
   children and display all of their main properties, as shown in the following:

```
pr_info("now move through all properties...\n");
for_each_property_of_node(node, prop)
    pr_info("-> %s\n", prop->name);

/* Move through node's children... */
pr_info("Now move through children...\n");
for_each_child_of_node(node, child)
    print_main_prop(child);

/* Force module unloading... */
return -EINVAL;
}
```

How it works...

In step 1, it's quite obvious that if we insert the module into the kernel specifying path=<my_path>, we force the desired value; otherwise, we simply accept the default, which is the root (represented by the / character). The rest of the steps are quite self-explanatory.

Understanding the code should be very easy; in fact the get_dt_data_init() function simply calls of_find_node_by_path(), passing the device path name; no errors, we use print_main_prop() to display the node name and some main (or interesting) properties of the node:

```
static void print_main_prop(struct device_node *node)
{
    pr_info("+ node = %s\n", node->full_name);
    print_property_u32(node, "#address-cells");
    print_property_u32(node, "#size-cells");
    print_property_u32(node, "reg");
    print_property_string(node, "name");
    print_property_string(node, "compatible");
    print_property_string(node, "status");
}
```

Note that the print_property_u32() and print_property_string() functions are defined in such a way as to display nothing if the supplied property is not present:

```
static void print_property_u32(struct device_node *node, const char *name)
{
    u32 val32;
    if (of_property_read_u32(node, name, &val32) == 0)
        pr_info(" \%s = %d\n", name, val32);
}

static void print_property_string(struct device_node *node, const char
*name)
{
    const char *str;
    if (of_property_read_string(node, name, &str) == 0)
        pr_info(" \%s = %s\n", name, str);
}
```

Functions such as `of_property_read_u32()`/`of_property_read_string()` and `for_each_child_of_node()`/`for_each_property_of_node()` and friends are defined in the header file `linux/include/linux/of.h` of kernel sources.

Once compiled from the `get_dt_data.c` file, we should get its compiled version named `get_dt_data.ko`, which is suitable for loading into the ESPRESSObin:

```
$ make KERNEL_DIR=../../../linux
make -C ../../../linux \
            ARCH=arm64 \
            CROSS_COMPILE=aarch64-linux-gnu- \
SUBDIRS=/home/giometti/Projects/ldddc/github/chapter_4/get_dt_data modules
make[1]: Entering directory '/home/giometti/Projects/ldddc/linux'
  CC [M]
/home/giometti/Projects/ldddc/github/chapter_4/get_dt_data/get_dt_data.o
  Building modules, stage 2.
  MODPOST 1 modules
  CC
/home/giometti/Projects/ldddc/github/chapter_4/get_dt_data/get_dt_data.mod.
o
  LD [M]
/home/giometti/Projects/ldddc/github/chapter_4/get_dt_data/get_dt_data.ko
make[1]: Leaving directory '/home/giometti/Projects/ldddc/linux'
```

The following is what we should get if we use `modinfo` in our newly created kernel module:

```
# modinfo get_dt_data.ko
filename: /root/get_dt_data.ko
version: 0.1
description: Module to inspect device tree from the kernel
author: Rodolfo Giometti
license: GPL
srcversion: 6926CA8AD5E7F8B45C97CE6
depends:
name: get_dt_data
vermagic: 4.18.0 SMP preempt mod_unload aarch64
parm: path:a device tree pathname (default is "/") (charp)
```

There's more...

OK, so let's try using the default value for the path by using the following command:

```
# insmod get_dt_data.ko
```

We should get an output such as the following:

```
get_dt_data: path = "/"
get_dt_data: device-tree node found!
...
```

By using / as the path name, we obviously found a corresponding entry in the device tree, so the output continues as follows:

```
...
get_dt_data: now getting main properties...
get_dt_data: + node =
get_dt_data: #address-cells = 2
get_dt_data: #size-cells = 2
get_dt_data: name =
get_dt_data: compatible = globalscale,espressobin
get_dt_data: now move through all properties...
get_dt_data: -> model
get_dt_data: -> compatible
get_dt_data: -> interrupt-parent
get_dt_data: -> #address-cells
get_dt_data: -> #size-cells
get_dt_data: -> name
...
```

The following are all properties of the root node that can be verified against the original sources or in the `espressobin-reverted.dts` file:

```
/ {
    #address-cells = <0x2>;
    model = "Globalscale Marvell ESPRESSOBin Board";
    #size-cells = <0x2>;
    interrupt-parent = <0x1>;
    compatible = "globalscale,espressobin", "marvell,armada3720",
"marvell,armada3710";
```

Readers should notice that, in this case, the `name` property is empty due to the fact we are inspecting the root node, and for the `compatible` property only the first entry is displayed because we used the `of_property_read_string()` function instead of the corresponding array `of_property_read_string_array()` version and friends.

After all of the node's properties, our program will move through all of its children as reported in the following:

```
...
get_dt_data: Now move through children...
get_dt_data: + node = aliases
get_dt_data: name = aliases
get_dt_data: + node = cpus
get_dt_data: #address-cells = 1
get_dt_data: #size-cells = 0
get_dt_data: name = cpus
...
get_dt_data: + node = soc
get_dt_data: #address-cells = 2
get_dt_data: #size-cells = 2
get_dt_data: name = soc
get_dt_data: compatible = simple-bus
get_dt_data: + node = chosen
get_dt_data: name = chosen
get_dt_data: + node = memory@0
get_dt_data: reg = 0
get_dt_data: name = memory
get_dt_data: + node = regulator
get_dt_data: name = regulator
get_dt_data: compatible = regulator-gpio
...
```

At this point, the `get_dt_data_init()` function does a `return -EINVAL`, not to return an error condition, but to force a module to unload; in fact, as the last printed out message, we see the following:

```
insmod: ERROR: could not insert module get_dt_data.ko: Invalid parameters
```

Now, just to show a different usage, we can try to ask for information regarding the system's CPUs by specifying the `path=/cpus` command in the command line:

```
# insmod get_dt_data.ko path=/cpus
```

The program says that a node is found:

```
get_dt_data: path = "/cpus"
get_dt_data: device-tree node found!
```

Then it starts printing the node's information:

```
get_dt_data: now getting main properties...
get_dt_data: + node = cpus
get_dt_data: #address-cells = 1
get_dt_data: #size-cells = 0
get_dt_data: name = cpus
```

Finally, it displays all of the children's properties:

```
get_dt_data: now move through all properties...
get_dt_data: -> #address-cells
get_dt_data: -> #size-cells
get_dt_data: -> name
get_dt_data: Now move through children...
get_dt_data: + node = cpu@0
get_dt_data: reg = 0
get_dt_data: name = cpu
get_dt_data: compatible = arm,cortex-a53
get_dt_data: + node = cpu@1
get_dt_data: reg = 1
get_dt_data: name = cpu
get_dt_data: compatible = arm,cortex-a53
```

Note that the following error message can be safely ignored because we force it to automatically retrieve the module to be unloaded by the insmod command:

```
insmod: ERROR: could not insert module get_dt_data.ko:
Invalid parameters
```

In a similar manner, we can obtain information regarding the I2C controller as shown in the following:

```
# insmod get_dt_data.ko path=/soc/internal-regs@d0000000/i2c@11000
get_dt_data: path = "/soc/internal-regs@d0000000/i2c@11000"
get_dt_data: device-tree node found!
get_dt_data: now getting main properties...
get_dt_data: + node = i2c@11000
get_dt_data: #address-cells = 1
get_dt_data: #size-cells = 0
get_dt_data: reg = 69632
get_dt_data: name = i2c
get_dt_data: compatible = marvell,armada-3700-i2c
```

```
get_dt_data: status = disabled
get_dt_data: now move through all properties...
...
```

See also

- To see all available functions for inspecting a device tree, the reader can take a look at the included `linux/include/linux/of.h` file, which is well documented.

Using a device tree to describe a character driver

At this point, we have all the information needed to define a new character device by using a device tree. In particular, this time, to register our `chrdev` device, we can use the new API that we skipped in `Chapter 3`, *Working with Char Drivers*.

Getting ready

As stated in the previous paragraph, we can use a device tree node to add a new device to our system. In particular, we can obtain a definition as reported in the following:

```
chrdev {
    compatible = "ldddc,chrdev";
    #address-cells = <1>;
    #size-cells = <0>;

    chrdev@2 {
        label = "cdev-eeprom";
        reg = <2>;
    };

    chrdev@4 {
        label = "cdev-rom";
        reg = <4>;
        read-only;
    };
};
```

All these modifications can be applied using
the `add_chrdev_devices.dts.patch` file in the root directory of the
kernel sources, as shown in the following:

```
$ patch -p1 <
../github/chapter_04/chrdev/add_chrdev_devices.dts.patch
```

Then the kernel must be recompiled and reinstalled (with the
ESPRESSObin's DTB file) in order to take effect.

In this example, we are defining a `chrdev` node, which defines a new set of devices
compatible with `"ldddc,chrdev"` and with two subnodes; each subnode defines a
particular device with its own settings. The first subnode defines a `"ldddc,chrdev"`
device labeled `"cdev-eeprom"` with a `reg` property equal to 2, while the second subnode
defines another `"ldddc,chrdev"` device labeled `"cdev-rom"` with a `reg` property equal
to 4, and with a `read-only` property.

The `#address-cells` and `#size-cells` properties must be 1 and 0 because the
subdevice's `reg` property holds a single value representing something as the "device
address". In fact, devices that are addressable use `#address-cells`, `#size-cells`, and
the `reg` property to encode address information into the device tree.

Each addressable device obtains a `reg` property, which is a list as shown in the following:

```
reg = <address1 length1 [address2 length2] [address3 length3] ... >
```

Each tuple represents an address range used by the device and each address or length value
is a list of one or more 32-bit integers called **cells** (the length can also be empty as in our
example).

Since both the address and length fields may vary and be of variable size, the `#address-
cells` and `#size-cells` properties in the parent node are used to state how many cells
are in each subnode's field.

For further information regarding the `#address-cells`, `#size-cells`,
and `reg` properties, you can take a look at the device tree specification at
`https://www.devicetree.org/specifications/`.

How to do it...

Now it's time to see how we can use the preceding device tree definition to create our char devices (note that this time we're going to create more than one device!).

1. Both of the module's `init()` and `exit()` functions must be rewritten as shown in the following code. `chrdev_init()` looks as follows:

```
static int __init chrdev_init(void)
{
    int ret;

    /* Create the new class for the chrdev devices */
    chrdev_class = class_create(THIS_MODULE, "chrdev");
    if (!chrdev_class) {
        pr_err("chrdev: failed to allocate class\n");
        return -ENOMEM;
    }

    /* Allocate a region for character devices */
    ret = alloc_chrdev_region(&chrdev_devt, 0, MAX_DEVICES,
"chrdev");
    if (ret < 0) {
        pr_err("failed to allocate char device region\n");
        goto remove_class;
    }

    pr_info("got major %d\n", MAJOR(chrdev_devt));

    return 0;

remove_class:
    class_destroy(chrdev_class);

    return ret;
}
```

2. The `chrdev_exit()` function looks like this:

```
static void __exit chrdev_exit(void)
{
    unregister_chrdev_region(chrdev_devt, MAX_DEVICES);
    class_destroy(chrdev_class);
}
```

All code can be retrieved from GitHub sources in the `chrdev.c` file.

3. If we try to insert the module into the kernel, we should get something like the following:

```
# insmod chrdev.ko
chrdev: loading out-of-tree module taints kernel.
chrdev:chrdev_init: got major 239
```

4. To create the character device, we must use the next `chrdev_device_register()` function, but we must first do some checks regarding whether the device has already been created or not:

```
int chrdev_device_register(const char *label, unsigned int id,
                unsigned int read_only,
                struct module *owner, struct device *parent)
{
    struct chrdev_device *chrdev;
    dev_t devt;
    int ret;

    /* First check if we are allocating a valid device... */
    if (id >= MAX_DEVICES) {
        pr_err("invalid id %d\n", id);
        return -EINVAL;
    }
    chrdev = &chrdev_array[id];

    /* ... then check if we have not busy id */
    if (chrdev->busy) {
        pr_err("id %d\n is busy", id);
        return -EBUSY;
    }
```

Then we do something a little bit more complicated than we've done in the previous chapter, in which we simply called the `register_chrdev()` function; now the really important thing is the calling sequence of the `cdev_init()`, `cdev_add()`, and `device_create()` functions, which actually do the job, as shown in the following:

```
/* Create the device and initialize its data */
cdev_init(&chrdev->cdev, &chrdev_fops);
chrdev->cdev.owner = owner;
```

```
devt = MKDEV(MAJOR(chrdev_devt), id);
ret = cdev_add(&chrdev->cdev, devt, 1);
if (ret) {
    pr_err("failed to add char device %s at %d:%d\n",
            label, MAJOR(chrdev_devt), id);
    return ret;
}

chrdev->dev = device_create(chrdev_class, parent, devt, chrdev,
                "%s@%d", label, id);
if (IS_ERR(chrdev->dev)) {
    pr_err("unable to create device %s\n", label);
    ret = PTR_ERR(chrdev->dev);
    goto del_cdev;
}
```

Once the `device_create()` function returns success, we use the
`dev_set_drvdata()` function to save a pointer to our driver data, which is then
initialized like this:

```
    dev_set_drvdata(chrdev->dev, chrdev);

 /* Init the chrdev data */
 chrdev->id = id;
 chrdev->read_only = read_only;
 chrdev->busy = 1;
 strncpy(chrdev->label, label, NAME_LEN);
 memset(chrdev->buf, 0, BUF_LEN);

 dev_info(chrdev->dev, "chrdev %s with id %d added\n", label, id);

 return 0;

del_cdev:
 cdev_del(&chrdev->cdev);

 return ret;
}
EXPORT_SYMBOL(chrdev_device_register);
```

All these functions operate on `struct chrdev_device`, defined as the
following:

```
/* Main struct */
struct chrdev_device {
    char label[NAME_LEN];
    unsigned int busy : 1;
    char buf[BUF_LEN];
```

```
        int read_only;

        unsigned int id;
        struct module *owner;
        struct cdev cdev;
        struct device *dev;
    };
```

How it works...

In *step 1*, within `chrdev_init()` function, this time, we use the
`alloc_chrdev_region()` function, which asks the kernel to reserve some character
devices named `chrdev` (in our case, this number is equivalent to
the `MAX_DEVICES` definition). The `chrdev` information is then stored in
the `chrdev_devt` variable.

Here, we should be careful and notice that we also create a device class by calling the
`class_create()` function. Each device defined for the device tree must belong to a
proper class and, since our `chrdev` driver is new, we need a dedicated class.

> In the next steps, I will be more clear about the reason we need to do it
> this way; for the moment, we should consider it as a compulsory data
> allocation.
> It's quite clear that the `unregister_chrdev_region()` function just
> releases all of the `chrdev` data allocated in `with`
> `alloc_chrdev_region()`.

In *step 3*, if we take a look at the `/proc/devices` file, we get the following:

```
# grep chrdev /proc/devices
239 chrdev
```

Good! Now we've got something similar to Chapter 3, *Working with Char Drivers*! However,
this time, if we try to create a special character file by using `mknod` and try to read from it,
we get an error!

```
# mknod /dev/chrdev c 239 0
# cat /dev/chrdev
cat: /dev/chrdev: No such device or address
```

The kernel tells us that the device doesn't exist! This is because we have not yet created
anything, but just reserved some kernel internal data.

In *step 4*, the first fields are just relative to our specific implementation, while the last four are present in almost every character driver implementation: the `id` field is just a unique identifier of each `chrdev` (remember that our implementation supports `MAX_DEVICES` instances), the `owner` pointer is used to store the owner of our driver's module, the `cdev` structure holds all of the kernel data about our character device, and the `dev` pointer points to a kernel `struct device` related to the one we specify in the device tree.

So, `cdev_init()` is used to initialize `cdev` with our file operations; `cdev_add()` is used to define major and minor numbers of our driver; `device_create()` is used to glue the `devt` data to the data pointed to by `dev`; and our `chrdev` class (represented by the `chrdev_class` pointer) actually creates the character device.

However, the `chrdev_device_register()` function is not called by any function in the `chrdev.c` file; this is why it has been declared as an exported symbol using the `EXPORT_SYMBOL()` definition. In fact, this function is called the `chrdev_req_probe()` function, defined in another module as a file named `chrdev-req.c`, which is reported in the following snippet. The function first understands how many devices we have to register:

```
static int chrdev_req_probe(struct platform_device *pdev)
{
    struct device *dev = &pdev->dev;
    struct fwnode_handle *child;
    struct module *owner = THIS_MODULE;
    int count, ret;

    /* If we are not registering a fixed chrdev device then get
     * the number of chrdev devices from DTS
     */
    count = device_get_child_node_count(dev);
    if (count == 0)
        return -ENODEV;
    if (count > MAX_DEVICES)
        return -ENOMEM;
```

Then, for each device, after reading the device's properties, the `chrdev_device_register()` calls to register the device on the system (and it will do for every device reported in the device tree as illustrated in the preceding code):

```
device_for_each_child_node(dev, child) {
        const char *label;
        unsigned int id, ro;

        /*
         * Get device's properties
```

```
        */

        if (fwnode_property_present(child, "reg")) {
            fwnode_property_read_u32(child, "reg", &id);
        } else {
...

        }
        ro = fwnode_property_present(child, "read-only");

        /* Register the new chr device */
        ret = chrdev_device_register(label, id, ro, owner, dev);
        if (ret) {
            dev_err(dev, "unable to register");
        }
    }

    return 0;
}
```

But how can the system know when the `chrdev_req_probe()` function must be called?
Well, it's quite clear if we keep reading `chrdev-req.c`; in fact, near the end, we find the
following code:

```
static const struct of_device_id of_chrdev_req_match[] = {
    {
        .compatible = "ldddc,chrdev",
    },
    { /* sentinel */ }
};
MODULE_DEVICE_TABLE(of, of_chrdev_req_match);

static struct platform_driver chrdev_req_driver = {
    .probe = chrdev_req_probe,
    .remove = chrdev_req_remove,
    .driver = {
        .name = "chrdev-req",
        .of_match_table = of_chrdev_req_match,
    },
};
module_platform_driver(chrdev_req_driver);
```

When we insert the `chrdev-req.ko` module into the kernel, we define a new platform driver by using `module_platform_driver()`, then the kernel starts looking for a node with the `compatible` property set to `"ldddc,chrdev"`; if found, it executes the function pointed at by the `probe` pointer we set to `chrdev_req_probe()`. This causes a new driver to be registered.

Before showing how it works, let's take a look at the opposite steps, intended to deallocate whatever we requested from the kernel during character driver allocation. When we remove the `chrdev-req.ko` module, the kernel invokes the platform driver's `remove` function, that is `chrdev_req_remove()` in the `chrdev-req.c` file, as partially reported in the following:

```
static int chrdev_req_remove(struct platform_device *pdev)
{
    struct device *dev = &pdev->dev;
    struct fwnode_handle *child;
    int ret;

    device_for_each_child_node(dev, child) {
        const char *label;
        int id;

        /*
         * Get device's properties
         */

        if (fwnode_property_present(child, "reg"))
            fwnode_property_read_u32(child, "reg", &id);
        else
            BUG();
        if (fwnode_property_present(child, "label"))
            fwnode_property_read_string(child, "label", &label);
        else
            BUG();

        /* Register the new chr device */
        ret = chrdev_device_unregister(label, id);
        if (ret)
            dev_err(dev, "unable to unregister");
    }

    return 0;
}
```

This function, which is inside the `chrdev.c` file, calls `chrdev_device_unregister()` (for each `chrdev` node in the device tree) and is reported in the following; and it starts by doing some sanity checks:

```
int chrdev_device_unregister(const char *label, unsigned int id)
{
    struct chrdev_device *chrdev;

    /* First check if we are deallocating a valid device... */
    if (id >= MAX_DEVICES) {
        pr_err("invalid id %d\n", id);
        return -EINVAL;
    }
    chrdev = &chrdev_array[id];

    /* ... then check if device is actualy allocated */
    if (!chrdev->busy || strcmp(chrdev->label, label)) {
        pr_err("id %d is not busy or label %s is not known\n",
                        id, label);
        return -EINVAL;
    }
```

But then it unregisters the driver by using the `device_destroy()` and `cdev_del()` functions:

```
        /* Deinit the chrdev data */
        chrdev->id = 0;
        chrdev->busy = 0;
        dev_info(chrdev->dev, "chrdev %s with id %d removed\n", label, id);

        /* Dealocate the device */
        device_destroy(chrdev_class, chrdev->dev->devt);
        cdev_del(&chrdev->cdev);

        return 0;
}
EXPORT_SYMBOL(chrdev_device_unregister);
```

There's more...

Using a device tree is not just useful for describing a peripheral (and then the whole system); by using it, we can also gain access to several ready-to-use features that Linux offers to kernel developers. So let's take a look at the most important (and useful) ones.

How device files are created in /dev

In `Chapter 3`, *Working with Char Drivers*, when we created a new character device nothing happened in the user space and we had to create a character device file by hand using the `mknod` command; however, in this chapter, when we inserted the second kernel module, which created our new `chrdev` devices. By getting their properties from the device tree, in the `/dev` directory, two new character files were automatically created.

It's Linux's kernel object mechanism that implements this magic; let's see how.

Whenever a new device is created in the kernel, a new kernel event is generated and sent to the user space; this new event is then captured by a dedicated application that interprets it. These special applications may vary but the most famous application of this type used by almost all important Linux distributions is the `udev` application.

The `udev` daemon is born to replace and create a mechanism to automatically create special device files under the `/dev` directory, and it works so well that it is now used for several different tasks. In fact, the `udev` daemon receives device kernel events (called **uevents**) directly from the kernel whenever a device is added or removed from the system (or when it changes its state), and for each event, it executes a set of rules according to its configuration files. A rule is executed if it matches various device attributes and it then creates new files in the `/dev` directory accordingly; a matching rule may also provide additional device information to be used to create meaningful symlink names, execute scripts, and much more!

> For further information regarding `udev` rules, a good starting point is a related page in the Debian Wiki at `https://wiki.debian.org/udev`.

To monitor these events, we can use the `udevadm` tool, which comes within the `udev` package as reported in the following command line:

```
# udevadm monitor -k -p -s chrdev
monitor will print the received events for:
KERNEL - the kernel uevent
```

By using the `monitor` subcommand, we select the `udevadm` monitor features (since `udevadm` can do several other tasks) and by specifying the `-k` option argument we ask for kernel-generated messages only to be displayed (since some messages may come from the userspace too); also, by using the `-p` option argument, we ask for event properties to be displayed and, with the `-s` option argument, we select messages from the subsystem matching the `chrdev` string only.

To see all kernel messages, during the chrdev module insertion the kernel sends just execute udevadm monitor command, dropping all of these option arguments.

To see new events, just execute the above command, and, in another terminal (or directly from the serial console) repeat the kernel module insertion. After inserting the chrdev-req.ko module we see the same kernel messages as before:

```
# insmod chrdev-req.ko
chrdev cdev-eeprom@2: chrdev cdev-eeprom with id 2 added
chrdev cdev-rom@4: chrdev cdev-rom with id 4 added
```

However, in the terminal where we executed the udevadm message, we should now see something like the following:

```
KERNEL[14909.624343] add /devices/platform/chrdev/chrdev/cdev-eeprom@2
(chrdev)
ACTION=add
DEVNAME=/dev/cdev-eeprom@2
DEVPATH=/devices/platform/chrdev/chrdev/cdev-eeprom@2
MAJOR=239
MINOR=2
SEQNUM=2297
SUBSYSTEM=chrdev

KERNEL[14909.631813] add /devices/platform/chrdev/chrdev/cdev-rom@4
(chrdev)
ACTION=add
DEVNAME=/dev/cdev-rom@4
DEVPATH=/devices/platform/chrdev/chrdev/cdev-rom@4
MAJOR=239
MINOR=4
SEQNUM=2298
SUBSYSTEM=chrdev
```

These are the kernel messages informing udev that two new devices named /dev/cdev-eeprom@2 and /dev/cdev-rom@4 have been created (with other properties), so udev has all the information it needs to create new files under the /dev directory.

Downloading the firmware

By using the device tree, we're now able to specify a lot of different settings for our driver, but there is still one last thing we have to see: how to load firmware into our device. In fact, some devices may require a program for themselves to work which, for license reasons, cannot be linked within the kernel.

In this section, we're going to see some examples of how we can ask the kernel to load firmware for our device.

Getting ready

Some peripherals need firmware to work and then we need a mechanism to load such binary data into them. Linux provides us with different mechanisms to do this job and they all refer to the `request_firmware()` function.

Whenever we use a `request_firmware(..., "filename", ...)` function call (or one of its friends) in our driver (specifying a filename), the kernel starts looking at different locations:

- First of all, it takes a look at the boot image file and, in case, the firmware is loaded from it; this is because we can bundle binary code with the kernel during compilation. However, this solution is permitted only if the firmware is free software; otherwise it cannot be linked to Linux. It is also not very flexible when changing firmware data if we have to recompile the kernel too.
- If no data has been stored within the kernel, it starts to load the firmware data directly from the filesystem by looking for the `filename` in several path locations starting from the one specified for the kernel command line with the `firmware_class.path="<path>"` option argument, then in `/lib/firmware/updates/<UTS_RELEASE>`, then into `/lib/firmware/updates`, then into `/lib/firmware/<UTS_RELEASE>`, and, finally, in the `/lib/firmware` directory.

`<UTS_RELEASE>` is the kernel release version number, which can be obtained directly from the kernel by using the `uname -r` command as in the following:
```
$ uname -r
4.15.0-45-generic
```

- If this last step fails too, then the kernel may try a fallback procedure, which consists of enabling the firmware loader user helper. This last chance to load firmware must be enabled for the kernel configuration by enabling the following kernel configuration settings:

```
CONFIG_FW_LOADER_USER_HELPER=y
CONFIG_FW_LOADER_USER_HELPER_FALLBACK=y
```

By using the usual make menuconfig method, we have to go through **Device Drivers**, then **Generic Driver Options**, and **Firmware loader entries** to enable them (see the following screenshot).

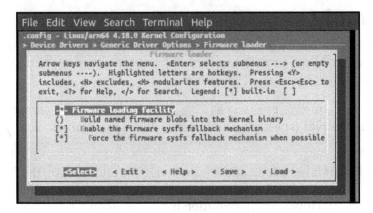

After we have enabled these settings and recompiled the kernel, we can explore, in detail, how we can load custom firmware for our driver within the kernel.

How to do it...

First, we need a modified version of the chrdev-req.c file focused on firmware loading; that's why it's better to use another file.

1. To do our job, we can use the chrdev-fw.c file with the following device definitions:

```
static const struct of_device_id of_chrdev_req_match[] = {
    {
        .compatible = "ldddc,chrdev-fw_wait",
    },
    {
        .compatible = "ldddc,chrdev-fw_nowait",
    },
```

```
        { /* sentinel */ }
};
MODULE_DEVICE_TABLE(of, of_chrdev_req_match);

static struct platform_driver chrdev_req_driver = {
    .probe = chrdev_req_probe,
    .remove = chrdev_req_remove,
    .driver = {
        .name = "chrdev-fw",
        .of_match_table = of_chrdev_req_match,
    },
};
module_platform_driver(chrdev_req_driver);
```

 The `chrdev-fw.c` file can be found in the GitHub sources for this chapter.

2. In this situation, our probing function can be implemented as follows, where at the beginning of the `chrdev_req_probe()` function we read some of the device's properties:

```
static int chrdev_req_probe(struct platform_device *pdev)
{
    struct device *dev = &pdev->dev;
    struct device_node *np = dev->of_node;
    struct fwnode_handle *fwh = of_fwnode_handle(np);
    struct module *owner = THIS_MODULE;
    const char *file;
    int ret = 0;

    /* Read device properties */
    if (fwnode_property_read_string(fwh, "firmware", &file)) {
        dev_err(dev, "unable to get property \"firmware\"!");
        return -EINVAL;
    }

    /* Load device firmware */
    if (of_device_is_compatible(np, "ldddc,chrdev-fw_wait"))
        ret = chrdev_load_fw_wait(dev, file);
    else if (of_device_is_compatible(np, "ldddc,chrdev-fw_nowait"))
        ret = chrdev_load_fw_nowait(dev, file);
    if (ret)
        return ret;
```

We then register the char device:

```
/* Register the new chr device */
ret = chrdev_device_register("chrdev-fw", 0, 0, owner, dev);
if (ret) {
    dev_err(dev, "unable to register");
    return ret;
}

return 0;
}
```

3. A former device type calls the `chrdev_load_fw_wait()` function, which carries out the next steps. It starts by requesting the firmware's data structure:

```
static int chrdev_load_fw_wait(struct device *dev, const char
*file)
{
    char fw_name[FIRMWARE_NLEN];
    const struct firmware *fw;
    int ret;

    /* Compose firmware filename */
    if (strlen(file) > (128 - 6 - sizeof(FIRMWARE_VER)))
        return -EINVAL;
    sprintf(fw_name, "%s-%s.bin", file, FIRMWARE_VER);

    /* Do the firmware request */
    ret = request_firmware(&fw, fw_name, dev);
    if (ret) {
        dev_err(dev, "unable to load firmware\n");
        return ret;
    }
```

It then dumps the data received and finally releases the firmware's previously allocated data structure:

```
dump_data(fw->data, fw->size);

/* Firmware data has been read, now we can release it */
release_firmware(fw);

return 0;
}
```

The `FIRMWARE_VER` and `FIRMWARE_NLEN` macros have been defined within the `chrdev-fw.c` file as shown in the following:

```
#define FIRMWARE_VER      "1.0.0"
#define FIRMWARE_NLEN     128
```

How it works...

In *step 1*, in the `of_chrdev_req_match[]` array, we now have two devices that we can use to test different ways of loading firmware. One device, named `ldddc,chrdev-fw_wait` can be used to test direct firmware loading from the filesystem, while the other, named `ldddc,chrdev-fw_nowait`, can be used to test the firmware loader's user helper. I used these two examples to show the reader two different firmware loading techniques but, in reality, these two methods can be used for different purposes; the former can be used whenever our device needs its firmware since the startup otherwise it cannot work (this forces the driver not being built-in), while the former can be used when our device can be partially used even without any firmware and it can be loaded later after device initialization (which removes the mandatory built-in form).

In *step 2*, after reading the `firmware` property (holding the firmware file name) we check if the device is compatible with the `ldddc,chrdev-fw_wait` or `ldddc,chrdev-fw_nowait` device and then we call the proper firmware loading function, accordingly, before registering the new device.

In *step 3*, the `chrdev_load_fw_wait()` function builds up a filename in the `<name>-<version>.bin` form and then calls the effective firmware loading function named `request_firmware()`. In response, this function may return an error, which causes an error during the driver loading, or it can return a proper structure holding the firmware into the `buffer fw->data` pointer with the `long fw->size` size bytes. The `dump_data()` function simply dumps firmware data by printing it into kernel messages, but the `release_firmware()` function is important and must be called to inform the kernel we have read all data and finished with it, and then it can release the resource.

On the other hand, if we specify the `ldddc`, `chrdev-fw_nowait` device in the device tree, then the `chrdev_load_fw_nowait()` function is called instead. This function operates in a similar manner as before, but at the end, it calls `request_firmware_nowait()`, which works like `request_firmware()`. However, if the firmware is not loaded directly from the filesystem, it executes the fallback procedure, which involves the firmware loader's user helper. This special helper sends a uevent message to the `udev` tool (or similar), which causes automatic firmware loading, or the creation of an entry within sysfs, which can be used by the user to manually load the kernel.

The `chrdev_load_fw_nowait()` function has the following body:

```
static int chrdev_load_fw_nowait(struct device *dev, const char *file)
{
    char fw_name[FIRMWARE_NLEN];
    int ret;

    /* Compose firmware filename */
    if (strlen(file) > (128 - 6 - sizeof(FIRMWARE_VER)))
        return -EINVAL;
    sprintf(fw_name, "%s-%s.bin", file, FIRMWARE_VER);

    /* Do the firmware request */
    ret = request_firmware_nowait(THIS_MODULE, false, fw_name, dev,
            GFP_KERNEL, dev, chrdev_fw_cb);
    if (ret) {
        dev_err(dev,
            "unable to register call back for firmware loading\n");
        return ret;
    }

    return 0;
}
```

Some important difference
between `request_firmware_nowait()` and `request_firmware()` is that the former defines a callback function, which is invoked whenever the firmware is actually loaded from the user space, and it has, as a second parameter, a Boolean, which can be used to ask the kernel to send, or not, a uevent message to the userspace. By using a value, we achieve functionality similar to `request_firmware()`, while if we specify a false value (as in our case), we force manual firmware loading.

Then, when a userspace process takes the required steps to load the desired firmware, the callback function is used and we can actually load firmware data as shown in the following example:

```
static void chrdev_fw_cb(const struct firmware *fw, void *context)
{
    struct device *dev = context;

    dev_info(dev, "firmware callback executed!\n");
    if (!fw) {
        dev_err(dev, "unable to load firmware\n");
        return;
    }

    dump_data(fw->data, fw->size);

    /* Firmware data has been read, now we can release it */
    release_firmware(fw);
}
```

In this function, we actually take the same steps as before to dump firmware data within kernel messages.

There's more

Let's just verify how everything works in this recipe. As the first step, let's try using the `ldddc,chrdev-fw_wait` device, which uses the `request_firmware()` function; we need the next entry in the device tree:

```
--- a/arch/arm64/boot/dts/marvell/armada-3720-espressobin.dts
+++ b/arch/arm64/boot/dts/marvell/armada-3720-espressobin.dts
@@ -41,6 +41,11 @@
                3300000 0x0>;
            enable-active-high;
        };
+
+        chrdev {
+            compatible = "ldddc,chrdev-fw_wait";
+            firmware = "chrdev-wait";
+        };
    };

    /* J9 */
```

Then we have to compile the code, and we can do this by simply adding our new `chrdev-fw.c` file into the `makefile` as shown in the following:

```
--- a/chapter_4/chrdev/Makefile
+++ b/chapter_4/chrdev/Makefile
@@ -6,7 +6,7 @@ ARCH ?= arm64
 CROSS_COMPILE ?= aarch64-linux-gnu-

 obj-m = chrdev.o
-obj-m += chrdev-req.o
+obj-m += chrdev-fw.o

 all: modules
```

Once we have our new modules within ESPRESSObin's filesystem, we can try inserting them into the kernel as shown here:

```
# insmod chrdev.ko
chrdev: loading out-of-tree module taints kernel.
chrdev:chrdev_init: got major 239
# insmod chrdev-fw.ko
chrdev-fw chrdev: Direct firmware load for chrdev-wait-1.0.0.bin
failed with error -2
chrdev-fw chrdev: Falling back to syfs fallback for: chrdev-wait-1.0.0.bin
chrdev-fw chrdev: unable to load firmware
chrdev-fw: probe of chrdev failed with error -11
```

As we can see, the kernel tries to load the `chrdev-wait-1.0.0.bin` file, but it cannot find it since it simply doesn't exist in the filesystem; then, the kernel moves to sysfs fallback, but since it fails again we get an error and the driver loading fails too.

To get a positive result, we must add a file named `chrdev-wait-1.0.0.bin` into one of the search paths; for instance, we can put it in `/lib/firmware/` as seen in the following example:

```
# echo "THIS IS A DUMMY FIRMWARE FOR CHRDEV DEVICE" > \
        /lib/firmware/chrdev-wait-1.0.0.bin
```

If the `/lib/firmware` directory doesn't exist, we can just create it using the `mkdir /lib/firmware` command.

Now we can retry loading our `chrdev-fw.ko` module as follows:

```
# rmmod chrdev-fw
# insmod chrdev-fw.ko
chrdev_fw:dump_data: 54[T] 48[H] 49[I] 53[S] 20[ ] 49[I] 53[S] 20[ ]
chrdev_fw:dump_data: 41[A] 20[ ] 44[D] 55[U] 4d[M] 4d[M] 59[Y] 20[ ]
chrdev_fw:dump_data: 46[F] 49[I] 52[R] 4d[M] 57[W] 41[A] 52[R] 45[E]
chrdev_fw:dump_data: 20[ ] 46[F] 4f[O] 52[R] 20[ ] 43[C] 48[H] 52[R]
chrdev_fw:dump_data: 44[D] 45[E] 56[V] 20[ ] 44[D] 45[E] 56[V] 49[I]
chrdev_fw:dump_data: 43[C] 45[E] 0a[-]
chrdev chrdev-fw@0: chrdev chrdev-fw with id 0 added
```

Perfect! Now the firmware has been loaded as desired and the `chrdev` device has been correctly created.

Now we can try using the second device by modifying the device tree as follows and then rebooting the ESPRESSObin with the new DTB file:

```
--- a/arch/arm64/boot/dts/marvell/armada-3720-espressobin.dts
+++ b/arch/arm64/boot/dts/marvell/armada-3720-espressobin.dts
@@ -41,6 +41,11 @@
                3300000 0x0>;
           enable-active-high;
      };
+
+     chrdev {
+         compatible = "lddc,chrdev-fw_nowait";
+         firmware = "chrdev-nowait";
+     };
  };

 /* J9 */
```

With these new configuration settings, if we try to load the `chrdev` module, we get the following messages:

```
# insmod chrdev.ko
chrdev: loading out-of-tree module taints kernel.
chrdev:chrdev_init: got major 239
# insmod chrdev-fw.ko
chrdev-fw chrdev: Direct firmware load for chrdev-nowait-1.0.0.bin failed
with error -2
chrdev-fw chrdev: Falling back to syfs fallback for: chrdev-
nowait-1.0.0.bin
chrdev chrdev-fw@0: chrdev chrdev-fw with id 0 added
```

This time, the kernel still tries to directly load firmware from the filesystem, but it fails because no file named `chrdev-nowait-1.0.0.bin` exists; it then falls back to the fallback firmware loader user helper, which we've forced into manual mode. However, the driver's probing function successfully registers our `chrdev` driver, which is now fully functional even if no firmware has been loaded yet.

To manually load firmware, we can use special sysfs entries in the `/sys/class/firmware/` directory as shown in the following:

```
# ls /sys/class/firmware/
chrdev-nowait-1.0.0.bin  timeout
```

The `chrdev-nowait-1.0.0.bin` directory is called as the string passed as `fw_name` parameter to `request_firmware_nowait()` function, and, inside it, we find the following files:

```
# ls /sys/class/firmware/chrdev-nowait-1.0.0.bin
data  device  loading  power  subsystem  uevent
```

Now, the required steps to automatically load firmware are as follows:

```
# echo 1 > /sys/class/firmware/chrdev-nowait-1.0.0.bin/loading
# echo "THIS IS A DUMMY FIRMWARE" > /sys/class/firmware/chrdev-
nowait-1.0.0.bin/data
# echo 0 > /sys/class/firmware/chrdev-nowait-1.0.0.bin/loading
chrdev-fw chrdev: firmware callback executed!
chrdev_fw:dump_data: 54[T] 48[H] 49[I] 53[S] 20[ ] 49[I] 53[S] 20[ ]
chrdev_fw:dump_data: 41[A] 20[ ] 44[D] 55[U] 4d[M] 4d[M] 59[Y] 20[ ]
chrdev_fw:dump_data: 46[F] 49[I] 52[R] 4d[M] 57[W] 41[A] 52[R] 45[E]
chrdev_fw:dump_data: 0a[-]
```

We start the download procedure by writing 1 into the `loading` file, then we have to copy all the firmware data into the `data` file; we then finish the download by writing 0 in the `loading` file. As soon as we do this, the kernel calls our driver's callback and the firmware is loaded.

See also

- For further information regarding firmware loading, a good starting point is the Linux driver implementer's API guide, available online at `https://www.kernel.org/doc/html/v5.0/driver-api/firmware/request_firmware.html`.

Configuring CPU pins for specific peripherals

As the device driver developer, this task is really important because to be able to talk with external devices (or internal ones but with external signal lines) we must be sure that each CPU pin is properly configured to talk with these external signals. In this recipe, we will look at how we can use the device tree to configure CPU pins.

How to do it...

Just as a simple example, let's try to modify the pin configuration for our ESPRESSObin.

1. First of all, we should take a look at the current configuration by looking at sysfs in the `/sys/bus/platform/drivers/mvebu-uart/` directory, where we verify that only one UART is currently enabled:

```
# ls /sys/bus/platform/drivers/mvebu-uart/
d0012000.serial   uevent
# ls /sys/bus/platform/drivers/mvebu-uart/d0012000.serial/tty/
ttyMV0
```

Then the `mvebu-uart` drivers manage the `d0012000.serial` device, which can be accessed using the `/dev/ttyMV0` file. We can also verify how the CPU's pins are configured by taking a look at the `/sys/kernel/debug/pinctrl/d0013800.pinctrl-armada_37xx-pinctrl/pinmux-pins` file in debugfs, where we can see that only the `uart1` group is enabled:

```
# cat /sys/kernel/debug/pinctrl/d0013800.pinctrl-armada_37xx-p
inctrl/pinmux-pins
Pinmux settings per pin
Format: pin (name): mux_owner gpio_owner hog?
pin 0 (GPIO1-0): (MUX UNCLAIMED) (GPIO UNCLAIMED)
pin 1 (GPIO1-1): (MUX UNCLAIMED) (GPIO UNCLAIMED)
pin 2 (GPIO1-2): (MUX UNCLAIMED) (GPIO UNCLAIMED)
pin 3 (GPIO1-3): (MUX UNCLAIMED) GPIO1:479
pin 4 (GPIO1-4): (MUX UNCLAIMED) GPIO1:480
pin 5 (GPIO1-5): (MUX UNCLAIMED) (GPIO UNCLAIMED)
...
pin 24 (GPIO1-24): (MUX UNCLAIMED) (GPIO UNCLAIMED)
pin 25 (GPIO1-25): d0012000.serial (GPIO UNCLAIMED) function uart
group uart1
pin 26 (GPIO1-26): d0012000.serial (GPIO UNCLAIMED) function uart
```

```
group uart1
pin 27 (GPIO1-27): (MUX UNCLAIMED) (GPIO UNCLAIMED)
...
```

For further information about debugfs, see `https://en.wikipedia.org/wiki/Debugfs` and then following some external links.

2. We should then try to modify ESPRESSObin's DTS file to enable another UART device named `uart1` with its own pins defined in the `uart2_pins` group as follows:

```
--- a/arch/arm64/boot/dts/marvell/armada-3720-espressobin.dts
+++ b/arch/arm64/boot/dts/marvell/armada-3720-espressobin.dts
@@ -97,6 +97,13 @@
     status = "okay";
  };

+/* Exported on extension connector P9 at pins 24(UA2_TXD) and
26(UA2_RXD) */
+&uart1 {
+    pinctrl-names = "default";
+    pinctrl-0 = <&uart2_pins>;
+    status = "okay";
+};
+
  /*
   * Connector J17 and J18 expose a number of different features.
Some pins are
   * multiplexed. This is the case for instance for the following
features:
```

This pin group is defined in the `linux/arch/arm64/boot/dts/marvell/armada-37xx.dtsi` file as follows:

```
uart2_pins: uart2-pins {
    groups = "uart2";
    function = "uart";
};
```

How it works...

Let's check how this works by testing our pinctrl modification. For this, we have to regenerate ESPRESSObin's DTB file, as usual, and restart the system. If everything works well, we should now have two UART devices as follows:

```
# ls /sys/bus/platform/drivers/mvebu-uart/
d0012000.serial d0012200.serial uevent
# ls /sys/bus/platform/drivers/mvebu-uart/d0012200.serial/tty/
ttyMV1
```

Also, if we take another look in the `/sys/kernel/debug/pinctrl/d0013800.pinctrl-armada_37xx-pinctrl/pinmux-pins` file, we see that this time the `uart2` pins group has been added and then our new serial port is available on extension connector P9 at pins 24 and 26.

See also

- For further information regarding the pinctrl subsystem, a good starting point is `https://www.kernel.org/doc/Documentation/pinctrl.txt`.

5
Managing Interrupts and Concurrency

When implementing a device driver, a developer has to resolve two main problems:

- How to exchange data with peripherals
- How to manage interrupts that peripherals generate to the CPU

The first point was covered (at least for char drivers) in previous chapters, while the second one (and its related matter) will be the main topic of this chapter.

In the kernel, we can consider the CPU (or the internal core executing some code) running in two main execution contexts — the **interrupt context** and the **process context**. The interrupt context is very easy to understand; in fact, the CPU is in this context each time it executes an interrupt handler (that is, special code the kernel executes each time an interrupt occurs). In addition to this, interrupts can be generated by the hardware or even by the software; that's why we talk about hardware interrupts and software interrupts (we'll take a closer look at software interrupts in the following sections), which in turn define the **hardware interrupt context** and the **software interrupt context**.

On the other hand, the **process context** is when the CPU (or one of its internal cores) executes some code of a process in the kernel space (processes also execute in the user space, but we are not covering that here), that is, when the CPU executes the code of a system call that has been invoked by a process (see `Chapter 3`, *Working with Char Drivers*). In this situation, it's very common to yield the CPU and then suspend the current process because some data from the peripheral is not ready to be read; for instance; this can be done by asking to the scheduler to take the CPU and then assign it to another process. When this happens we usually say that the current **process has gone to sleep,** and when data is newly available we say that a **process has been awakened**, and, it restarts its execution where it was previously interrupted.

In this chapter, we'll see how to do all these actions, how a device driver developer can ask the kernel to suspend the current reading process because the peripheral is not ready to serve the request, and also how to wake up a sleeping process. We'll also see how to manage concurrent access to our driver's methods to avoid data corruption due to a race condition, and how to manage time flow in order to do a specific action after a well-defined amount of time, respecting the possible time constraints a peripheral may require.

We will also look at how to exchange data between a char driver and the userspace, and how to handle those kernel events a driver should be able to manage. The first (and probably the most important) example is how to manage interrupts, followed by how to defer a job "later in time," and how to wait for an event. We can do all these using the following recipes:

- Implementing an interrupt handler
- Deferring jobs
- Managing time with kernel timers
- Waiting for an event
- Doing atomic operations

Technical requirements

For more information on this chapter, you can visit the *Appendix*.

The code and other files used in this chapter can be downloaded from GitHub at `https://github.com/giometti/linux_device_driver_development_cookbook/tree/master/chapter_05`.

Implementing an interrupt handler

Inside the kernel, an **interrupt handler** is a function associated with a CPU interrupt line (or pin) that Linux executes whenever the peripheral connected with this line changes the pin status; when this happens, an interrupt request is generated for the CPU, and it's captured by the kernel, which in turn executes the proper handler.

In this recipe, we will see how to install an interrupt handler which the kernel executes each time an interrupt occurs on a well-defined line.

Getting ready

The simplest code to implement an interrupt handler is the code in
`linux/drivers/misc/dummy-irq.c`. Here is the handler:

```
static int irq = -1;

static irqreturn_t dummy_interrupt(int irq, void *dev_id)
{
    static int count = 0;

    if (count == 0) {
        printk(KERN_INFO "dummy-irq: interrupt occurred on IRQ %d\n",
                irq);
        count++;
    }

    return IRQ_NONE;
}
```

Here is the code to install or to remove it:

```
static int __init dummy_irq_init(void)
{
    if (irq < 0) {
        printk(KERN_ERR "dummy-irq: no IRQ given. Use irq=N\n");
        return -EIO;
    }
    if (request_irq(irq, &dummy_interrupt, IRQF_SHARED, "dummy_irq", &irq))
{
        printk(KERN_ERR "dummy-irq: cannot register IRQ %d\n", irq);
        return -EIO;
    }
    printk(KERN_INFO "dummy-irq: registered for IRQ %d\n", irq);
    return 0;
}

static void __exit dummy_irq_exit(void)
{
    printk(KERN_INFO "dummy-irq unloaded\n");
    free_irq(irq, &irq);
}
```

This code is really simple, and, as we can see, it calls the `request_irq()` function in the `dummy_irq_init()` module initialization function, and the `free_irq()` function in the `dummy_irq_exit()` module exit function. Then, these two functions respectively ask the kernel to connect the `dummy_interrupt()` interrupt handler to the `irq` interrupt line and, in the opposite operation, to detach the handler from it.

This code briefly shows how to install an interrupt handler; however, it doesn't show how a device driver's developer can install its own handler; that's why in the next section we're going to do a practical example using a real interrupt line simulated with a General Purpose Input Output line (GPIO).

In order to implement a management for our first **interrupt request (IRQ)** handler, we can use a normal GPIO as an interrupt line; however, before doing so, we have to verify that our GPIO line correctly detects high and low input levels.

To manage GPIOs we're going to use its sysfs interface so, first of all, we have to verify that it is currently enabled for our kernel by checking if the `/sys/class/gpio` directory exists. If not we'll have to enable the `CONFIG_GPIO_SYSFS` kernel configuration entry by using the kernel configuration menu (`make menuconfig`); the can be done by going to **Device Drivers**, then **GPIO Support,** and enabling the **/sys/class/gpio/... (sysfs interface)** menu entry.

A way to quickly check if the entry is enabled is by using the following command line:

```
$ rgrep CONFIG_GPIO_SYSFS .config
CONFIG_GPIO_SYSFS=y
```

Otherwise, if it is not enabled, we'll get the following output, and then we must enable it:

```
$ rgrep CONFIG_GPIO_SYSFS .config
# CONFIG_GPIO_SYSFS is not set
```

If everything is in place, we should get something something similar to the following:

```
# ls /sys/class/gpio/
export   gpiochip446   gpiochip476   unexport
```

The `gpiochip446` and `gpiochip476` directories represent the two ESPRESSObin's GPIOs controller as we saw in the previous chapter describing the device tree. (See *The Armada 3720* section in Appendix of `Chapter 4`, *Using the Device Tree, Configuring CPU's pins for specific peripherals* section). The `export` and `unexport` files are used to get access to GPIO lines.

To do our job, we need to get access to the MPP2_20 CPU line, which is mapped on pin 12 of the ESPRESSObin extension #2; that is, the connector P8 (or J18) on the ESPRESSObin schematics. (See the *Technical requirements* section in `Chapter 1`, I*nstalling the Development System*). In the CPU datasheet, we discover that the MPP2_20 line is attached to the second pinctrl controller (named south bridge and mapped as `pinctrl_sb: pinctrl@18800` in the device tree). To know which is the right gpiochip device to use, we can still use the sysfs as follows:

```
# ls -l /sys/class/gpio/gpiochip4*
lrwxrwxrwx 1 root root 0 Mar 7 20:20 /sys/class/gpio/gpiochip446 ->
  ../../devices/platform/soc/soc:internal-
regs@d0000000/d0018800.pinctrl/gpio/gpiochip446
lrwxrwxrwx 1 root root 0 Mar 7 20:20 /sys/class/gpio/gpiochip476 ->
  ../../devices/platform/soc/soc:internal-
regs@d0000000/d0013800.pinctrl/gpio/gpiochip476
```

It's now clear that we have to use `gpiochip446`. In that directory, we will find the `base` file that tells us the corresponding number of the first GPIO line, and, since we're using the 20th line, we should export the `base+20` GPIO line as follows:

```
# cat /sys/class/gpio/gpiochip446/base
446
# echo 466 > /sys/class/gpio/export
```

If everything works well, a new `gpio466` entry is now present in the `/sys/class/gpio` directory, corresponding to our just exported GPIO line:

```
# ls /sys/class/gpio/
export   gpio466   gpiochip446   gpiochip476   unexport
```

Great! The `gpio466` directory is now ready to be used, and, by taking a look inside it, we get the following files:

```
# ls /sys/class/gpio/gpio466/
active_low device direction edge power subsystem uevent value
```

To see if we are able to modify our GPIO line, we can simply use the following command:

```
cat /sys/class/gpio/gpio466/value
1
```

 Note that the line is set to 1, even if unconnected, because this pin is normally configured with an internal pull-up that forces the pin state to the high level.

This output tells us that the GPIO line 20 is currently high, but, if we connect pin 12 of the P8 connector to the ground (pin 1 or 2) of the same connector (P8/J8), the GPIO line should go to the downstate and the preceding command should now return 0, instead, as follows:

```
# cat /sys/class/gpio/gpio466/value
0
```

If the line doesn't change, you should verify that you're working on the correct pins/connector. Also, you should take a look at the `/sys/class/gpio/gpio466/direction` file, which should hold the `in` string, shown as follows:
```
# cat /sys/class/gpio/gpio466/direction
in
```

OK. Now we are ready to generate our interrupts!

How to do it...

Let's see how to do it by following these steps:

1. Now, let's assume that we have a dedicated platform driver named `irqtest`, defined as follows in the ESPRESSObin device tree:

```
irqtest {
    compatible = "ldddc,irqtest";

    gpios = <&gpiosb 20 GPIO_ACTIVE_LOW>;
};
```

Remember that the ESPRESSObin device tree file is `linux/arch/arm64/boot/dts/marvell/armada-3720-espressobin.dts`.

2. Then we have to add a platform driver to the kernel as we did in the previous chapter with the following code:

```
static const struct of_device_id irqtest_dt_ids[] = {
    { .compatible = "ldddc,irqtest", },
    { /* sentinel */ }
};
MODULE_DEVICE_TABLE(of, irqtest_dt_ids);

static struct platform_driver irqtest_driver = {
    .probe = irqtest_probe,
```

```
    .remove = irqtest_remove,
    .driver = {
        .name = "irqtest",
        .of_match_table = irqtest_dt_ids,
    },
};

module_platform_driver(irqtest_driver);
```

 Note that all code presented here can be obtained from the GitHub repository by applying the add_irqtest_module.patch patch within the root directory of kernel sources by executing the patch command, as follows:

$ patch –p1 <
../linux_device_driver_development_cookbook/chapter_5/add
_irqtest_module.patch

3. Now, we know that, once the kernel detects in the device tree that a driver is compatible with lddddc, irqtest, the following irqtest_probe() probing function should be executed. This function is very similar to the one in the preceding linux/drivers/misc/dummy-irq.c file, even if a bit more complex. In fact, first we have to read from the device tree which is the GPIO line where interrupts will come from, by using the of_get_gpio() function:

```
static int irqtest_probe(struct platform_device *pdev)
{
    struct device *dev = &pdev->dev;
    struct device_node *np = dev->of_node;
    int ret;

    /* Read gpios property (just the first entry) */
    ret = of_get_gpio(np, 0);
    if (ret < 0) {
        dev_err(dev, "failed to get GPIO from device tree\n");
        return ret;
    }
    irqinfo.pin = ret;
    dev_info(dev, "got GPIO %u from DTS\n", irqinfo.pin);
```

4. Then, we have to ask the kernel for the GPIO line, by using the devm_gpio_request() function:

```
    /* Now request the GPIO and set the line as an input */
    ret = devm_gpio_request(dev, irqinfo.pin, "irqtest");
    if (ret) {
        dev_err(dev, "failed to request GPIO %u\n", irqinfo.pin);
```

```
        return ret;
    }
    ret = gpio_direction_input(irqinfo.pin);
    if (ret) {
        dev_err(dev, "failed to set pin input direction\n");
        return -EINVAL;
    }

    /* Now ask to the kernel to convert GPIO line into an IRQ line
*/
    ret = gpio_to_irq(irqinfo.pin);
    if (ret < 0) {
        dev_err(dev, "failed to map GPIO to IRQ!\n");
        return -EINVAL;
    }
    irqinfo.irq = ret;
    dev_info(dev, "GPIO %u correspond to IRQ %d\n",
                irqinfo.pin, irqinfo.irq);
```

5. After we are sure that the GPIO is for us only, we have to set it up as an input (interrupts are incoming signals) using the gpio_direction_input() function, and then we have to get the corresponding interrupt line number (which, very often, is a different number) by using the gpio_to_irq() function:

```
    ret = gpio_direction_input(irqinfo.pin);
    if (ret) {
        dev_err(dev, "failed to set pin input direction\n");
        return -EINVAL;
    }

    /* Now ask to the kernel to convert GPIO line into an IRQ line
*/
    ret = gpio_to_irq(irqinfo.pin);
    if (ret < 0) {
        dev_err(dev, "failed to map GPIO to IRQ!\n");
        return -EINVAL;
    }
    irqinfo.irq = ret;
    dev_info(dev, "GPIO %u correspond to IRQ %d\n",
                irqinfo.pin, irqinfo.irq);
```

6. After that, we have all the necessary information to install our interrupt handler using the `request_irq()` function defined in the `linux/include/linux/interrupt.h` header file, as follows:

```
extern int __must_check
request_threaded_irq(unsigned int irq, irq_handler_t handler,
            irq_handler_t thread_fn,
            unsigned long flags, const char *name, void *dev);

static inline int __must_check
request_irq(unsigned int irq, irq_handler_t handler, unsigned long
flags,
            const char *name, void *dev)
{
    return request_threaded_irq(irq, handler, NULL, flags, name,
dev);
}

extern int __must_check
request_any_context_irq(unsigned int irq, irq_handler_t handler,
            unsigned long flags, const char *name, void *dev_id);
```

7. Finally, the `handler` parameter specifies the function to be executed as an interrupt handler and `dev` is a pointer, which the kernel will pass as-is to the handler when executed. In our example, the interrupt handler is defined as follows:

```
static irqreturn_t irqtest_interrupt(int irq, void *dev_id)
{
    struct irqtest_data *info = dev_id;
    struct device *dev = info->dev;

    dev_info(dev, "interrupt occurred on IRQ %d\n", irq);

    return IRQ_HANDLED;
}
```

How it works...

In *step 1*, the node declares a device compatible with the driver named ldddc, irqtest, that requires for its usage the GPIO line 20 of the gpiosb node, defined as follows in the Armada 3270 device tree arch/arm64/boot/dts/marvell/armada-37xx.dtsi file:

```
pinctrl_sb: pinctrl@18800 {
    compatible = "marvell,armada3710-sb-pinctrl",
            "syscon", "simple-mfd";
    reg = <0x18800 0x100>, <0x18C00 0x20>;
    /* MPP2[23:0] */
    gpiosb: gpio {
        #gpio-cells = <2>;
        gpio-ranges = <&pinctrl_sb 0 0 30>;
        gpio-controller;
        interrupt-controller;
        #interrupt-cells = <2>;
        interrupts =
        <GIC_SPI 160 IRQ_TYPE_LEVEL_HIGH>,
        <GIC_SPI 159 IRQ_TYPE_LEVEL_HIGH>,
        <GIC_SPI 158 IRQ_TYPE_LEVEL_HIGH>,
        <GIC_SPI 157 IRQ_TYPE_LEVEL_HIGH>,
        <GIC_SPI 156 IRQ_TYPE_LEVEL_HIGH>;
    };
    . . .
```

Here, we have the confirmation that the gpiosb node is related to MPP2 lines.

In *step 2* we just declare the driver within the kernel while in *step 3*, the function gets GPIO information from the gpio property, and, by using the second argument set to 0, we simply ask for the first entry. The return value is saved into the module's data structure, which is now defined as follows:

```
static struct irqtest_data {
    int irq;
    unsigned int pin;
    struct device *dev;
} irqinfo;
```

In step 4, in reality, the devm_gpio_request() call is not strictly needed since we're in the kernel and nobody can stop us using a resource; however, if all drivers do this, we can ensure that we're informed if someone else is holding the resource!

We should now notice that the `devm_gpio_request()` function does not have a counterpart in the module's `exit()` function `irqtest_remove()`. This is because functions with the `devm` prefix are related to managed devices that are able to automatically deallocate resources when the owner device is removed from the system.

In the `linux/drivers/gpio/devres.c` file, where this function is defined, we see the following comment, which explains how this function works:

```
/**
 * devm_gpio_request - request a GPIO for a managed device
 * @dev: device to request the GPIO for
 * @gpio: GPIO to allocate
 * @label: the name of the requested GPIO
 *
 * Except for the extra @dev argument, this function takes the
 * same arguments and performs the same function as
 * gpio_request(). GPIOs requested with this function will be
 * automatically freed on driver detach.
 *
 * If an GPIO allocated with this function needs to be freed
 * separately, devm_gpio_free() must be used.
 */
```

This is advanced resource management and beyond the scope of this book. However, if you are interested, there is a lot of information on the internet, and the following is a good article to start with: `https://lwn.net/Articles/222860/`.

Anyway the normal counterparts of the `devm_gpio_request()` function are the `gpio_request()` and `gpio_free()` functions.

In step 5, note that a GPIO line number almost never corresponds to an interrupt line number; that's why we need to invoke the `gpio_to_irq()` function in order to get the correct IRQ line related to our GPIO line.

In step 6, we can see the `request_irq()` function is a special case of the `request_threaded_irq()` function, which informs us that an interrupt handler can run in an interrupt context, or inside a kernel thread that is in a process context.

At the moment, we still don't know what kernel threads are (they will be explained in `Chapter 6`, *Miscellaneous Kernel Internals*), but it should be easy to understand that they are something like a thread (or process) executed in the kernel space.

Also the `request_any_context_irq()` function can be used to delegate the kernel to automatically request a normal interrupt handler or a threaded one depending of the IRQ line characteristics.

This a really advanced use of interrupt handlers, which is fundamental when we have to manage peripherals (such as I2C or SPI devices) where we need to suspend the interrupt handler to be able to read from, or write data to, the peripheral's registers.

Apart from these aspects, all the `request_irq*()` functions take several parameters. First of all, the `irq` line, then a symbolic `name` describing the interrupt line we can find in the `/proc/interrupts` file, and then we can use the `flags` argument to specify some special settings, shown as follows (see the `linux/include/linux/interrupt.h` file for a complete list):

```
/*
 * These correspond to the IORESOURCE_IRQ_* defines in
 * linux/ioport.h to select the interrupt line behaviour. When
 * requesting an interrupt without specifying a IRQF_TRIGGER, the
 * setting should be assumed to be "as already configured", which
 * may be as per machine or firmware initialisation.
 */
#define IRQF_TRIGGER_NONE 0x00000000
#define IRQF_TRIGGER_RISING 0x00000001
#define IRQF_TRIGGER_FALLING 0x00000002
#define IRQF_TRIGGER_HIGH 0x00000004
#define IRQF_TRIGGER_LOW 0x00000008
...
/*
 * IRQF_SHARED - allow sharing the irq among several devices
 * IRQF_ONESHOT - Interrupt is not reenabled after the hardirq
handler finished.
 * Used by threaded interrupts which need to keep the
 * irq line disabled until the threaded handler has been run.
 * IRQF_NO_SUSPEND - Do not disable this IRQ during suspend. Does
not guarantee
 * that this interrupt will wake the system from a suspended
 * state. See Documentation/power/suspend-and-interrupts.txt
 */
```

The `IRQF_SHARED` flag should be used when the IRQ line is shared with more than one peripheral. (Nowadays it is quite useless but, in the past, it was very useful, especially on x86 machines.) The `IRQF_ONESHOT` flag is used by the system to be sure that even threaded interrupt handlers can run with their own IRQ line disabled. The `IRQF_NO_SUSPEND` flag can be used to allow our peripheral to wake the system from a suspended state, by sending a proper interrupt request. (See the `linux/Documentation/power/suspend-and-interrupts.txt` file for more details.)

Then the `IRQF_TRIGGER_*` flag can be used to specify the IRQ trigger mode for our peripheral, that is, if the interrupt must be generated on high or low levels or during a rising or falling transition.

 These last flag groups should be carefully checked against the device tree pinctrl settings; otherwise, we might see some unexpected behavior.

In step 7, since in the `request_irq()` function we set the `dev` parameter to the pointer of the `struct irqtest_data` module, when the `irqtest_interrupt()` interrupt handler executes, it will find in the `dev_id` argument the same pointer we supplied to `request_irq()`. By using this trick, we can get back the `dev` value we got from the probing function, and we can safely reuse it as an argument of the `dev_info()` function, as earlier.

In our example, the interrupt handler does almost nothing but display a message. However, usually in the interrupt handler, we have to acknowledge the peripheral, read from or write data to it, and then wake up all the sleeping processes that are waiting for peripheral activities. In any case, at the end, the handler should return one value from the ones listed in the `linux/include/linux/irqreturn.h` file:

```
/**
 * enum irqreturn
 * @IRQ_NONE       interrupt was not from this device or was not handled
 * @IRQ_HANDLED    interrupt was handled by this device
 * @IRQ_WAKE_THREAD handler requests to wake the handler thread
 */
```

The `IRQ_NONE` value is useful in case we're working on a shared interrupt to inform the system that the current IRQ is not for us, and that it must be propagated to the next handler, while `IRQ_WAKE_THREAD` should be used in the case of threaded IRQ handlers. Of course, `IRQ_HANDLED` must be used to report to the system that the IRQ has been served.

There's more...

If you wish to check how this works, we can do so by testing our example. We have to compile it and then reinstall the kernel with our code compiled as built-in, so let's use the usual `make menuconfig` command and enable our testing code, or just use `make oldconfig`, answering `y` when the system asks for a choice, as follows:

```
Simple IRQ test (IRQTEST_CODE) [N/m/y/?] (NEW)
```

After that, we've just to recompile and reinstall the kernel and then reboot the ESPRESSObin. If everything works well during the boot sequence, we should see kernel messages as follows:

```
irqtest irqtest: got GPIO 466 from DTS
irqtest irqtest: GPIO 466 correspond to IRQ 40
irqtest irqtest: interrupt handler for IRQ 40 is now ready!
```

Now, the MPP2_20 line has been taken by the kernel and converted into the number 40 interrupt line. To verify it, we can take a look at the `/proc/interrupts` file, which holds all registered interrupt lines within the kernel. Earlier, we used the `irqtest` label in the `request_irq()` function during an interrupt handler registration, so we have to search for it within the file with `grep` as follows:

```
# grep irqtest /proc/interrupts
  40:      0      0     GPIO2    20    Edge    irqtest
```

OK. The interrupt line 40 has been assigned to our module, and we notice that this IRQ line corresponds to the GPIO line 20 of the GPIO2 group (that is, the MPP2_20 line). If we take a look at the beginning of the `/proc/interrupts` file, we should get an output as follows:

```
# head -4 /proc/interrupts
            CPU0    CPU1
    1:         0       0    GICv3    25    Level    vgic
    3:      5944   20941    GICv3    30    Level    arch_timer
    4:         0       0    GICv3    27    Level    kvm guest timer
...
```

The first number is the interrupt line; the second and third ones show how many interrupts have been served by the CPU0 and CPU1, respectively, so we can use this information to verify which CPU served our interrupt.

OK. Now we're ready to go. Just connect pin 12 to pin 1 of the P8 extension connector; at least one interrupt should be generated and a message, such as the following, should appear in the kernel messages:

```
irqtest irqtest: interrupt occurred on IRQ 40
```

Note that you may get several messages due to the fact that, during the short circuit operation, the electrical signal may generate several oscillations, which in turn will generate several interrupts.

As a final note, let's take a look at what happens if we try to export the number 466 GPIO line, as we did earlier, using the sysfs interface:

```
# echo 466 > /sys/class/gpio/export
-bash: echo: write error: Device or resource busy
```

Now, we correctly get a busy error due to the fact such a GPIO has been requested by the kernel when we used the `devm_gpio_request()` function.

See also

- For further information about interrupts handlers, a good starting point (even if it is slightly outdated) is The Linux Kernel Module Programming Guide at `https://www.tldp.org/LDP/lkmpg/2.4/html/x1210.html`.

Deferring work

Interrupts are events generated by peripherals, but, as said earlier, they are not the only events that the kernel can handle. In fact, software interrupts exist, which are similar to hardware interrupts but generated by software. In this book, we'll see two examples of such software interrupts; both of them can be used to safely defer a job for a future time. We'll also have a look at a useful mechanism that a device driver developer can use to catch special kernel events and perform actions as a consequence (for instance, when a network device is enabled, or the system is doing a reboot, and so on).

In this recipe, we will see how to defer a job when a specific event happens within the kernel.

Getting ready

Since tasklets and workqueues were implemented to defer jobs, their main usage is in an interrupt handler where we just acknowledge the Interrupt Request (usualy named IRQ), and then we invoke the tasklet/workqueue to finish the job.

However, don't forget that this is just only one of the several possible usage of tasklets and workqueues that, of course, can be used even without interrupts.

How to do it...

In this section, we're going to present simple examples regarding both tasklets and workqueues by using patches against the previous `irqtest.c` example.

In the next chapters, whenever needed, we're going to present more complex usages of these mechanisms, but, for the moment, we're interested in understanding their basic usage only.

Tasklets

Let's see how to do it by following these steps:

1. The following modifications are needed to add a custom tasklet invocation to our `irqtest_interrupt()` interrupt handler:

```
--- a/drivers/misc/irqtest.c
+++ b/drivers/misc/irqtest.c
@@ -26,9 +26,19 @@ static struct irqtest_data {
 } irqinfo;

 /*
- * The interrupt handler
+ * The interrupt handlers
  */

+static void irqtest_tasklet_handler(unsigned long flag)
+{
+       struct irqtest_data *info = (struct irqtest_data *) flag;
+       struct device *dev = info->dev;
+
+       dev_info(dev, "tasklet executed after IRQ %d", info->irq);
+}
+DECLARE_TASKLET(irqtest_tasklet, irqtest_tasklet_handler,
+                (unsigned long) &irqinfo);
+
 static irqreturn_t irqtest_interrupt(int irq, void *dev_id)
 {
        struct irqtest_data *info = dev_id;
@@ -36,6 +46,8 @@ static irqreturn_t irqtest_interrupt(int irq,
void *dev_id)
```

```
        dev_info(dev, "interrupt occurred on IRQ %d\n", irq);

+       tasklet_schedule(&irqtest_tasklet);
+
        return IRQ_HANDLED;
 }

@@ -98,6 +110,7 @@ static int irqtest_remove(struct platform_device
*pdev)
 {
        struct device *dev = &pdev->dev;

+       tasklet_kill(&irqtest_tasklet);
        free_irq(irqinfo.irq, &irqinfo);
        dev_info(dev, "IRQ %d is now unmanaged!\n", irqinfo.irq);
```

 The previous patch can be found in the GitHub resources in the
`add_tasklet_to_irqtest_module.patch` file, and it can be applied as
usual with the
`patch -p1 < add_tasklet_to_irqtest_module.patch` command.

2. Once the tasklet has been defined, it can be invoked by using the
`tasklet_schedule()` function as shown previously. To stop it, we can use the
`tasklet_kill()` function, which was in our example for the
`irqtest_remove()` function to stop the tasklet before unloading the module
from the kernel. In fact, we must make sure that every resource previously
allocated and/or enabled by our driver has been disabled and/or released before
unloading our module or a memory corruption can occur.
Note that the compile-time usage of `DECLARE_TASKLET()` is not the only way to
declare a tasklet. In fact, the following is an alternate way:

```
--- a/drivers/misc/irqtest.c
+++ b/drivers/misc/irqtest.c
@@ -23,12 +23,21 @@ static struct irqtest_data {
        int irq;
        unsigned int pin;
        struct device *dev;
+       struct tasklet_struct task;
 } irqinfo;

 /*
- * The interrupt handler
+ * The interrupt handlers
  */

+static void irqtest_tasklet_handler(unsigned long flag)
```

```
+{
+       struct irqtest_data *info = (struct irqtest_data *) flag;
+       struct device *dev = info->dev;
+
+       dev_info(dev, "tasklet executed after IRQ %d", info->irq);
+}
+
 static irqreturn_t irqtest_interrupt(int irq, void *dev_id)
 {
       struct irqtest_data *info = dev_id;
@@ -36,6 +45,8 @@ static irqreturn_t irqtest_interrupt(int irq,
void *dev_id)

       dev_info(dev, "interrupt occurred on IRQ %d\n", irq);

+       tasklet_schedule(&info->task);
+
       return IRQ_HANDLED;
 }

@@ -80,6 +91,10 @@ static int irqtest_probe(struct platform_device
*pdev)
       dev_info(dev, "GPIO %u correspond to IRQ %d\n",
                                 irqinfo.pin, irqinfo.irq);
```

Then, we create our tasklet as follows:

```
+       /* Create our tasklet */
+       tasklet_init(&irqinfo.task, irqtest_tasklet_handler,
+                               (unsigned long) &irqinfo);
+
        /* Request IRQ line and setup corresponding handler */
        irqinfo.dev = dev;
        ret = request_irq(irqinfo.irq, irqtest_interrupt, 0,
@@ -98,6 +113,7 @@ static int irqtest_remove(struct platform_device
*pdev)
 {
       struct device *dev = &pdev->dev;

+       tasklet_kill(&irqinfo.task);
       free_irq(irqinfo.irq, &irqinfo);
       dev_info(dev, "IRQ %d is now unmanaged!\n", irqinfo.irq);
```

The preceding patch can be found in the GitHub resources in the `add_tasklet_2_to_irqtest_module.patch` file, and it can be applied as usual with the `patch -p1 < add_tasklet_2_to_irqtest_module.patch` command.

This second form is useful when we have to embed a tasklet inside a device structure and then generate it dynamically.

Workqueues

Let's now take a look at workqueues. In the following example, we add a custom workqueue referenced by the `irqtest_wq` pointer and named `irqtest`, which, in turn, executes two different works described by the `work` and `dwork` structures: the former is a normal work, while the latter represents a delayed work, that is, a work that is executed after a well-known delay.

1. First of all, we have to add our data structures:

```
a/drivers/misc/irqtest.c
+++ b/drivers/misc/irqtest.c
@@ -14,6 +14,7 @@
 #include <linux/gpio.h>
 #include <linux/irq.h>
 #include <linux/interrupt.h>
+#include <linux/workqueue.h>

 /*
  * Module data
@@ -23,12 +24,37 @@ static struct irqtest_data {
        int irq;
        unsigned int pin;
        struct device *dev;
+       struct work_struct work;
+       struct delayed_work dwork;
 } irqinfo;

+static struct workqueue_struct *irqtest_wq;
 ...
```

All these modifications can be found in the GitHub resources in the `add_workqueue_to_irqtest_module.patch` file and it can be applied as usual with the
`patch -p1 < add_workqueue_to_irqtest_module.patch` command.

2. Then, we have to create the workqueue and it works. For the workqueue creation, we can use the `create_singlethread_workqueue()` function, while the two works can be initialized by using `INIT_WORK()` and `INIT_DELAYED_WORK()`,, shown as follows:

```
@@ -80,24 +108,40 @@ static int irqtest_probe(struct
platform_device *pdev)
         dev_info(dev, "GPIO %u correspond to IRQ %d\n",
                                 irqinfo.pin, irqinfo.irq);

+        /* Create our work queue and init works */
+        irqtest_wq = create_singlethread_workqueue("irqtest");
+        if (!irqtest_wq) {
+            dev_err(dev, "failed to create work queue!\n");
+            return -EINVAL;
+        }
+        INIT_WORK(&irqinfo.work, irqtest_work_handler);
+        INIT_DELAYED_WORK(&irqinfo.dwork, irqtest_dwork_handler);
+
         /* Request IRQ line and setup corresponding handler */
         irqinfo.dev = dev;
         ret = request_irq(irqinfo.irq, irqtest_interrupt, 0,
                                 "irqtest", &irqinfo);
         if (ret) {
             dev_err(dev, "cannot register IRQ %d\n", irqinfo.irq);
-            return -EIO;
+            goto flush_wq;
         }
         dev_info(dev, "interrupt handler for IRQ %d is now ready!\n",
                                 irqinfo.irq);

         return 0;
+
+flush_wq:
+        flush_workqueue(irqtest_wq);
+        return -EIO;
 }
```

To create a workqueue, we can also use the `create_workqueue()` function; however, this creates a workqueue that has a dedicated thread for each processor on the system. In many cases, all those threads are simply overkilled and the single worker thread obtained with `create_singlethread_workqueue()` will suffice.

Note that the Concurrency Managed Workqueue API, available in the kernel's documentation file (`linux/Documentation/core-api/workqueue.rst`), states that the `create_*workqueue()` functions are deprecated and scheduled for removal. However, they seem to be still widely used with kernel sources.

3. Next are the handlers bodies representing the effective workloads for the normal workqueue and the delayed workqueue, as follows:

```
+static void irqtest_dwork_handler(struct work_struct *ptr)
+{
+       struct irqtest_data *info = container_of(ptr, struct
irqtest_data,
+                                                 dwork.work);
+       struct device *dev = info->dev;
+
+       dev_info(dev, "delayed work executed after work");
+}
+
+static void irqtest_work_handler(struct work_struct *ptr)
+{
+       struct irqtest_data *info = container_of(ptr, struct
irqtest_data,
+                                                 work);
+       struct device *dev = info->dev;
+
+       dev_info(dev, "work executed after IRQ %d", info->irq);
+
+       /* Schedule the delayed work after 2 seconds */
+       queue_delayed_work(irqtest_wq, &info->dwork, 2*HZ);
+}
```

Note that to specify a delay of two seconds we used the `2*HZ` code, where `HZ` is a define (see the next section for further information about `HZ`) representing how many jiffies are needed to compose one second. So, to have a delay of two seconds, we have to multiply `HZ` by two.

4. The interrupt handler now just uses the following `queue_work()` function to execute the first workqueue before returning:

```
@@ -36,6 +62,8 @@ static irqreturn_t irqtest_interrupt(int irq,
void *dev_id)

        dev_info(dev, "interrupt occurred on IRQ %d\n", irq);

+       queue_work(irqtest_wq, &info->work);
```

```
+
        return IRQ_HANDLED;
    }
```

So, when `irqtest_interrupt()` ends, the system invokes
`irqtest_work_handler()` which in turn, invokes `irqtest_dwork_handler()`
with a two-second delay by using `queue_delayed_work()`.

5. Finally, as for tasklets, before exiting the module, we have to cancel all works and
   workqueues (if created) by using `cancel_work_sync()` for normal work,
   `cancel_delayed_work_sync()` for delayed work, and (in our case)
   `flush_workqueue()` to stop the `irqtest` workqueue:

```
static int irqtest_remove(struct platform_device *pdev)
{
        struct device *dev = &pdev->dev;

+       cancel_work_sync(&irqinfo.work);
+       cancel_delayed_work_sync(&irqinfo.dwork);
+       flush_workqueue(irqtest_wq);
        free_irq(irqinfo.irq, &irqinfo);
        dev_info(dev, "IRQ %d is now unmanaged!\n", irqinfo.irq);
```

There's more...

We can check how it works, by testing our examples. So, we have to apply the desired
patch and then we have to recompile the kernel, reinstalling and rebooting the
ESPRESSObin.

Tasklets

To test tasklets, we can do exactly as before, that is, connecting pin 12 to pin 1 of extension
connector P8. The following are the kernel messages we should get:

```
irqtest irqtest: interrupt occurred on IRQ 40
irqtest irqtest: tasklet executed after IRQ 40
```

As expected, an IRQ is generated and then managed by the hardware
`irqtest_interrupt()` interrupt handler that, in turn, executes the
`irqtest_tasklet_handler()`. tasklet handler.

Workqueues

To test workqueues, we have to short circuit our well known pins, and we should have an output as follows:

```
[ 33.113008] irqtest irqtest: interrupt occurred on IRQ 40
[ 33.115731] irqtest irqtest: work executed after IRQ 40
...
[ 33.514268] irqtest irqtest: interrupt occurred on IRQ 40
[ 33.516990] irqtest irqtest: work executed after IRQ 40
[ 33.533121] irqtest irqtest: interrupt occurred on IRQ 40
[ 33.535846] irqtest irqtest: work executed after IRQ 40
[ 35.138114] irqtest irqtest: delayed work executed after work
```

 Note that, this time, I didn't remove the first part of kernel messages, in order to see timings, and to better evaluate delay between the normal work and delayed one.

As we can see, as soon as we connect ESPRESSObin pins, we have several interrupts followed by the work, but the delayed work is executed just once. This happens because, even if scheduled several times, it's just the first invocation that takes effect, and so here we can see that the delayed work has been finally executed 2.025106 seconds after its first `schedule_work()` invocation. This also means that it has been effectively executed 25.106 ms later than the required and expected two seconds. Such an apparent anomaly is due to the fact that, when you ask the kernel to schedule some work to happen at a later point in time with a delayed workqueue, the kernel will certainly schedule your work at the desired point in the future, but it won't guarantee you that it will be executed at exactly that point in time. It will only assure you that such work won't be executed any earlier than the requested deadline. The length of such an additional random delay depends on the level of system workload at the time.

See also

- Regarding tasklets, you may wish to take a look at `https://www.kernel.org/doc/htmldocs/kernel-hacking/basics-softirqs.html`.
- For workqueues, more information is available at `https://www.kernel.org/doc/html/v4.15/core-api/workqueue.html`.

Managing time with kernel timers

During the device driver development, it may be necessary to perform several repeated operations at specific moments in time, or we may have to postpone the execution of some code after a well-defined delay. In these situations, kernel timers come to help the device driver developer.

In this recipe, we will see how to use kernel timers to do repeated jobs at well-defined periods of time, or to defer a job until after a well-defined time interval.

Getting ready

For a simple example of kernel timers, we can still use a kernel module where we define a kernel timer during a module's initialization function.

In the `chapter_05/timer` directory of GitHub resources, there are two simple examples about **kernel timers (ktimer)** and **high-resolution timers (hrtimer)**, and in the next sections we're going to explain them in detail, starting with the new high-resolution implementation, which should be preferred in new drivers. An old API is also presented to complete the picture.

How to do it...

The following main parts of the `hires_timer.c` file contain a simple example about high resolution kernel timers.

1. Let's start from the end of the file, with the module `init()` function:

```
static int __init hires_timer_init(void)
{
    /* Set up hires timer delay */

    pr_info("delay is set to %dns\n", delay_ns);

    /* Setup and start the hires timer */
    hrtimer_init(&hires_tinfo.timer, CLOCK_MONOTONIC,
                 HRTIMER_MODE_REL | HRTIMER_MODE_SOFT);
    hires_tinfo.timer.function = hires_timer_handler;
    hrtimer_start(&hires_tinfo.timer, ns_to_ktime(delay_ns),
                 HRTIMER_MODE_REL | HRTIMER_MODE_SOFT);

    pr_info("hires timer module loaded\n");
```

```
        return 0;
    }
```

Let's see where the module `exit()` function is located:

```
    static void __exit hires_timer_exit(void)
    {
        hrtimer_cancel(&hires_tinfo.timer);

        pr_info("hires timer module unloaded\n");
    }

    module_init(hires_timer_init);
    module_exit(hires_timer_exit);
```

As we can see in module `hires_timer_init()` initialization function, we read the `delay_ns` parameter, and, using the `hrtimer_init()` function, we first initialize the timer by specifying some features:

```
    /* Initialize timers: */
    extern void hrtimer_init(struct hrtimer *timer, clockid_t
    which_clock,
                            enum hrtimer_mode mode);
```

Using the `which_clock` argument, we ask the kernel to use a particular clock. In our example, we used `CLOCK_MONOTONIC`, which is very useful for reliable timestamps and measuring short time intervals accurately (it starts at system boot time but stops during suspend), but we can use other values (see `linux/include/uapi/linux/time.h` header file for the complete list), for example:

- `CLOCK_BOOTTIME`: This clock is like `CLOCK_MONOTONIC` but does not stop when the system goes into suspend mode. This can be useful for key expiration times that need to be synchronized with other machines across a suspend operation.
- `CLOCK_REALTIME`: This clock uses the time as relative to the UNIX epoch starting in 1970 using the **Coordinated Universal Time (UTC)** as `gettimeofday()` does in userspace. This is used for all timestamps that need to persist across a reboot, since it can jump backward due to a leap second update, **Network Time Protocol (NTP)** adjustment with the `settimeofday()` operation from the userspace. However, this clock is rarely used for device drivers.

- CLOCK_MONOTONIC_RAW: Like CLOCK_MONOTONIC but runs at the same rate as the hardware clock source without adjustments for clock drift (like NTP has). This is also rarely needed in device drivers.

2. After the timer initialization, we have to set up the callback or handler function by using the function pointer as follows, where we've set timer.function to hires_timer_handler:

```
hires_tinfo.timer.function = hires_timer_handler;
```

This time, the hires_tinfo module data structure is defined as follows:

```
static struct hires_timer_data {
    struct hrtimer timer;
    unsigned int data;
} hires_tinfo;
```

3. After the timer has been initialized, we can start it by calling hrtimer_start() where we just set the expiry time with a function like ns_to_ktime(), in case we have a time interval, or by using ktime_set(), in case we have a seconds/nanoseconds value.

> See the linux/include/linux/ktime.h header for more of the ktime*() functions.

If we take a look at the linux/include/linux/hrtimer.h file, we discover that the main function to start a high-resolution timer is hrtimer_start_range_ns() and hrtimer_start() is a particular case of that function, as can be seen in the following:

```
/* Basic timer operations: */
extern void hrtimer_start_range_ns(struct hrtimer *timer, ktime_t tim,
                        u64 range_ns, const enum hrtimer_mode
mode);

/**
 * hrtimer_start - (re)start an hrtimer
 * @timer: the timer to be added
 * @tim: expiry time
 * @mode: timer mode: absolute (HRTIMER_MODE_ABS) or
 * relative (HRTIMER_MODE_REL), and pinned (HRTIMER_MODE_PINNED);
```

```
 * softirq based mode is considered for debug purpose only!
 */
static inline void hrtimer_start(struct hrtimer *timer, ktime_t
tim,
                                 const enum hrtimer_mode mode)
{
    hrtimer_start_range_ns(timer, tim, 0, mode);
}
```

We also discover that the `HRTIMER_MODE_SOFT` mode should not be used apart from for debugging purposes.

By using the `hrtimer_start_range_ns()` function, we allow a `range_ns` delta time, which gives the kernel the freedom to schedule the actual wake up to a time that is both power and performance friendly. The kernel gives the normal best effort behavior for expiry time plus delta, but may decide to fire the timer earlier, but no earlier than the `tim` expiry time.

4. The `hires_timer_handler()` function from the `hires_timer.c` file is an example of the callback function:

```
static enum hrtimer_restart hires_timer_handler(struct hrtimer
*ptr)
{
    struct hires_timer_data *info = container_of(ptr,
                    struct hires_timer_data, timer);

    pr_info("kernel timer expired at %ld (data=%d)\n",
            jiffies, info->data++);

    /* Now forward the expiration time and ask to be rescheduled */
    hrtimer_forward_now(&info->timer, ns_to_ktime(delay_ns));
    return HRTIMER_RESTART;
}
```

By using the `container_of()` operator, we can take a pointer to our data structure (defined in the example as `struct hires_timer_data`) and, then, having completed our job, we call `hrtimer_forward_now()` to set up a new expiry time, and, by returning the `HRTIMER_RESTART` value, we ask the kernel to restart the timer. For one-shot timers, we can return `HRTIMER_NORESTART`.

5. On the module exit, within the `hires_timer_exit()` function, we must use the `hrtimer_cancel()` function to wait for the timer to stop. It's really important to wait for the timer to stop, because timers are asynchronous events and it may happen that we remove the `struct hires_timer_data` module freeing structure while the timer callback is executing, which can result in a severe memory corruption!

Note that syncing is implemented as a sleep (or suspend) `process`, and it means that the `hrtimer_cancel()` function cannot be called when we're in interrupt context (hard or soft). However, in these situations, we can use `hrtimer_try_to_cancel()`, which simply returns a non-negative value if the timer has been correctly stopped (or is simply not active).

How it works...

To see how it works, we test our code by simply compiling it as usual and then move the code to our ESPRESSObin. When everything is in place, we just have to load the module into the kernel as follows:

```
# insmod hires_timer.ko
```

Then, in kernel messages, we should get something like the following:

```
[ 528.902156] hires_timer:hires_timer_init: delay is set to 1000000000ns
[ 528.911593] hires_timer:hires_timer_init: hires timer module loaded
```

In *steps 1, 2,* and *3* we set up the timer, and here we know that it has been started with a delay of one second.

When the timer expires, thanks to step 4, we execute the kernel timer's handler:

```
[ 529.911604] hires_timer:hires_timer_handler: kernel timer expired at
4295024749 (data=0)
[ 530.911602] hires_timer:hires_timer_handler: kernel timer expired at
4295024999 (data=1)
[ 531.911602] hires_timer:hires_timer_handler: kernel timer expired at
4295025249 (data=2)
[ 532.911602] hires_timer:hires_timer_handler: kernel timer expired at
4295025499 (data=3)
. . .
```

I've left the timings so you have an idea about kernel timer's precision.

As we can see, the expiration time is really accurate (a few microseconds).

Now, thanks to *step 5*, if we remove the module, the timer is stopped, as the following shows:

```
hires_timer:hires_timer_exit: hires timer module unloaded
```

There's more...

Just to complete your understanding, it could be interesting to take a look at the legacy kernel timer API.

Legacy kernel timers

The `ktimer.c` file contains a simple example of legacy kernel timers. As usual, let's start from the end of the file where the module `init()` and `exit()` functions are located:

```
static int __init ktimer_init(void)
{
    /* Save kernel timer delay */
    ktinfo.delay_jiffies = msecs_to_jiffies(delay_ms);
    pr_info("delay is set to %dms (%ld jiffies)\n",
                delay_ms, ktinfo.delay_jiffies);

    /* Setup and start the kernel timer */
    timer_setup(&ktinfo.timer, ktimer_handler, 0);
    mod_timer(&ktinfo.timer, jiffies + ktinfo.delay_jiffies);

    pr_info("kernel timer module loaded\n");
    return 0;
}

static void __exit ktimer_exit(void)
{
    del_timer_sync(&ktinfo.timer);

    pr_info("kernel timer module unloaded\n");
}
```

The module data structure with the handler function is as follows:

```
static struct ktimer_data {
    struct timer_list timer;
    long delay_jiffies;
    unsigned int data;
} ktinfo;

...

static void ktimer_handler(struct timer_list *t)
{
    struct ktimer_data *info = from_timer(info, t, timer);

    pr_info("kernel timer expired at %ld (data=%d)\n",
            jiffies, info->data++);

    /* Reschedule kernel timer */
    mod_timer(&info->timer, jiffies + info->delay_jiffies);
}
```

As we can see, this implementation is very similar to high-resolution timers. In fact in the `ktimer_init()` initialization function, we read the module `delay_ms` parameter and, by using `msecs_to_jiffies()`, we translate its value into jiffies, which are the unit of measurement of kernel timers. (Remember that legacy kernel timers have a lower time limit set to one jiffy.)

Then, we use the `timer_setup()` and `mod_timer()` functions to respectively set up the kernel timer and to start it. The `timer_setup()` function takes three arguments:

```
/**
 * timer_setup - prepare a timer for first use
 * @timer: the timer in question
 * @callback: the function to call when timer expires
 * @flags: any TIMER_* flags
 *
 * Regular timer initialization should use either DEFINE_TIMER() above,
 * or timer_setup(). For timers on the stack, timer_setup_on_stack() must
 * be used and must be balanced with a call to destroy_timer_on_stack().
 */
#define timer_setup(timer, callback, flags) \
    __init_timer((timer), (callback), (flags))
```

A variable `timer` of the `struct timer_list` type, a function `callback` (or handler), and some flags (within `flags` variable) which can be used to specify some particular features of our kernel timer. Just to give you an idea about available flags and their meanings, here are some flag definitions from the `linux/include/linux/timer.h` file:

```
/*
 * A deferrable timer will work normally when the system is busy, but
 * will not cause a CPU to come out of idle just to service it; instead,
 * the timer will be serviced when the CPU eventually wakes up with a
 * subsequent non-deferrable timer.
 *
 * An irqsafe timer is executed with IRQ disabled and it's safe to wait for
 * the completion of the running instance from IRQ handlers, for example,
 * by calling del_timer_sync().
 *
 * Note: The irq disabled callback execution is a special case for
 * workqueue locking issues. It's not meant for executing random crap
 * with interrupts disabled. Abuse is monitored!
 */
#define TIMER_CPUMASK       0x0003FFFF
#define TIMER_MIGRATING     0x00040000
#define TIMER_BASEMASK      (TIMER_CPUMASK | TIMER_MIGRATING)
#define TIMER_DEFERRABLE    0x00080000
#define TIMER_PINNED        0x00100000
#define TIMER_IRQSAFE       0x00200000
```

With regard to the callback function, let's look at `ktimer_handler()` from our example:

```
static void ktimer_handler(struct timer_list *t)
{
    struct ktimer_data *info = from_timer(info, t, timer);

    pr_info("kernel timer expired at %ld (data=%d)\n",
                jiffies, info->data++);

    /* Reschedule kernel timer */
    mod_timer(&info->timer, jiffies + info->delay_jiffies);
}
```

By using `from_timer()`, we can take a pointer to our data structure (defined in the example as `struct ktimer_data`), then, after having completed our job, we can call again `mod_timer()` to reschedule a new timer execution; otherwise, everything will stop.

Note that the `from_timer()` function still uses `container_of()` to do its job, as the following definition from the `linux/include/linux/timer.h` file shows:

```
#define from_timer(var, callback_timer, timer_fieldname) \
container_of(callback_timer, typeof(*var), timer_fieldname).
```

On the module exit, within the `ktimer_exit()` function, we must use the `del_timer_sync()` function to wait for the timer to stop. Whatever we stated previously regarding waiting for exit is still valid, so, to stop a kernel timer from an interrupt context, we can use `try_to_del_timer_sync()`, which simply returns a non-negative value if the timer has been correctly stopped.

To test our code, we simply need to compile and then move it to our ESPRESSObin, then we can load the module into the kernel as follows:

```
# insmod ktimer.ko
```

Then, in the kernel messages, we should get something like this:

```
[ 122.174020] ktimer:ktimer_init: delay is set to 1000ms (250 jiffies)
[ 122.180519] ktimer:ktimer_init: kernel timer module loaded
[ 123.206222] ktimer:ktimer_handler: kernel timer expired at 4294923072
(data=0)
[ 124.230222] ktimer:ktimer_handler: kernel timer expired at 4294923328
(data=1)
[ 125.254218] ktimer:ktimer_handler: kernel timer expired at 4294923584
(data=2)
```

Again, I've left the timings to give you an idea about kernel timer's precision.

Here, we discover that 1,000 ms is equal to 250 jiffies; that is, 1 jiffy is 4 ms, and also we can see that timer's handler is executed more or less every second. (With a jitter very near to 4 ms, that is 1 jiffy.)

When we remove the module the timer is stopped as shown as follows:

```
ktimer:ktimer_exit: kernel timer module unloaded
```

See also

- Interesting documentation about high-resolution kernel timers is in the kernel sources at `linux/Documentation/timers/hrtimers.txt`.

Waiting for an event

In previous sections, we saw how to manage an interrupt directly in its handler or by deferring the interrupt activities by using tasklets, workqueues, and so on. Also, we saw how to do periodic operations or how to delay an action forward in time; however, a device driver may need to wait for a specific event, such as waiting for some data, waiting for a buffer to become full, or a for a variable to reach a desired value.

 Please don't confuse events managed by the notifiers, we saw before, which are kernel related, with generic events for a specific driver.

When there is no data to be read from a peripheral, the reading process must be put on sleep and then awakened when the "data ready" event arrives. Another example is when we start a complex job and we wish to be signaled when it's finished; in this case, we start the job and then we go to sleep until the "job finished" event arrives. All these tasks can be done by using **waiting queues** (waitqueues) or **completions** (which are still implemented by waitqueues).

A waiting queue (or a completion) is just a queue where one or more processes stays waiting for the event related to the queue; when the event arrives, one, more than one, or even all sleeping processes are awakened in order to allow someone to manage it. In this recipe, we will learn how to use a waitqueue.

Getting ready

In order to prepare a simple example about waiting queues, we can again use a kernel module where we define a kernel timer during the module initialization function, which has the task of generating our event, and then we use a waitqueue or completion to wait for it.

In the `chapter_05/wait_event` directory of GitHub resources, there are two simple examples about waitqueues and completions, then, in the *How it works...* section, we're going to explain them in detail.

How to do it...

First, let's see a simple example regarding a waitqueue used to wait for the "data is greater then 5" event.

Waitqueues

The following is the main part of the `waitqueue.c` file, which holds a simple example about waitqueues.

1. Again let's start from the end, to see the module `init()` function:

```
static int __init waitqueue_init(void)
{
    int ret;

    /* Save kernel timer delay */
    wqinfo.delay_jiffies = msecs_to_jiffies(delay_ms);
    pr_info("delay is set to %dms (%ld jiffies)\n",
                delay_ms, wqinfo.delay_jiffies);

    /* Init the wait queue */
    init_waitqueue_head(&wqinfo.waitq);

    /* Setup and start the kernel timer */
    timer_setup(&wqinfo.timer, ktimer_handler, 0);
    mod_timer(&wqinfo.timer, jiffies + wqinfo.delay_jiffies);
```

After the kernel timer has been started, we can use the `wait_event_interruptible()` function to wait for the `wqinfo.data > 5` event on the `wqinfo.waitq` waitqueue, shown as follows:

```
    /* Wait for the wake up event... */
    ret = wait_event_interruptible(wqinfo.waitq, wqinfo.data > 5);
    if (ret < 0)
        goto exit;

    pr_info("got event data > 5\n");

    return 0;
```

```
exit:
    if (ret == -ERESTARTSYS)
        pr_info("interrupted by signal!\n");
    else
        pr_err("unable to wait for event\n");

    del_timer_sync(&wqinfo.timer);

    return ret;
}
```

2. The data structure is now defined, as follows:

```
static struct ktimer_data {
    struct wait_queue_head waitq;
    struct timer_list timer;
    long delay_jiffies;
    unsigned int data;
} wqinfo;
```

3. However, before any action can happen on the waitqueue, it must initialized, so, before starting the kernel timer, we use the `init_waitqueue_head()` function to properly set up `struct wait_queue_head waitq` stored in `struct ktimer_data`.

   If we take a look in the `linux/include/linux/wait.h` header, we can see how `wait_event_interruptible()` works:

```
/**
 * wait_event_interruptible - sleep until a condition gets true
 * @wq_head: the waitqueue to wait on
 * @condition: a C expression for the event to wait for
 *
 * The process is put to sleep (TASK_INTERRUPTIBLE) until the
 * @condition evaluates to true or a signal is received.
 * The @condition is checked each time the waitqueue @wq_head is
woken up.
 *
 * wake_up() has to be called after changing any variable that
could
 * change the result of the wait condition.
 *
 * The function will return -ERESTARTSYS if it was interrupted by a
 * signal and 0 if @condition evaluated to true.
 */
#define wait_event_interruptible(wq_head, condition) \
```

4. To see how to awake the sleeping processes, we should consider the kernel timer handler in the `waitqueue.c` file named `ktimer_handler()`:

```c
static void ktimer_handler(struct timer_list *t)
{
    struct ktimer_data *info = from_timer(info, t, timer);

    pr_info("kernel timer expired at %ld (data=%d)\n",
                jiffies, info->data++);

    /* Wake up all sleeping processes */
    wake_up_interruptible(&info->waitq);

    /* Reschedule kernel timer */
    mod_timer(&info->timer, jiffies + info->delay_jiffies);
}
```

Completions

If we wish to wait for a job to complete, we still can use a waitqueue, but it's better to use a completion that (as the name says) is specifically designed to carry out such activities. Here is a simple example, which can be retrieved from the `completion.c` file of GitHub resources about competitions.

1. First of all, let's see the module `init()` and `exit()` functions:

```c
static int __init completion_init(void)
{
    /* Save kernel timer delay */
    cinfo.delay_jiffies = msecs_to_jiffies(delay_ms);
    pr_info("delay is set to %dms (%ld jiffies)\n",
                delay_ms, cinfo.delay_jiffies);

    /* Init the wait queue */
    init_completion(&cinfo.done);

    /* Setup and start the kernel timer */
    timer_setup(&cinfo.timer, ktimer_handler, 0);
    mod_timer(&cinfo.timer, jiffies + cinfo.delay_jiffies);

    /* Wait for completition... */
    wait_for_completion(&cinfo.done);

    pr_info("job done\n");

    return 0;
```

```
    }

    static void __exit completion_exit(void)
    {
        del_timer_sync(&cinfo.timer);

        pr_info("module unloaded\n");
    }
```

2. The module data structure is now like the following:

```
static struct ktimer_data {
    struct completion done;
    struct timer_list timer;
    long delay_jiffies;
    unsigned int data;
} cinfo;
```

3. When the job is done, we can signal it as done to the `ktimer_handler ()` kernel timer handler by using the `complete()` function:

```
static void ktimer_handler(struct timer_list *t)
{
    struct ktimer_data *info = from_timer(info, t, timer);

    pr_info("kernel timer expired at %ld (data=%d)\n",
                jiffies, info->data++);

    /* Signal that job is done */
    complete(&info->done);
}
```

When `complete()` is called, a single thread waiting on the completion is signaled:

```
/**
 * complete: - signals a single thread waiting on this completion
 * @x: holds the state of this particular completion
 *
 * This will wake up a single thread waiting on this completion.
Threads will be
 * awakened in the same order in which they were queued.
 *
 * See also complete_all(), wait_for_completion() and related
routines.
 *
 * It may be assumed that this function implies a write memory
barrier before
```

```
 * changing the task state if and only if any tasks are woken up.
 */
void complete(struct completion *x)
```

While if we call `complete_all()`, all threads waiting for the completion are signaled:

```
/**
 * complete_all: - signals all threads waiting on this completion
 * @x: holds the state of this particular completion
 *
 * This will wake up all threads waiting on this particular
completion
 * event.
 * It may be assumed that this function implies a write memory
barrier
 * before changing the task state if and only if any tasks are
 * woken up.
 * Since complete_all() sets the completion of @x permanently to
done
 * to allow multiple waiters to finish, a call to
reinit_completion()
 * must be used on @x if @x is to be used again. The code must make
 * sure that all waiters have woken and finished before
reinitializing
 * @x. Also note that the function completion_done() can not be
used
 * to know if there are still waiters after complete_all() has been
 * called.
 */
void complete_all(struct completion *x)
```

How it works...

Let's see how this works in the following sections:

Waitqueues

In step 3, the calling process simply continues its execution if the condition is true; otherwise, it goes to sleep until the condition becomes true or a signal is received. (In this case the function returns the `-ERESTARTSYS` value.)

For a complete understanding, we should notice that there are two other variants of waiting event functions defined in the `linux/include/linux/wait.h` header. The first variant is just the `wait_event()` function, which works exactly as `wait_event_interruptible()`, but it cannot be interrupted by any signal:

```
/**
 * wait_event - sleep until a condition gets true
 * @wq_head: the waitqueue to wait on
 * @condition: a C expression for the event to wait for
 *
 * The process is put to sleep (TASK_UNINTERRUPTIBLE) until the
 * @condition evaluates to true. The @condition is checked each time
 * the waitqueue @wq_head is woken up.
 *
 * wake_up() has to be called after changing any variable that could
 * change the result of the wait condition.
 */
#define wait_event(wq_head, condition) \
```

While the second is `wait_event_timeout()` or `wait_event_interruptible_timeout()`, which works in the same way until a timeout elapses:

```
/** * wait_event_interruptible_timeout - sleep until a condition
 *     gets true or a timeout elapses
 * @wq_head: the waitqueue to wait on
 * @condition: a C expression for the event to wait for
 * @timeout: timeout, in jiffies
 *
 * The process is put to sleep (TASK_INTERRUPTIBLE) until the
 * @condition evaluates to true or a signal is received.
 * The @condition is checked each time the waitqueue @wq_head
 * is woken up.
 * wake_up() has to be called after changing any variable that could
 * change the result of the wait condition.
 * Returns:
 * 0 if the @condition evaluated to %false after the @timeout elapsed,
 * 1 if the @condition evaluated to %true after the @timeout elapsed,
 * the remaining jiffies (at least 1) if the @condition evaluated
 * to %true before the @timeout elapsed, or -%ERESTARTSYS if it was
 * interrupted by a signal.
 */
#define wait_event_interruptible_timeout(wq_head, condition, timeout) \
```

In *step 4*, in this function, we change the value stored into data and then we use `wake_up_interruptible()` on the waitqueue in order to signal a sleeping process that the data has been changed, and it should awake to test if the conditions are true.

In the `linux/include/linux/wait.h` header, there are several functions defined that are used to wake up one, more than one, or just all waiting processes (interruptible or not) by using a common `__wake_up()` function:

```
#define wake_up(x)          __wake_up(x, TASK_NORMAL, 1, NULL)
#define wake_up_nr(x, nr)   __wake_up(x, TASK_NORMAL, nr, NULL)
#define wake_up_all(x)      __wake_up(x, TASK_NORMAL, 0, NULL)
...
#define wake_up_interruptible(x) __wake_up(x, TASK_INTERRUPTIBLE, 1,
NULL)
#define wake_up_interruptible_nr(x, nr) __wake_up(x,
TASK_INTERRUPTIBLE, nr, NULL)
#define wake_up_interruptible_all(x) __wake_up(x, TASK_INTERRUPTIBLE,
0, NULL)
...
```

In our example, we asked for data greater than five, so the first five calls of `wake_up_interruptible()` should not awake our process; let's verify it in the next section!

> Note that the process that will go to sleep is just the `insmod` command, which is the one that calls the module initialization function.

Completions

In *step 1*, we can see the code is quite similar to the previous waitqueue example; we simply use the `init_completion()` function to initialize the completion as usual, and then we call `wait_for_completion()` on `struct completion done` within the `struct ktimer_data` structure to wait for the job ending.

As for waitqueues, inside the `linux/include/linux/completion.h` header, we can find several variants of the `wait_for_completion()` function:

```
extern void wait_for_completion(struct completion *);
extern int wait_for_completion_interruptible(struct completion *x);
extern unsigned long wait_for_completion_timeout(struct completion *x,
                                                 unsigned long
timeout);
extern long wait_for_completion_interruptible_timeout(
        struct completion *x, unsigned long timeout);
```

There's more...

Now, to test our code in both cases, we have to compile the kernel modules and then move them on the ESPRESSObin; moreover, in order to better understand how the example works, we should use an SSH connection and then look for the kernel messages on the serial console from another terminal window.

Waitqueues

When we insert the `waitqueue.ko` module with `insmod`, as follows, we should notice that the process is suspended until the data becomes greater than five:

 # insmod waitqueue.ko

When the `insmod` process is suspended, you should not get the prompt until the test is finished.

On the serial console, we should get the following messages:

```
waitqueue:waitqueue_init: delay is set to 1000ms (250 jiffies)
waitqueue:ktimer_handler: kernel timer expired at 4295371304 (data=0)
waitqueue:ktimer_handler: kernel timer expired at 4295371560 (data=1)
waitqueue:ktimer_handler: kernel timer expired at 4295371816 (data=2)
waitqueue:ktimer_handler: kernel timer expired at 4295372072 (data=3)
waitqueue:ktimer_handler: kernel timer expired at 4295372328 (data=4)
waitqueue:ktimer_handler: kernel timer expired at 4295372584 (data=5)
waitqueue:waitqueue_init: got event data > 5
waitqueue:ktimer_handler: kernel timer expired at 4295372840 (data=6)
...
```

As soon as the `got event data > 5` message is shown on the screen, the `insmod` process should return, and a new prompt should be displayed.

To verify that `wait_event_interruptible()` returns with `-ERESTARTSYS`, when a signal arrives, we can unload the module and the reload it, then just press *CTRL+C* keys before data reaches 5:

```
# rmmod waitqueue
# insmod waitqueue.ko
^C
```

This time in the kernel messages, we should get something like the following:

```
waitqueue:waitqueue_init: delay is set to 1000ms (250 jiffies)
waitqueue:ktimer_handler: kernel timer expired at 4295573632 (data=0)
waitqueue:ktimer_handler: kernel timer expired at 4295573888 (data=1)
waitqueue:waitqueue_init: interrupted by signal!
```

Completions

To test completions, we have to insert the `completion.ko` module into the kernel. Now you should notice that if we press *CTRL+C* nothing happens because we used `wait_for_completion()` instead of `wait_for_completion_interruptible()`:

```
# insmod completion.ko
^C^C^C^C
```

Then the prompt returns after five seconds and the kernel messages are something like the following:

```
completion:completion_init: delay is set to 5000ms (1250 jiffies)
completion:ktimer_handler: kernel timer expired at 4296124608 (data=0)
completion:completion_init: job done
```

See also

- Although slightly outdated, there is some good information about waitqueues at URL `https://lwn.net/Articles/577370/`.

Performing atomic operations

Atomic operations are a crucial step during device driver development. In fact, a driver is not like a normal program that executes from the beginning till the end, as it provides several methods (for example, read or write data to a peripheral, or set some communication parameters), which can be called asynchronously one to another. All these methods operate concurrently on common data structures that must be modified in a consistent manner. That's why we need to be able to perform atomic operations.

The Linux kernel uses a large variety of atomic operations. Each is used for different operations, depending on whether the CPU is running in an interrupt or process context.

When the CPU is in the process context, we can safely use **mutexes,** which can put the current running process to sleep if the mutex is locked; however, in an interrupt context "going to sleep" is not allowed so we need another mechanism, and Linux gives us **spinlocks**, which allow locking everywhere, but for short periods of time. This happens because spinlocks get their job done performing a busy-waiting tight-loop on the current CPU, and, if we stay too long, we can lose performance.

In this recipe, we'll see how to do operations on data in an uninterruptible manner in order to avoid data corruption.

Getting ready

Again, to build our examples, we can use a kernel module that defines a kernel timer during the module `init()` function, which has the task of generating an asynchronous execution where we can use our mutual exclusion mechanism to protect our data.

In the `chapter_05/atomic` directory of GitHub resources, there are simple examples of mutexes, spinlocks, and atomic data, and, in the next sections, we're going to explain them in detail.

How to do it...

In this paragraph, we're going to present two examples of how to use mutexes and spinlocks. We should consider them as just a demonstration about how to use the API, because, in real drivers, their usage is a bit different, and it will be covered in `Chapter 7`, *Advanced Char Driver Operations*, and the following chapters.

Mutexes

The following is the end of mutex.c file where mutexes are defined and initialized for the module init() function:

```
static int __init mut_init(void)
{
    /* Save kernel timer delay */
    minfo.delay_jiffies = msecs_to_jiffies(delay_ms);
    pr_info("delay is set to %dms (%ld jiffies)\n",
            delay_ms, minfo.delay_jiffies);

    /* Init the mutex */
    mutex_init(&minfo.lock);

    /* Setup and start the kernel timer */
    timer_setup(&minfo.timer, ktimer_handler, 0);
    mod_timer(&minfo.timer, jiffies);

    mutex_lock(&minfo.lock);
    minfo.data++;
    mutex_unlock(&minfo.lock);

    pr_info("mutex module loaded\n");
    return 0;
}
```

And here is the initialization for the module exit() function:

```
static void __exit mut_exit(void)
{
    del_timer_sync(&minfo.timer);

    pr_info("mutex module unloaded\n");
}

module_init(mut_init);
module_exit(mut_exit);
```

1. In the module initialization mut_init() function, we use mutex_init() to initialize the lock mutex; then we can safely start the timer.
   The module data structure is defined as follows:

   ```
   static struct ktimer_data {
       struct mutex lock;
       struct timer_list timer;
       long delay_jiffies;
   ```

```
        int data;
    } minfo;
```

2. We use `mutex_trylock()` to try to acquire the lock safely:

```
static void ktimer_handler(struct timer_list *t)
{
    struct ktimer_data *info = from_timer(info, t, timer);
    int ret;

    pr_info("kernel timer expired at %ld (data=%d)\n",
                jiffies, info->data);
    ret = mutex_trylock(&info->lock);
    if (ret) {
        info->data++;
        mutex_unlock(&info->lock);
    } else
        pr_err("cannot get the lock!\n");

    /* Reschedule kernel timer */
    mod_timer(&info->timer, jiffies + info->delay_jiffies);
}
```

Spinlocks

1. As usual, the `spinlock.c` file is shown as an example of spinlock usage. Here is the module `init()` function:

```
static int __init spin_init(void)
{
    unsigned long flags;

    /* Save kernel timer delay */
    sinfo.delay_jiffies = msecs_to_jiffies(delay_ms);
    pr_info("delay is set to %dms (%ld jiffies)\n",
                delay_ms, sinfo.delay_jiffies);

    /* Init the spinlock */
    spin_lock_init(&sinfo.lock);

    /* Setup and start the kernel timer */
    timer_setup(&sinfo.timer, ktimer_handler, 0);
    mod_timer(&sinfo.timer, jiffies);

    spin_lock_irqsave(&sinfo.lock, flags);
    sinfo.data++;
```

```
        spin_unlock_irqrestore(&sinfo.lock, flags);

        pr_info("spinlock module loaded\n");
        return 0;
    }
```

And here is the module `exit()` function:

```
static void __exit spin_exit(void)
{
    del_timer_sync(&sinfo.timer);

    pr_info("spinlock module unloaded\n");
}

module_init(spin_init);
module_exit(spin_exit);
```

The module data structure is as follows:

```
static struct ktimer_data {
    struct spinlock lock;
    struct timer_list timer;
    long delay_jiffies;
    int data;
} sinfo;
```

2. In the example, we use `spin_lock_init()` to initialize the spinlock, and then we use two different function pairs to protect our data: `spin_lock()` and `spin_unlock()`; both of these just use the spinlock to avoid race conditions, while `spin_lock_irqsave()` and `spin_unlock_irqrestore()` use the spinlock while the current CPU interrupts are disabled:

```
static void ktimer_handler(struct timer_list *t)
{
    struct ktimer_data *info = from_timer(info, t, timer);

    pr_info("kernel timer expired at %ld (data=%d)\n",
                jiffies, info->data);
    spin_lock(&sinfo.lock);
    info->data++;
    spin_unlock(&info->lock);

    /* Reschedule kernel timer */
    mod_timer(&info->timer, jiffies + info->delay_jiffies);
}
```

> By using `spin_lock_irqsave()` and `spin_unlock_irqrestore()`, we can be sure that nobody can interrupt us because the IRQs are disabled, and that no other CPU can execute our code (thanks to the spinlock).

How it works...

Let's see how mutexes and spinlocks work in the following two sections.

Mutexes

In *step 2*, each time we have to modify our data, we can protect it by calling the `mutex_lock()` and `mutex_unlock()` pair, passing a pointer to the mutex to lock as a parameter; of course, we cannot do it in an interrupt context (as the kernel timer handler is), and that's why we use `mutex_trylock()` to try to acquire the lock safely.

Spinlocks

In step 1, the example is very similar to the previous one, but it shows a really important difference between mutexes and spinlocks: the former protects code from the process's concurrency while the latter protects code from the CPU's concurrency! In fact, if the kernel has no symmetric multiprocessing support (`CONFIG_SMP=n` in the kernel `.config` file), then spinlocks just vanish into void code.

This is a really important concept, which device driver developers should understand very well; otherwise, a driver may not work at all, or lead to a severe bug.

There's more...

Since the last example is only meant to present the mutexes and spinlocks, API testing is quite useless. However, if we wish to do it anyway, the procedure is the same: compile modules and then move them to the ESPRESSObin.

Mutexes

When we insert the `mutex.ko` module, the output should be something like the following:

```
# insmod mutex.ko
mutex:mut_init: delay is set to 1000ms (250 jiffies)
mutex:mut_init: mutex module loaded
```

In step 1, we execute the module `init()` function where we increase `minfo.data` within a mutex protected area.

```
mutex:ktimer_handler: kernel timer expired at 4294997916 (data=1)
mutex:ktimer_handler: kernel timer expired at 4294998168 (data=2)
mutex:ktimer_handler: kernel timer expired at 4294998424 (data=3)
...
```

When we execute the handler, we can be sure that it cannot increase `minfo.data` if the module `init()` function is currently holding the mutex.

Spinlocks

When we insert the `spinlock.ko` module, the output should be something like the following:

```
# insmod spinlock.ko
spinlock:spin_init: delay is set to 1000ms (250 jiffies)
spinlock:spin_init: spinlock module loaded
```

As before, in *step 1*, we execute the module `init()` function where we increase `minfo.data` within a spinlock protected area.

```
spinlock:ktimer_handler: kernel timer expired at 4295019195 (data=1)
spinlock:ktimer_handler: kernel timer expired at 4295019448 (data=2)
spinlock:ktimer_handler: kernel timer expired at 4295019704 (data=3)
...
```

Again, when we execute the handler, we can be sure that it cannot increase `minfo.data` if the module `init()` function is currently holding the spinlock.

 Note that, in the case of mono core machines, spinlocks vanish, and we assure the `minfo.data` lock by just disabling interrupts.

By using mutexes and spinlocks, we have whatever we need to protect our data from race conditions; however, Linux offers us another API, **atomic operations**.

The atomic data type

During device driver development, we may need to atomically increment or decrement a variable, or more simply, set one or more bits in a variable. To do so, instead of using a complex mutual exclusion mechanism, we can use a set of variables and operations that are guaranteed to be atomic by the kernel.

In the `atomic.c` file from GitHub resources, we can see a simple example about them, where the atomic variables can be defined as follows:

```
static atomic_t bitmap = ATOMIC_INIT(0xff);

static struct ktimer_data {
    struct timer_list timer;
    long delay_jiffies;
    atomic_t data;
} ainfo;
```

Additionally, the following is the module `init()` function:

```
static int __init atom_init(void)
{
    /* Save kernel timer delay */
    ainfo.delay_jiffies = msecs_to_jiffies(delay_ms);
    pr_info("delay is set to %dms (%ld jiffies)\n",
                delay_ms, ainfo.delay_jiffies);

    /* Init the atomic data */
    atomic_set(&ainfo.data, 10);

    /* Setup and start the kernel timer after required delay */
    timer_setup(&ainfo.timer, ktimer_handler, 0);
    mod_timer(&ainfo.timer, jiffies + ainfo.delay_jiffies);

    pr_info("data=%0x\n", atomic_read(&ainfo.data));
    pr_info("bitmap=%0x\n", atomic_fetch_and(0x0f, &bitmap));

    pr_info("atomic module loaded\n");
    return 0;
}
```

And here is the module `exit()` function:

```
static void __exit atom_exit(void)
{
    del_timer_sync(&ainfo.timer);

    pr_info("atomic module unloaded\n");
}
```

In the preceding code, we use `ATOMIC_INIT()` to statically define and initialize an atomic variable, while the `atomic_set()` function can be used to do the same dynamically. Subsequently, atomic variables can be manipulated by using functions with the `atomic_*()` prefix, which are in the `linux/include/linux/atomic.h` and `linux/include/asm-generic/atomic.h` files.

Finally, the kernel timer handler can be implemented as follows:

```
static void ktimer_handler(struct timer_list *t)
{
    struct ktimer_data *info = from_timer(info, t, timer);

    pr_info("kernel timer expired at %ld (data=%d)\n",
                jiffies, atomic_dec_if_positive(&info->data));

    /* Compute an atomic bitmap operation */
    atomic_xor(0xff, &bitmap);
    pr_info("bitmap=%0x\n", atomic_read(&bitmap));

    /* Reschedule kernel timer */
    mod_timer(&info->timer, jiffies + info->delay_jiffies);
}
```

Atomic data can be added or subtracted by specific values, incremented, decremented, OR-ed, AND-ed, XOR-ed, and so on, and all these operations are guaranteed to be atomic by the kernel, so their usage is really simple.

Again, testing the code is quite useless. However, if we compile and then insert the `atomic.ko` module in the ESPRESSObin, the output is as follows:

```
# insmod atomic.ko
atomic:atom_init: delay is set to 1000ms (250 jiffies)
atomic:atom_init: data=a
atomic:atom_init: bitmap=ff
atomic:atom_init: atomic module loaded
atomic:ktimer_handler: kernel timer expired at 4295049912 (data=9)
atomic:ktimer_handler: bitmap=f0
atomic:ktimer_handler: kernel timer expired at 4295050168 (data=8)
```

```
atomic:ktimer_handler: bitmap=f
...
atomic:ktimer_handler: kernel timer expired at 4295051960 (data=1)
atomic:ktimer_handler: bitmap=f0
atomic:ktimer_handler: kernel timer expired at 4295052216 (data=0)
atomic:ktimer_handler: bitmap=f
atomic:ktimer_handler: kernel timer expired at 4295052472 (data=-1)
```

At this point, `data` stays at `-1` and doesn't decrement any further.

See also

- For several examples about kernel locking mechanisms, refer to `https://www.kernel.org/doc/htmldocs/kernel-locking/locks.html`.
- For more information about atomic operations, have a look at `https://www.kernel.org/doc/html/v4.12/core-api/atomic_ops.html`.

Miscellaneous Kernel Internals 6

When developing inside the kernel, we may need to do some miscellaneous activities to implement our device drivers, such as dynamically allocating memory and using specific data types in order to store register data, or simply actively waiting some time in order to be sure that a peripheral has completed its reset procedure.

To perform all these tasks, Linux offers to kernel developers a rich set of useful functions, macros, and data types that we'll try to present in this chapter through the means of very simple example codes, because we wish to point out to the reader how he/she can use them to simplify device driver development. That's why, in this chapter, we will cover the following recipes:

- Using kernel data types
- Managing helper functions
- Dynamic memory allocation
- Managing kernel linked lists
- Using kernel hash tables
- Getting access to I/O memory
- Spending time in the kernel

Technical requirements

For more information on this chapter, you can visit the *Appendix*.

The code and other files used in this chapter can be downloaded from GitHub at `https://github.com/giometti/linux_device_driver_development_cookbook/tree/master/chapter_06`.

Using kernel data types

Often, data items of a particular size are required by the kernel code to match predefined binary structures, to hold peripheral's register data, to communicate with userspace or to simply to align data within structures by inserting padding fields.

Sometimes, kernel code requires data items of a specific size, perhaps to match predefined binary structures, to communicate with userspace, to hold peripheral's register data, or simply to align data within structures by inserting padding fields.

In this section, we're going to see some special data types that can be used by kernel developers to simplify their everyday job. In the following, we're going to see an example with **fixed-size data types**, which are very useful to define some kind of data that is intended to match exactly the structure of data expected by a device or by a communication protocol; a careful reader will recognize that it wouldn't be possible indeed to define such fixed-size data entities by using standard C types, since the C standard does not explicitly guarantee a fixed-size representation across all the architectures, when we make use of similar standard C types such as int, short, or long.

The kernel offers the following data types to use whenever we need to know the size of our data (their actual definition depends on the currently used architecture, but they are named the same across different architectures):

- u8: Unsigned byte (8 bits)
- u16: Unsigned word (16 bits)
- u32: Unsigned 32-bit (32 bits)
- u64: Unsigned 64-bit (64 bits)
- s8: Signed byte (8 bits)
- s16: Signed word (16 bits)
- s32: Signed 32-bit (32 bits)
- s64: Signed 64-bit (64 bits)

It may also happen that fixed-size data types must be used to exchange data with user space; however, in this last case, we cannot use the preceding types, but we'll have to instead opt for the following alternative data types, which are equivalent to the preceding ones, but which can be used indifferently within both kernel and userspace (this concept will become clearer in the *Using the ioctl() method* recipe in Chapter 7, *Advanced Char Driver Operations*):

- __u8: Unsigned byte (8 bits)
- __u16: Unsigned word (16 bits)

- __u32: Unsigned 32-bit (32 bits)
- __u64: Unsigned 64-bit (64 bits)
- __s8: Signed byte (8 bits)
- __s16: Signed word (16 bits)
- __s32: Signed 32-bit (32 bits)
- __s64: Signed 64-bit (64 bits)

All these fixed-size types are defined in the header file, `linux/include/linux/types.h`.

Getting ready

In order to show how to use the preceding data types, we can again use a kernel module to execute some kernel code, which uses them to define a register mapping within a structure.

How to do it...

Let's see how to do it by following these steps:

1. Let's take a look at the `data_type.c` file, where we put all code into the module's `init()` function as follows:

```
static int __init data_types_init(void)
{
    struct dtypes_s *ptr = (struct dtypes_s *) base_addr;

    pr_info("\tu8\tu16\tu32\tu64\n");
    pr_info("size\t%ld\t%ld\t%ld\t%ld\n",
        sizeof(u8), sizeof(u16), sizeof(u32), sizeof(u64));

    pr_info("name\tptr\n");
    pr_info("reg0\t%px\n", &ptr->reg0);
    pr_info("reg1\t%px\n", &ptr->reg1);
    pr_info("reg2\t%px\n", &ptr->reg2);
    pr_info("reg3\t%px\n", &ptr->reg3);
    pr_info("reg4\t%px\n", &ptr->reg4);
    pr_info("reg5\t%px\n", &ptr->reg5);

    return -EINVAL;
}
```

How it works...

After performing *step 1*, the pointer `ptr` is then initialized according to the `base_addr` value in such a way that, by simply referencing a field of the `struct dtypes_s` (defined in the following code), we can point to the right memory address:

```
struct dtypes_s {
    u32 reg0;
    u8 pad0[2];
    u16 reg1;
    u32 pad1[2];
    u8 reg2;
    u8 reg3;
    u16 reg4;
    u32 reg5;
} __attribute__ ((packed));
```

During a structure definition, we should be aware that the compiler may quietly insert padding into the structure itself to ensure that every field is properly aligned in order to attain good performances on the target processor; a workaround to avoid this behavior is to tell the compiler that the structure must be packed, with no fillers added. This, of course, can be done by using `__attribute__ ((packed))`, as before.

There's more...

If we wish to verify the step, we can do this by testing the code. We just need to compile the module as usual, then move it to the ESPRESSObin, and finally insert into the kernel as follows:

 # insmod data_types.ko

You should also get an error message as follows:
```
insmod: ERROR: could not insert module data_types.ko:
Invalid parameters
```
However, this is due to the last `return -EINVAL` in the function `data_types_init()`; we used this as a trick, here and in the following, to force the kernel to remove the module after the module's `init()` function execution.

The first lines we get into kernel messages are about the dimensions of type u8, u16, u32, and u64 as follows:

```
data_types:data_types_init:       u8 u16 u32 u64
data_types:data_types_init: size 1  2   4   8
```

Then, the following lines (still among kernel messages) show to us the perfect padding we can achieve by using a struct definition with u8, u16, u32, and u64, and the __attribute__ ((packed)) statement:

```
data_types:data_types_init: name ptr
data_types:data_types_init: reg0 0000000080000000
data_types:data_types_init: reg1 0000000080000006
data_types:data_types_init: reg2 0000000080000010
data_types:data_types_init: reg3 0000000080000011
data_types:data_types_init: reg4 0000000080000012
data_types:data_types_init: reg5 0000000080000014
```

See also

- A good reference for kernel data types can be found at `https://kernelnewbies.org/InternalKernelDataTypes`.

Managing helper functions

During device driver development, we may need to concatenate a string or to compute its length or just copy or move a memory region (or a string). To do these common operations in the user space, we can use several functions, such as strcat(), strlen(), memcpy() (or strcpy()), and so on, and Linux offers us similarly named functions, which, of course, are safely usable in the kernel. (Note that kernel code cannot be linked against userspace glibc libraries.)

In this recipe, we will see how to use some kernel helpers in order to manage strings within the kernel.

Getting ready

If we take a look inside kernel sources at the include file
`linux/include/linux/string.h`, we can see a long list of usual userspace look-alike
utility functions, as follows:

```
#ifndef __HAVE_ARCH_STRCPY
extern char * strcpy(char *,const char *);
#endif
#ifndef __HAVE_ARCH_STRNCPY
extern char * strncpy(char *,const char *, __kernel_size_t);
#endif
#ifndef __HAVE_ARCH_STRLCPY
size_t strlcpy(char *, const char *, size_t);
#endif
#ifndef __HAVE_ARCH_STRSCPY
ssize_t strscpy(char *, const char *, size_t);
#endif
#ifndef __HAVE_ARCH_STRCAT
extern char * strcat(char *, const char *);
#endif
#ifndef __HAVE_ARCH_STRNCAT
extern char * strncat(char *, const char *, __kernel_size_t);
#endif
...
```

 Note that each function is enclosed into `#ifndef`/`#endif` preprocessor
condition clauses, because some of these functions can be implemented
with some form of optimization for an architecture; therefore, their
implementation may vary across different platforms.

In order to show how to use the preceding helper functions, we can again use a kernel
module to execute a kernel code that uses some of them.

How to do it...

Let's see how to do it by following these steps:

1. In the `helper_funcs.c` file, we can see some really silly code that exemplifies how we can use these helper functions.

You are encouraged to modify this code to play with different kernel helper functions.

2. All the work is done inside the module's `init()` function as it was in the preceding section. Here we can use the kernel functions `strlen()` and `strncpy()` as their userspace counterparts:

```
static int __init helper_funcs_init(void)
{
    char str2[STR2_LEN];

    pr_info("str=\"%s\"\n", str);
    pr_info("str size=%ld\n", strlen(str));

    strncpy(str2, str, STR2_LEN);

    pr_info("str2=\"%s\"\n", str2);
    pr_info("str2 size=%ld\n", strlen(str2));

    return -EINVAL;
}
```

These functions are special kernel implementations and they are not the userspace functions we usually use in normal programming. We cannot link a kernel module with the glibc!

3. The `str` string is defined as a module parameter as follows, and it can be used to try different strings:

```
static char *str = "default string";
module_param(str, charp, S_IRUSR | S_IWUSR);
MODULE_PARM_DESC(str, "a string value");
```

There's more...

If you wish to test the code in the recipe, you can do so by compiling it and then moving it into the ESPRESSObin.

First of all, we have to insert the module into the kernel:

```
# insmod helper_funcs.ko
```

 You can safely ignore the following error message, as discussed previously:
insmod: ERROR: could not insert module helper_funcs.ko: Invalid parameters

The kernel messages should now look as follows:

```
helper_funcs:helper_funcs_init: str="default string"
helper_funcs:helper_funcs_init: str size=14
helper_funcs:helper_funcs_init: str2="default string"
helper_funcs:helper_funcs_init: str2 size=14
```

In the preceding output, we can see that string `str2` is just a copy of `str`.

However, if we use the following `insmod` command, the output will change as follows:

```
# insmod helper_funcs.ko str=\"very very very looooooooong string\"
helper_funcs:helper_funcs_init: str="very very very looooooooong string"
helper_funcs:helper_funcs_init: str size=35
helper_funcs:helper_funcs_init: str2="very very very looooooooong str"
helper_funcs:helper_funcs_init: str2 size=32
```

Again, string `str2` is a copy of `str`, but with its maximum size `STR2_LEN` defined as follows:

```
#define STR2_LEN    32
```

See also

- For a more complete list of string manipulation functions, a good starting point is at https://www.kernel.org/doc/htmldocs/kernel-api/ch02s02.html.
- While regarding string conversion, you can take a look at https://www.kernel.org/doc/htmldocs/kernel-api/libc.html#id-1.4.3.

Dynamic memory allocation

A good device driver should support neither more than one peripheral and (possibly) not a fixed number of them! However, even if we decide to restrict driver usage to just one peripheral, it may happen that we need to manage a variable number of data chunks so, in any case, we need to be able to manage **dynamic memory allocation**.

In this recipe, we will see how we can dynamically (and safely) allocate chunks of memory in the kernel space.

How to do it...

In order to show how we can allocate from memory within the kernel by using kmalloc(), vmalloc(), and kvmalloc(), we can again use a kernel module.

Inside the mem_alloc.c file, we can see some really simple code that shows how memory allocation works together with the related memory deallocation functions:

1. All the work gets done inside the module's init() function as before. The first step is using kmalloc() with two different flags, that is GFP_KERNEL (which can sleep) and GFP_ATOMIC (which doesn't sleep and then it can be safely used inside the interrupt context):

```
static int __init mem_alloc_init(void)
{
    void *ptr;

    pr_info("size=%ldkbytes\n", size);

    ptr = kmalloc(size << 10, GFP_KERNEL);
    pr_info("kmalloc(..., GFP_KERNEL) =%px\n", ptr);
    kfree(ptr);

    ptr = kmalloc(size << 10, GFP_ATOMIC);
    pr_info("kmalloc(..., GFP_ATOMIC) =%px\n", ptr);
    kfree(ptr);
```

2. Then, we try allocating memory by using vmalloc():

```
ptr = vmalloc(size << 10);
pr_info("vmalloc(...) =%px\n", ptr);
vfree(ptr);
```

3. Finally, we try two different allocations by using `kvmalloc()` with two different flags, that is `GFP_KERNEL` (which can sleep) and `GFP_ATOMIC` (which doesn't sleep and then it can be safely used inside the interrupt context):

```
ptr = kvmalloc(size << 10, GFP_KERNEL);
pr_info("kvmalloc(..., GFP_KERNEL)=%px\n", ptr);
kvfree(ptr);

ptr = kvmalloc(size << 10, GFP_ATOMIC);
pr_info("kvmalloc(..., GFP_ATOMIC)=%px\n", ptr);
kvfree(ptr);

return -EINVAL;
}
```

 Note that, for each allocation function, we must use the related `free()` function!

The size of the memory chunk to allocate is passed as a kernel parameter as follows:

```
static long size = 4;
module_param(size, long, S_IRUSR | S_IWUSR);
MODULE_PARM_DESC(size, "memory size in Kbytes");
```

There's more...

OK, as you did before, just compile the module and then move it to the ESPRESSObin.

If we try inserting the module with the default memory size (that is, 4 KB), we should get the following kernel messages:

```
# insmod mem_alloc.ko
mem_alloc:mem_alloc_init: size=4kbytes
mem_alloc:mem_alloc_init: kmalloc(..., GFP_KERNEL) =ffff800079831000
mem_alloc:mem_alloc_init: kmalloc(..., GFP_ATOMIC) =ffff800079831000
mem_alloc:mem_alloc_init: vmalloc(...) =ffff000009655000
mem_alloc:mem_alloc_init: kvmalloc(..., GFP_KERNEL)=ffff800079831000
mem_alloc:mem_alloc_init: kvmalloc(..., GFP_ATOMIC)=ffff800079831000
```

You can safely ignore the following error message as discussed earlier:
`insmod: ERROR: could not insert module mem_alloc.ko:`
`Invalid parameters`

This shows us that all allocation functions successfully complete their job.

However, if we try to increase the memory chunk as follows, something changes:

```
root@espressobin:~# insmod mem_alloc.ko size=5000
mem_alloc:mem_alloc_init: size=5000kbytes
mem_alloc:mem_alloc_init: kmalloc(..., GFP_KERNEL) =0000000000000000
mem_alloc:mem_alloc_init: kmalloc(..., GFP_ATOMIC) =0000000000000000
mem_alloc:mem_alloc_init: vmalloc(...) =ffff00000b9fb000
mem_alloc:mem_alloc_init: kvmalloc(..., GFP_KERNEL)=ffff00000c135000
mem_alloc:mem_alloc_init: kvmalloc(..., GFP_ATOMIC)=0000000000000000
```

Now the `kmalloc()` functions fail, while `vmalloc()` is still successful due to the fact it allocates on the virtual memory space over non-contiguous physical addresses. On the other hand, `kvmalloc()` succeeds when invoked with the flag `GFP_KERNEL` while it fails with the flag `GFP_ATOMIC`. (This is due to the fact that it cannot use `vmalloc()` as a fallback in this special situation.)

See also

- For further information about memory allocation, a good starting point is
  `https://www.kernel.org/doc/html/latest/core-api/memory-allocation.html`.

Managing kernel linked lists

When programming inside the kernel, it could be useful to have the ability to manage lists of data, so, to reduce the amount of duplicated code, kernel developers have created a standard implementation of circular, doubly linked lists.

In this recipe, we will see how to use lists in our code by using the Linux API.

Getting ready

To demonstrate how the list API works, we can again use a kernel module where we do some operations inside the module's init() function, as done previously.

How to do it...

In the list.c file, there is our example code where all games are played inside list_init() function:

1. As the first step, let's take a look at the declaration of the structure implementing a list element and the head of the list:

```
static LIST_HEAD(data_list);

struct l_struct {
    int data;
    struct list_head list;
};
```

2. Now, in list_init(), we define our elements:

```
static int __init list_init(void)
{
    struct l_struct e1 = {
        .data = 5
    };
    struct l_struct e2 = {
        .data = 1
    };
    struct l_struct e3 = {
        .data = 7
    };
```

3. Then, we add the first element to the list and we print it:

```
pr_info("add e1...\n");
add_ordered_entry(&e1);
print_entries();
```

4. Next, we continue adding elements and print the list:

```
pr_info("add e2, e3...\n");
add_ordered_entry(&e2);
add_ordered_entry(&e3);
print_entries();
```

5. Finally, we delete an element:

```
pr_info("del data=5...\n");
del_entry(5);
print_entries();

return -EINVAL;
}
```

6. Now, let's see the local function definition; to add an element in ordered mode, we can do the following:

```
static void add_ordered_entry(struct l_struct *new)
{
    struct list_head *ptr;
    struct l_struct *entry;

    list_for_each(ptr, &data_list) {
        entry = list_entry(ptr, struct l_struct, list);
        if (entry->data < new->data) {
            list_add_tail(&new->list, ptr);
            return;
        }
    }
    list_add_tail(&new->list, &data_list);
}
```

7. Meanwhile, the entry deletion can be done as follows:

```
static void del_entry(int data)
{
    struct list_head *ptr;
    struct l_struct *entry;

    list_for_each(ptr, &data_list) {
        entry = list_entry(ptr, struct l_struct, list);
        if (entry->data == data) {
            list_del(ptr);
            return;
        }
    }
}
```

8. Finally, the printing of all elements in the list can be achieved as follows:

```
static void print_entries(void)
{
    struct l_struct *entry;
```

```
        list_for_each_entry(entry, &data_list, list)
            pr_info("data=%d\n", entry->data);
}
```

In this last function, we use the macro `list_for_each_entry()` instead of the pair `list_for_each()` and `list_entry()`, to get more compact and readable code, which essentially performs the same steps.

The macro is defined in the `linux/include/linux/list.h` file as follows:

```
/**
 * list_for_each_entry - iterate over list of given type
 * @pos: the type * to use as a loop cursor.
 * @head: the head for your list.
 * @member: the name of the list_head within the struct.
 */
#define list_for_each_entry(pos, head, member) \
        for (pos = list_first_entry(head, typeof(*pos), member); \
            &pos->member != (head); \
            pos = list_next_entry(pos, member))
```

There's more...

We can test the code after compilation and insertion into ESPRESSObin's kernel. To insert the kernel, we do the usual `insmod` command:

```
# insmod list.ko
```

You can safely ignore the following error message as discussed earlier:
`insmod: ERROR: could not insert module list.ko: Invalid parameters`

Then, after the first insertion, we have the following kernel message:

```
list:list_init: add e1...
list:print_entries: data=5
```

In *step 1* and *step 2*, we have defined the elements of our list, while, in *step 3* we have done the first insert into the list, and the preceding message is what we get after the insertion.

After the second insertion in *step 4*, we get the following instead:

```
list:list_init: add e2, e3...
list:print_entries: data=7
list:print_entries: data=5
list:print_entries: data=1
```

Finally, after the deletion of *step 5*, the list becomes as follows:

```
list:list_init: del data=5...
list:print_entries: data=7
list:print_entries: data=1
```

Note that, in *step 6*, we presented a possible implementation of element insertion within the list in ordered mode but, of course, it's up to the developer use the best solution. The same considerations can be done for *step 7*, where we have implemented the element removal, while in *step 8*, we have the printing function.

See also

- For a more complete function list regarding Linux's list API, a good reference can be found at https://www.kernel.org/doc/htmldocs/kernel-api/adt.html#id-1.3.2.

Using kernel hash tables

As for kernel lists, Linux offers to kernel developers a common interface to manage hash tables. Their implementation is based on a special version of the kernel lists seen in the preceding section and named `hlist` (which is still a doubly linked list but with a single pointer list head). This API is defined in the header file, `linux/include/linux/hashtable.h`.

In this recipe, we will show how we can use hash tables in our kernel code by using the Linux API.

Getting ready

Even in this recipe, we can use a kernel module to see how a test code works.

How to do it...

In the `hashtable.c` file, an example is implemented that is very similar to the one proposed in the preceding section with kernel lists:

1. As the first step, we declare the hash table, the data structure, and the hash function as follows:

```
static DEFINE_HASHTABLE(data_hash, 1);

struct h_struct {
    int data;
    struct hlist_node node;
};

static int hash_func(int data)
{
    return data % 2;
}
```

Our hash table has only two buckets just to be able to easily hit a collision, so the hash function implementation is very trivial; it must return only values 0 or 1.

2. Then, in the module's `init()` function, we define our nodes:

```
static int __init hashtable_init(void)
{
    struct h_struct e1 = {
        .data = 5
    };
    struct h_struct e2 = {
        .data = 2
    };
    struct h_struct e3 = {
        .data = 7
    };
```

3. Then, we do a first insertion followed by a data printing:

```
pr_info("add e1...\n");
add_node(&e1);
print_nodes();
```

4. Next, we continue node insertion:

```
pr_info("add e2, e3...\n");
add_node(&e2);
```

```
add_node(&e3);
print_nodes();
```

5. Finally, we try a node deletion:

```
pr_info("del data=5\n");
del_node(5);
print_nodes();

return -EINVAL;
}
```

6. As the final step, we can have a look at nodes' insertion and removal functions:

```
static void add_node(struct h_struct *new)
{
    int key = hash_func(new->data);
    hash_add(data_hash, &new->node, key);
}

static void del_node(int data)
{
    int key = hash_func(data);
    struct h_struct *entry;

    hash_for_each_possible(data_hash, entry, node, key) {
        if (entry->data == data) {
            hash_del(&entry->node);
            return;
        }
    }
}
```

These two functions need key generation in order to be sure to add or remove the node to or from the right bucket.

7. The hash table printing can be done by using the `hash_for_each()` macro as follows:

```
static void print_nodes(void)
{
    int key;
    struct h_struct *entry;
    hash_for_each(data_hash, key, entry, node)
        pr_info("data=%d\n", entry->data);
}
```

There's more...

Again, to test the code, just compile and then insert the kernel module into the ESPRESSObin.

After module insertion, in kernel messages, we should see the first output lines:

```
# insmod ./hashtable.ko
hashtable:hashtable_init: add e1...
hashtable:print_nodes: data=5
```

 You can safely ignore the following error message as discussed earlier:
```
insmod: ERROR: could not insert module hashtable.ko:
Invalid parameters
```

In *step 1* and *step 2*, we have defined the nodes of our hash table, while in *step 3* we have done the first insert into the table, and the preceding code is what we get after the insertion.

Then, we perform the second insertion within *step 4* where we add two nodes with the data fields set to 7 and 2:

```
hashtable:hashtable_init: add e2, e3...
hashtable:print_nodes: data=7
hashtable:print_nodes: data=2
hashtable:print_nodes: data=5
```

And finally, in *step 5* we remove the node having the `data` field set to 5:

```
hashtable:hashtable_init: del data=5
hashtable:print_nodes: data=7
hashtable:print_nodes: data=2
```

Note that in *step 6*, we presented a possible implementation of the node insertion within the hash table. In *step 7*, we have the printing function.

See also

- For further information about kernel hash tables, a good starting point (even if a bit outdated) is `https://lwn.net/Articles/510202/`.

Getting access to I/O memory

In this recipe, we will see how to get access to the internal peripherals of a CPU or to any other memory mapped device that is connected to the CPU.

Getting ready

This time, we'll present an example using an already existing piece of code in the kernel sources, so now there is nothing to compile, but we can go directly to the root directory of ESPRESSObin's kernel sources.

How to do it...

1. A good and really simple example about how to do a memory remap is reported in the linux/drivers/reset/reset-sunxi.c file in the sunxi_reset_init() function as follows:

```
static int sunxi_reset_init(struct device_node *np)
{
    struct reset_simple_data *data;
    struct resource res;
    resource_size_t size;
    int ret;

    data = kzalloc(sizeof(*data), GFP_KERNEL);
    if (!data)
        return -ENOMEM;

    ret = of_address_to_resource(np, 0, &res);
    if (ret)
        goto err_alloc;
```

By using the of_address_to_resource() function, we ask the device tree that is the memory mapping of our device and we get the result in the res structure.

2. Then, we request the memory mapping size by using the `resource_size()` function and then we call the `request_mem_region()` function in order to ask the kernel to get exclusive access to the memory addresses between `res.start` and `res.start+size-1`:

```
size = resource_size(&res);
if (!request_mem_region(res.start, size, np->name)) {
        ret = -EBUSY;
        goto err_alloc;
}
```

If nobody has already issued this same request, the region is marked as used by us with the labeling name stored into `np->name`.

> The name and memory region is now reserved for us and all this information can be retrieved from the `/proc/iomem` file, as will be shown in the next section.

3. After all the preceding preliminary operations, we can finally call the `ioremap()` function that actually does the remap:

```
data->membase = ioremap(res.start, size);
if (!data->membase) {
    ret = -ENOMEM;
    goto err_alloc;
}
```

In `data->membase`, is stored the virtual address we can use to get access to our device's registers.

The prototype of `ioremap()` and its counterpart `iounmap()`, which must be used when we have finished using this mapping, is defined in the header file, `linux/include/asm-generic/io.h`, as follows:

```
void __iomem *ioremap(phys_addr_t phys_addr, size_t size);

void iounmap(void __iomem *addr);
```

> Note that in `linux/include/asm-generic/io.h`, it is just reported that the implementation for systems that do not have an MMU due to the fact that each platform has its own implementation under the `linux/arch` directory.

How it works...

To have an idea about how to use `ioremap()`, we can compare the preceding code and the
Universal Asynchronous Receiver/Transmitter (UART) driver of our ESPRESSObin within
the `linux/drivers/tty/serial/mvebu-uart.c` file, shown in the following snippet:

```
    . . .
        port->membase = devm_ioremap_resource(&pdev->dev, reg);
        if (IS_ERR(port->membase))
            return -PTR_ERR(port->membase);
    . . .
        /* UART Soft Reset*/
        writel(CTRL_SOFT_RST, port->membase + UART_CTRL(port));
        udelay(1);
        writel(0, port->membase + UART_CTRL(port));
    . . .
```

The preceding code is part of the `mvebu_uart_probe()` function, which, at some time,
calls the `devm_ioremap_resource()` function, which performs similar steps as the
combined execution of functions presented in *step 1*, *step 2*, and *step 3*, that is, the
functions `of_address_to_resource()`, `request_mem_region()`, and `ioremap()` at
once: it takes information from the device tree and does a memory remap, reserving those
registers for its exclusive usage only.

This registration (done previously in *step 2*) can be checked in the procfs file `/proc/iomem`
as follows, where we see that the memory area `d0012000-d00121ff` is assigned to
`serial@12000`:

```
root@espressobin:~# cat /proc/iomem
00000000-7fffffff : System RAM
00080000-00faffff : Kernel code
010f0000-012a9fff : Kernel data
d0010600-d0010fff : spi@10600
d0012000-d00121ff : serial@12000
d0013000-d00130ff : nb-periph-clk@13000
d0013200-d00132ff : tbg@13200
d0013c00-d0013c1f : pinctrl@13800
d0018000-d00180ff : sb-periph-clk@18000
d0018c00-d0018c1f : pinctrl@18800
d001e808-d001e80b : sdhci@d0000
d0030000-d0033fff : ethernet@30000
d0058000-d005bfff : usb@58000
d005e000-d005ffff : usb@5e000
d0070000-d008ffff : pcie@d0070000
d00d0000-d00d02ff : sdhci@d0000
d00e0000-d00e1fff : sata@e0000
e8000000-e8ffffff : pcie@d0070000
```

As already stated several times in this book, when we're in the kernel, nobody can really stop us from doing something; therefore, when I talk about *exclusive usage* of a memory area, the reader should imagine that this is true, if all programmers voluntarily refrain from issuing memory accesses on that area if a previous access request (like the ones issued previously) to an I/O memory area had failed.

See also

- For further information about memory mapping, a good starting point is `https:/ /linux-kernel-labs.github.io/master/labs/memory_mapping.html`.

Spending time in the kernel

In this recipe, we will take a look at how we can delay the execution after some time in the future by using busy loops or more complex functions that may involve a suspension.

Getting ready

Even in this recipe, we can use a kernel module to see how a test code works.

How to do it...

In the `time.c` file, we can find a simple example exemplifying how the preceding functions work:

1. As the first step, we declare a utility function to get the execution time in nanoseconds, of a line of code:

```
#define print_time(str, code)      \
    do {                           \
        u64 t0, t1;                \
        t0 = ktime_get_real_ns(); \
        code;                      \
        t1 = ktime_get_real_ns(); \
        pr_info(str " -> %lluns\n", t1 - t0); \
    } while (0)
```

This is an easy trick to define a macro that executes a line of code while taking its execution time by using the `ktime_get_real_ns()` function, which returns the current system time in nanoseconds.

 For further information regarding `ktime_get_real_ns()` and related functions, you can take a look at `https://www.kernel.org/doc/html/latest/core-api/timekeeping.html`.

2. Now, for the module's `init()` function, we can use our macro and then call all the preceding delaying functions as follows:

```
static int __init time_init(void)
{
    pr_info("*delay() functions:\n");
    print_time("10ns", ndelay(10));
    print_time("10000ns", udelay(10));
    print_time("10000000ns", mdelay(10));

    pr_info("*sleep() functions:\n");
    print_time("10000ns", usleep_range(10, 10));
    print_time("10000000ns", msleep(10));
    print_time("10000000ns", msleep_interruptible(10));
    print_time("10000000000ns", ssleep(10));

    return -EINVAL;
}
```

There's more...

We can test our code by compiling it and then inserting it into the ESPRESSObin kernel:

```
# insmod time.ko
```

The following kernel messages should be printed out by using the macro defined in *step 1*. This macro simply takes the execution time of the delay function passed into the `code` parameter by using the `ktime_get_real_ns()` function, which is useful for getting the current kernel time in nanoseconds:

```
time:time_init: *delay() functions:
time:time_init: 10ns -> 480ns
time:time_init: 10000us -> 10560ns
time:time_init: 10000000ms -> 10387920ns
time:time_init: *sleep() functions:
time:time_init: 10000us -> 580720ns
```

```
time:time_init: 10000000ms -> 17979680ns
time:time_init: 10000000ms -> 17739280ns
time:time_init: 10000000000ms -> 10073738800ns
```

 You can safely ignore the following error message as discussed earlier:
`insmod: ERROR: could not insert module time.ko: Invalid`
`parameters`

 Note that the prompt will take 10 seconds before returning, due to the last call of the `ssleep(10)` function, which is not interruptible; so, even if we press *Ctrl* + *C*, we cannot stop the execution.

Examining the preceding output (from *step 2*), we notice that `ndelay()` is not as reliable as expected for a small amount of time, while `udelay()` and `mdelay()` work better. Regarding `*sleep()` functions, instead, we have to say that they are heavily affected by the machine load due to the fact they can sleep.

See also

- For further information about delaying functions, a good starting point is provided in the kernel documentation within the `linux/Documentation/timers/timers-howto.txt` file.

Advanced Char Driver Operations

7

In previous chapters, we learned several useful things that can be handy in device driver development; however, a final step is needed. We must see how to add advanced functionalities to our character device and fully understand how we can synchronize user space processes with the peripheral I/O activity.

In this chapter, we'll see how to implement system calls for the `lseek()`, `ioctl()`, and `mmap()` functions, and we'll also get to know several techniques to put a process to sleep, just in case our peripheral does not yet have data to return to it; therefore, in this chapter, we will cover the following recipes:

- Going up and down within a file with lseek()
- Using ioctl() for custom commands
- Accessing I/O memory with mmap()
- Locking with the process context
- Locking (and syncing) with the interrupt context
- Waiting for I/O operations with poll() and select()
- Managing asynchronous notifications with fasync()

Technical requirements

Please check the appendix section of this chapter for more information.

The code and other files used in this chapter can be downloaded from GitHub at `https://github.com/giometti/linux_device_driver_development_cookbook/tree/master/chapter_07`.

Going up and down within a file with lseek()

In this recipe, we're going to take a better look at how we can manipulate the ppos pointer (described in the *Exchanging data with a char driver* recipe in Chapter 3, *Working with Char Drivers*), which is related to the read() and write() system call implementations.

Getting ready

To provide a simple example about lseek() implementation, we can reuse our chrdev driver in Chapter 4, *Using the Device Tree* in the chapter_04/chrdev directory (we need both of the chrdev.c and chrdev-req.c files of GitHub repository), where we can simply add our custom llseek() method according to our device memory layout.

 For simplicity, I just copied these files in the chapter_07/chrdev/ directory, and reworked them.

We also need to modify the ESPRESSObin's DTS file as we did in chapter 4 with the chapter_04/chrdev/add_chrdev_devices.dts.patch file in order to enable the chrdev device, and then, finally, we can reuse the chrdev_test.c program created in Chapter 3, *Working with Char Drivers* within the chapter_03/chrdev_test.c file as a base program for our lseek() implementation testing.

Regarding the ESPRESSObin's DTS file, we can patch it by going in the kernel sources and then executing the patch command, as follows:

```
$ patch -p1 < ../github/chapter_04/chrdev/add_chrdev_devices.dts.patch
patching file arch/arm64/boot/dts/marvell/armada-3720-espressobin.dts
```

Then, we have to recompile the kernel and reinstall it with the preceding DTS as we did in Chapter 1, *Installing the Development System*, and, finally, reboot the system.

How to do it...

Let's see how to do it by following these steps:

1. First, we can simply redefine `struct file_operations` by adding our `chrdev_llseek` method:

```
static const struct file_operations chrdev_fops = {
    .owner   = THIS_MODULE,
    .llseek  = chrdev_llseek,
    .read    = chrdev_read,
    .write   = chrdev_write,
    .open    = chrdev_open,
    .release = chrdev_release
};
```

2. Then, we define the method's body by using a big switch, where the `SEEK_SET`, `SEEK_CUR`, and `SEEK_END` possible values are managed, according to the memory layout of the driver:

```
static loff_t chrdev_llseek(struct file *filp, loff_t offset, int
whence)
{
    struct chrdev_device *chrdev = filp->private_data;
    loff_t newppos;

    dev_info(chrdev->dev, "should move *ppos=%lld by whence %d
off=%lld\n",
                filp->f_pos, whence, offset);

    switch (whence) {
    case SEEK_SET:
        newppos = offset;
        break;

    case SEEK_CUR:
        newppos = filp->f_pos + offset;
        break;

    case SEEK_END:
        newppos = BUF_LEN + offset;
        break;

    default:
        return -EINVAL;
    }
```

3. Finally, we have to verify that `newppos` is still between 0 and `BUF_LEN` and, in a positive case, we have to update `filp->f_pos` with the `newppos` value as follows:

```
if ((newppos < 0) || (newppos >= BUF_LEN))
    return -EINVAL;

filp->f_pos = newppos;
dev_info(chrdev->dev, "return *ppos=%lld\n", filp->f_pos);

return newppos;
}
```

Note that the new version of the `chrdev.c` driver can be retrieved from GitHub sources within the `chapter_07/` directory related to this chapter.

How it works...

In *step 2*, we should remember that we have a memory buffer of `BUF_LEN` bytes per device, so we can compute the new `newppos` position within the device by simply executing some simple operations.

So, for `SEEK_SET`, which sets `ppos` to `offset`, we can simply perform an assignment; for `SEEK_CUR`, which moves `ppos` from its current location (which is `filp->f_pos`) plus `offset` bytes, we execute a sum; and, finally, for `SEEK_END`, which set `ppos` to the end of the file plus `offset` bytes, we still perform a sum with the `BUF_LEN` buffer size since we are expecting a negative value or zero from the userspace.

There's more...

If you wish to test the `lseek()` system call now, we can modify the `chrdev_test.c` program as reported previously, and then try to execute it on our new driver version.

So, let's modify chrdev_test.c using the `modify_lseek_to_chrdev_test.patch` file, as follows:

```
$ cd github/chapter_03/
$ patch -p2 < ../chapter_07/chrdev/modify_lseek_to_chrdev_test.patch
```

Then, we have to recompile it as follows:

```
$ make CFLAGS="-Wall -O2" \
        CC=aarch64-linux-gnu-gcc \
            chrdev_test
aarch64-linux-gnu-gcc -Wall -O2 chrdev_test.c -o chrdev_test
```

Note that this command can be executed in the ESPRESSObin by simply removing the `CC=aarch64-linux-gnu-gcc` setting.

Then we have to move both the new `chrdev_test` executable and the `chrdev.ko` (the one with `lseek()` support) and `chrdev-req.ko` kernel modules on the ESPRESSObin, and then insert them into the kernel:

```
# insmod chrdev.ko
chrdev:chrdev_init: got major 239
# insmod chrdev-req.ko
chrdev cdev-eeprom@2: chrdev cdev-eeprom with id 2 added
chrdev cdev-rom@4: chrdev cdev-rom with id 4 added
```

This output is from a serial console, so we also get kernel messages. If you execute these commands over an SSH connection, you'll get no output and you will have to use the `dmesg` command to get an output in the preceding example.

Finally, we can execute the `chrdev_test` program on one chrdev device, as shown in the following:

```
# ./chrdev_test /dev/cdev-eeprom\@2
file /dev/cdev-eeprom@2 opened
wrote 11 bytes into file /dev/cdev-eeprom@2
data written are: 44 55 4d 4d 59 20 44 41 54 41 00
*ppos moved to 0
read 11 bytes from file /dev/cdev-eeprom@2
data read are: 44 55 4d 4d 59 20 44 41 54 41 00
```

As expected, the `lseek()` system call invokes the
driver's `chrdev_llseek()` method, which does what we expect. The kernel messages related to the preceding command are reported as follows:

```
chrdev cdev-eeprom@2: chrdev (id=2) opened
chrdev cdev-eeprom@2: should write 11 bytes (*ppos=0)
chrdev cdev-eeprom@2: got 11 bytes (*ppos=11)
chrdev cdev-eeprom@2: should move *ppos=11 by whence 0 off=0
```

```
chrdev cdev-eeprom@2: return *ppos=0
chrdev cdev-eeprom@2: should read 11 bytes (*ppos=0)
chrdev cdev-eeprom@2: return 11 bytes (*ppos=11)
chrdev cdev-eeprom@2: chrdev (id=2) released
```

So, ppos moved from byte 0 to byte 11 when the first write() system call is executed, then it moves back to 0 thanks to lseek(), and, finally, it moves again to 11 due to the execution of the read() system call.

Note that we can also invoke the lseek() method using the dd command, as follows:

```
# dd if=/dev/cdev-eeprom\@2 skip=11 bs=1 count=3 | od -tx1
3+0 records in
3+0 records out
3 bytes copied, 0.0530299 s, 0.1 kB/s
0000000 00 00 00
0000003
```

Here, we open the device, then we move ppos 11 bytes forward from the beginning, and then we do three 1-byte length reads for each.

In the following kernel messages, we can verify that the dd program behaves exactly as expected:

```
chrdev cdev-eeprom@2: chrdev (id=2) opened
chrdev cdev-eeprom@2: should move *ppos=0 by whence 1 off=0
chrdev cdev-eeprom@2: return *ppos=0
chrdev cdev-eeprom@2: should move *ppos=0 by whence 1 off=11
chrdev cdev-eeprom@2: return *ppos=11
chrdev cdev-eeprom@2: should read 1 bytes (*ppos=11)
chrdev cdev-eeprom@2: return 1 bytes (*ppos=12)
chrdev cdev-eeprom@2: should read 1 bytes (*ppos=12)
chrdev cdev-eeprom@2: return 1 bytes (*ppos=13)
chrdev cdev-eeprom@2: should read 1 bytes (*ppos=13)
chrdev cdev-eeprom@2: return 1 bytes (*ppos=14)
chrdev cdev-eeprom@2: chrdev (id=2) released
```

See also

- For further information about the lseek() system call, a good starting point is its man page, which can be obtained by using the man 2 lseek command.

Using ioctl() for custom commands

In this recipe, we will see how to add custom commands to configure or manage our peripheral in a very customized manner.

Getting ready

Now, in order to present a simple example about how we can implement an `ioctl()` system call within our driver, we can still use the chrdev driver presented earlier, where we add the `unlocked_ioctl()` method, as explained later.

How to do it...

Let's see how to do it by following these steps:

1. First of all, we have to add the `unlocked_ioctl()` method within the `chrdev_fops` structure:

```
static const struct file_operations chrdev_fops = {
    .owner          = THIS_MODULE,
    .unlocked_ioctl = chrdev_ioctl,
    .llseek         = chrdev_llseek,
    .read           = chrdev_read,
    .write          = chrdev_write,
    .open           = chrdev_open,
    .release        = chrdev_release
};
```

2. Then, we add the method's body where, at the beginning, we did some assignments and checks as follows:

```
static long chrdev_ioctl(struct file *filp,
            unsigned int cmd, unsigned long arg)
{
    struct chrdev_device *chrdev = filp->private_data;
    struct chrdev_info info;
    void __user *uarg = (void __user *) arg;
    int __user *iuarg = (int __user *) arg;
    int ret;

    /* Get some command information */
    if (_IOC_TYPE(cmd) != CHRDEV_IOCTL_BASE) {
        dev_err(chrdev->dev, "command %x is not for us!\n", cmd);
```

```
            return -EINVAL;
        }
        dev_info(chrdev->dev, "cmd nr=%d size=%d dir=%x\n",
                    _IOC_NR(cmd), _IOC_SIZE(cmd), _IOC_DIR(cmd));
```

3. Then, we can implement a big switch to execute the requested command, as follows:

```
        switch (cmd) {
        case CHRDEV_IOC_GETINFO:
            dev_info(chrdev->dev, "CHRDEV_IOC_GETINFO\n");

            strncpy(info.label, chrdev->label, NAME_LEN);
            info.read_only = chrdev->read_only;

            ret = copy_to_user(uarg, &info, sizeof(struct
chrdev_info));
            if (ret)
                return -EFAULT;

            break;

        case WDIOC_SET_RDONLY:
            dev_info(chrdev->dev, "WDIOC_SET_RDONLY\n");

            ret = get_user(chrdev->read_only, iuarg);
            if (ret)
                return -EFAULT;

            break;

        default:
            return -ENOIOCTLCMD;
        }

        return 0;
    }
```

4. For the last step, we have to define the `chrdev_ioctl.h` include file to be shared with the user space, holding the `ioctl()` commands defined in the preceding code block:

```
    /*
     * Chrdev ioctl() include file
     */

    #include <linux/ioctl.h>
    #include <linux/types.h>
```

```
#define CHRDEV_IOCTL_BASE      'C'
#define CHRDEV_NAME_LEN        32

struct chrdev_info {
    char label[CHRDEV_NAME_LEN];
    int read_only;
};

/*
 * The ioctl() commands
 */

#define CHRDEV_IOC_GETINFO _IOR(CHRDEV_IOCTL_BASE, 0, struct
chrdev_info)
#define WDIOC_SET_RDONLY _IOW(CHRDEV_IOCTL_BASE, 1, int)
```

How it works...

In *step 2*, the `info`, `uarg`, and `iuarg` variables will be used, while the usage of
the `_IOC_TYPE()` macro is to verify that the `cmd` command was effective for our driver by
checking the command's type against the `CHRDEV_IOCTL_BASE` definition.

A careful reader should note that this check is not fault-proof due to the
fact that a command's type is just a random number; however, it can be
enough for our purposes here.

Also, by using `_IOC_NR()`, `_IOC_SIZE()`, and `_IOC_DIR()`, we can extract other
information from the command, which can be useful for further checks.

In *step 3*, as we can see for each command, according to the fact it's a reading or writing (or
both) command, we have to get, or put, user data from the user space by utilizing the
proper access functions, as explained in `Chapter 3`, *Working with Char Drivers*, in order to
avoid memory corruption!

Now it should be also clear how the `info`, `uarg`, and `iuarg` variables are used. The first is
used to locally store `struct chrdev_info` data, while the others are used to have
properly typed data to be used with the `copy_to_user()` or `get_user()` functions.

There's more...

To test the code and see how it behaves, we need to realize a proper tool that executes our new `ioctl()` commands.

An example is provided in the `chrdev_ioctl.c` file, and in the following snippet, where the `ioctl()` calls are used:

```c
/* Try reading device info */
ret = ioctl(fd, CHRDEV_IOC_GETINFO, &info);
    if (ret < 0) {
        perror("ioctl(CHRDEV_IOC_GETINFO)");
        exit(EXIT_FAILURE);
    }
printf("got label=%s and read_only=%d\n", info.label, info.read_only);

/* Try toggling the device reading mode */
read_only = !info.read_only;
ret = ioctl(fd, WDIOC_SET_RDONLY, &read_only);
    if (ret < 0) {
        perror("ioctl(WDIOC_SET_RDONLY)");
        exit(EXIT_FAILURE);
    }
printf("device has now read_only=%d\n", read_only);
```

Now, let's compile the `chrdev_ioctl.c` program by using the next command line on our host PC:

```
$ make CFLAGS="-Wall -O2 -Ichrdev/" \
       CC=aarch64-linux-gnu-gcc \
           chrdev_ioctl
aarch64-linux-gnu-gcc -Wall -O2 chrdev_ioctl.c -o chrdev_ioctl
```

Note that this command can also be executed in the ESPRESSObin by simply removing the `CC=aarch64-linux-gnu-gcc` setting.

Now, if we try to execute the command on a chrdev device, we should get the following output:

```
# ./chrdev_ioctl /dev/cdev-eeprom\@2
file /dev/cdev-eeprom@2 opened
got label=cdev-eeprom and read_only=0
device has now read_only=1
```

Of course, for this to work, we'll have already loaded this new chrdev driver's version containing the `ioctl()` method.

While on the kernel messages we should get the following:

```
chrdev cdev-eeprom@2: chrdev (id=2) opened
chrdev cdev-eeprom@2: cmd nr=0 size=36 dir=2
chrdev cdev-eeprom@2: CHRDEV_IOC_GETINFO
chrdev cdev-eeprom@2: cmd nr=1 size=4 dir=1
chrdev cdev-eeprom@2: WDIOC_SET_RDONLY
chrdev cdev-eeprom@2: chrdev (id=2) released
```

As we can see, after the device opening, two `ioctl()` commands are executed as expected.

See also

- For further information about the `ioctl()` system call, a good starting point is its man page, which can be obtained by using the `man 2 ioctl` command.

Accessing I/O memory with mmap()

In this recipe, we will see how to map an I/O memory region within the process memory space to gain access to our peripheral's internal by simply using a pointer in memory.

Getting ready

Now, let's see how we can implement a custom `mmap()` system call for our chrdev driver.

Since we have a virtual device totally mapped into memory, we may suppose that the `buf` buffer within `struct chrdev_device` represents the memory areas to be mapped. Also, we need to dynamically allocate it for it to be remapped; this is due to the fact that kernel virtual memory addresses cannot be remapped using the `remap_pfn_range()` function.

This is the only limitation of `remap_pfn_range()`, which is unable to remap the kernel virtual memory addresses that are not dynamically allocated. These addresses can be remapped too, but by using another technique not covered in this book.

To prepare our driver, we must make the following modifications to `struct`
`chrdev_device`:

```
diff --git a/chapter_07/chrdev/chrdev.h b/chapter_07/chrdev/chrdev.h
index 6b925fe..40a244f 100644
--- a/chapter_07/chrdev/chrdev.h
+++ b/chapter_07/chrdev/chrdev.h
@@ -7,7 +7,7 @@

 #define MAX_DEVICES 8
 #define NAME_LEN     CHRDEV_NAME_LEN
-#define BUF_LEN      300
+#define BUF_LEN      PAGE_SIZE

 /*
  * Chrdev basic structs
@@ -17,7 +17,7 @@
 struct chrdev_device {
     char label[NAME_LEN];
     unsigned int busy : 1;
-    char buf[BUF_LEN];
+    char *buf;
     int read_only;

     unsigned int id;
```

Note that we also modified the buffer size to be at least a `PAGE_SIZE` long due to the fact
we cannot remap memory areas shorter than the `PAGE_SIZE` bytes.

Then, to dynamically allocate the memory buffer, we have to make the modifications listed
as follows:

```
diff --git a/chapter_07/chrdev/chrdev.c b/chapter_07/chrdev/chrdev.c
index 3717ad2..a8bffc3 100644
--- a/chapter_07/chrdev/chrdev.c
+++ b/chapter_07/chrdev/chrdev.c
@@ -7,6 +7,7 @@
 #include <linux/module.h>
 #include <linux/fs.h>
 #include <linux/uaccess.h>
+#include <linux/slab.h>
 #include <linux/mman.h>


@@ -246,6 +247,13 @@ int chrdev_device_register(const char *label, unsigned
int
id,
```

```
          return -EBUSY;
      }

+     /* First try to allocate memory for internal buffer */
+     chrdev->buf = kzalloc(BUF_LEN, GFP_KERNEL);
+     if (!chrdev->buf) {
+         dev_err(chrdev->dev, "cannot allocate memory buffer!\n");
+         return -ENOMEM;
+     }
+
      /* Create the device and initialize its data */
      cdev_init(&chrdev->cdev, &chrdev_fops);
      chrdev->cdev.owner = owner;
@@ -255,7 +263,7 @@ int chrdev_device_register(const char *label, unsigned
int id,
      if (ret) {
          pr_err("failed to add char device %s at %d:%d\n",
                          label, MAJOR(chrdev_devt), id);
-         return ret;
+         goto kfree_buf;
      }
  chrdev->dev = device_create(chrdev_class, parent, devt, chrdev,
```

Here is the continuation of the preceding `diff` file:

```
@@ -272,7 +280,6 @@ int chrdev_device_register(const char *label, unsigned
int id,
      chrdev->read_only = read_only;
      chrdev->busy = 1;
      strncpy(chrdev->label, label, NAME_LEN);
-     memset(chrdev->buf, 0, BUF_LEN);

      dev_info(chrdev->dev, "chrdev %s with id %d added\n", label, id);

@@ -280,6 +287,8 @@ int chrdev_device_register(const char *label, unsigned
int id,

  del_cdev:
      cdev_del(&chrdev->cdev);
+ kfree_buf:
+     kfree(chrdev->buf);

      return ret;
  }
@@ -309,6 +318,9 @@ int chrdev_device_unregister(const char *label,
unsigned int id)

      dev_info(chrdev->dev, "chrdev %s with id %d removed\n", label, id);
```

```
+        /* Free allocated memory */
+        kfree(chrdev->buf);
+

         /* Dealocate the device */
         device_destroy(chrdev_class, chrdev->dev->devt);
         cdev_del(&chrdev->cdev);
```

However, apart from this little note, we can proceed as we did previously, that is, by modifying our chrdev driver and adding the new method.

How to do it...

Let's see how to do it by following these steps:

1. Again, as in previous sections, the first step is adding our new `mmap()` method to the driver's `struct file_operations`:

   ```
   static const struct file_operations chrdev_fops = {
           .owner          = THIS_MODULE,
           .mmap           = chrdev_mmap,
           .unlocked_ioctl = chrdev_ioctl,
           .llseek         = chrdev_llseek,
           .read           = chrdev_read,
           .write          = chrdev_write,
           .open           = chrdev_open,
           .release        = chrdev_release
   };
   ```

2. Then, we add the `chrdev_mmap()` implementation, as explained in the previous section and reported in the following:

   ```
   static int chrdev_mmap(struct file *filp, struct vm_area_struct
   *vma)
   {
       struct chrdev_device *chrdev = filp->private_data;
       size_t size = vma->vm_end - vma->vm_start;
       phys_addr_t offset = (phys_addr_t) vma->vm_pgoff << PAGE_SHIFT;
       unsigned long pfn;

       /* Does it even fit in phys_addr_t? */
       if (offset >> PAGE_SHIFT != vma->vm_pgoff)
           return -EINVAL;

       /* We cannot mmap too big areas */
       if ((offset > BUF_LEN) || (size > BUF_LEN - offset))
           return -EINVAL;
   ```

3. Then, we must get the physical address of the `buf` buffer:

```
/* Get the physical address belong the virtual kernel address */
pfn = virt_to_phys(chrdev->buf) >> PAGE_SHIFT;
```

Note that this step won't be needed if we simply wanted to remap the physical address on which our peripheral is mapped.

4. Finally, we can do the remap:

```
        /* Remap-pfn-range will mark the range VM_IO */
        if (remap_pfn_range(vma, vma->vm_start,
                    pfn, size,
                    vma->vm_page_prot))
            return -EAGAIN;

        return 0;
    }
```

How it works...

In *step 2*, the function begins with some sanity checks in which we must verify that the memory region requested is compatible with the system and peripheral requirements. In our example, we must verify that the size of the memory region and the offset within it, and where the map starts from, are within the `buf` size, which is `BUF_LEN` bytes.

There's more...

To test our new `mmap()` implementation, we can use the `chrdev_mmap.c` program introduced earlier. where we talked about `textfile.txt`. To compile it, we can use the following command on the host PC:

```
$ make CFLAGS="-Wall -O2" \
        CC=aarch64-linux-gnu-gcc \
            chrdev_mmap
aarch64-linux-gnu-gcc -Wall -O2 chrdev_mmap.c -o chrdev_mmap
```

Note that this command can be executed in the ESPRESSObin by simply removing the `CC=aarch64-linux-gnu-gcc` setting.

Now, let's start by writing something in the driver:

```
# cp textfile.txt /dev/cdev-eeprom\@2
```

The kernel messages are as follows:

```
chrdev cdev-eeprom@2: chrdev (id=2) opened
chrdev cdev-eeprom@2: chrdev (id=2) released
chrdev cdev-eeprom@2: chrdev (id=2) opened
chrdev cdev-eeprom@2: should write 54 bytes (*ppos=0)
chrdev cdev-eeprom@2: got 54 bytes (*ppos=54)
chrdev cdev-eeprom@2: chrdev (id=2) released
```

Now, as expected, within our memory buffer we have the textfile.txt contents; in fact:

```
# cat /dev/cdev-eeprom\@2
This is a test file

This is line 3.

End of the file
```

Now we can try to execute the chrdev_mmap program on our device to verify whether everything works well:

```
# ./chrdev_mmap /dev/cdev-eeprom\@2 54
file /dev/cdev-eeprom@2 opened
got address=0xffff9896c000 and len=54
---
This is a test file

This is line 3.

End of the file
```

Note that we must be sure not to specify a size a value bigger than the device's buffer size, which is 4,096 in our example. In fact, if we do the following, we get an error:

```
./chrdev_mmap /dev/cdev-eeprom\@2 4097
file /dev/cdev-eeprom@2 opened
mmap: Invalid argument
```

This means we got it! Note that the chrdev_mmap program (as cp and cat) works exactly the same on both usual files and on our char device.

The kernel messages related to the `mmap()` execution are as follows:

```
chrdev cdev-eeprom@2: chrdev (id=2) opened
chrdev cdev-eeprom@2: mmap vma=ffff9896c000 pfn=79ead size=1000
chrdev cdev-eeprom@2: chrdev (id=2) released
```

Note that, after the remap, the program doesn't execute any system calls to gain access to the data. This leads to the possibility of better performances in obtaining access to the device's data rather than the case where we needed to use the `read()` or `write()` system calls.

We can also modify the buffer content by adding the optional argument, `0`, to the `chrdev_mmap` program, as follows:

```
./chrdev_mmap /dev/cdev-eeprom\@2 54 0
file /dev/cdev-eeprom@2 opened
got address=0xffff908ef000 and len=54
---
This is a test file

This is line 3.

End of the file
---
First character changed to '0'
```

Then, when we read the buffer again using the `read()` system call with, `cat` command, we can see that the first character within the file has changed to **0** as expected:

```
# cat /dev/cdev-eeprom\@2
0his is a test file

This is line 3.

End of the file
```

See also

- For further information regarding `mmap()`, a good starting point is its man page (`man 2 mmap`); then, looking at `https://linux-kernel-labs.github.io/master/labs/memory_mapping.html` would be even better.

Locking with the process context

In this recipe, we will see how to protect data against the concurrent access of two or more processes to avoid race conditions.

How to do it...

To present a simple example about how to add a mutex to the chrdev driver, we can make a few modifications to it, as reported in the following.

1. First, we have to add the `mux` mutex to the driver's main structure in the `chrdev.h` header file, as follows:

```
/* Main struct */
struct chrdev_device {
    char label[NAME_LEN];
    unsigned int busy : 1;
    char *buf;
    int read_only;

    unsigned int id;
    struct module *owner;
    struct cdev cdev;
    struct device *dev;

    struct mutex mux;
};
```

All modifications presented here can be applied to the chrdev code using the `patch` command in the `add_mutex_to_chrdev.patch` file, as follows:

```
$ patch -p3 < add_mutex_to_chrdev.patch
```

2. Then, in the `chrdev_device_register()` function, we have to initialize the mutex by using the `mutex_init()` function:

```
/* Init the chrdev data */
chrdev->id = id;
chrdev->read_only = read_only;
chrdev->busy = 1;
strncpy(chrdev->label, label, NAME_LEN);
mutex_init(&chrdev->mux);
```

```
dev_info(chrdev->dev, "chrdev %s with id %d added\n", label, id);

return 0;
```

3. Next, we can modify the `read()` and `write()` methods to protect them. The `read()` methods should then look like the following:

```
static ssize_t chrdev_read(struct file *filp,
                char __user *buf, size_t count, loff_t *ppos)
{
    struct chrdev_device *chrdev = filp->private_data;
    int ret;

    dev_info(chrdev->dev, "should read %ld bytes (*ppos=%lld)\n",
                count, *ppos);
    mutex_lock(&chrdev->mux); // Grab the mutex

    /* Check for end-of-buffer */
    if (*ppos + count >= BUF_LEN)
        count = BUF_LEN - *ppos;

    /* Return data to the user space */
    ret = copy_to_user(buf, chrdev->buf + *ppos, count);
    if (ret < 0) {
        count = -EFAULT;
        goto unlock;
    }

    *ppos += count;
    dev_info(chrdev->dev, "return %ld bytes (*ppos=%lld)\n", count,
*ppos);

unlock:
    mutex_unlock(&chrdev->mux); // Release the mutex

    return count;
}
```

The `write()` method is reported as follows:

```
static ssize_t chrdev_write(struct file *filp,
                const char __user *buf, size_t count, loff_t *ppos)
{
    struct chrdev_device *chrdev = filp->private_data;
    int ret;

    dev_info(chrdev->dev, "should write %ld bytes (*ppos=%lld)\n",
                count, *ppos);
```

```
        if (chrdev->read_only)
            return -EINVAL;

    mutex_lock(&chrdev->mux); // Grab the mutex

    /* Check for end-of-buffer */
    if (*ppos + count >= BUF_LEN)
        count = BUF_LEN - *ppos;

    /* Get data from the user space */
    ret = copy_from_user(chrdev->buf + *ppos, buf, count);
    if (ret < 0) {
        count = -EFAULT;
        goto unlock;
    }

    *ppos += count;
    dev_info(chrdev->dev, "got %ld bytes (*ppos=%lld)\n", count,
*ppos);

unlock:
    mutex_unlock(&chrdev->mux); // Release the mutex

    return count;
}
```

4. Finally, we have to protect the ioctl() method too, since the driver's read_only property may change:

```
static long chrdev_ioctl(struct file *filp,
            unsigned int cmd, unsigned long arg)
{
    struct chrdev_device *chrdev = filp->private_data;
    struct chrdev_info info;
    void __user *uarg = (void __user *) arg;
    int __user *iuarg = (int __user *) arg;
    int ret;

    ...

    /* Grab the mutex */
    mutex_lock(&chrdev->mux);

    switch (cmd) {
    case CHRDEV_IOC_GETINFO:
        dev_info(chrdev->dev, "CHRDEV_IOC_GETINFO\n");

    ...
```

```
        default:
            ret = -ENOIOCTLCMD;
            goto unlock;
        }
        ret = 0;

unlock:
        /* Release the mutex */
        mutex_unlock(&chrdev->mux);

        return ret;
}
```

This is really a silly example, but you should consider the case where even the `ioctl()` method may change the data buffer or other shared data of the driver.

This time, we removed all the `return` statements in favor of `goto`.

How it works...

It's really hard to show how the code works by simply executing it, due to the intrinsic difficulties in reproducing a race condition, so it's better to discuss what we may expect from it.

However, you are encouraged to test the code anyway, maybe by trying to write a more complex driver where the concurrency may be a real problem if not correctly managed by the use of mutexes.

In *step 1*, we added a mutex for each chrdev device we may have in the system. Then, after its initialization in *step 2*, we can effectively use it, as reported in *step 3* and *step 4*.

By using the `mutex_lock()` function we are, in fact, telling the kernel that no other process may go concurrently beyond this point to ensure that just one process can manage the driver's shared data. If some other process should effectively try to acquire the mutex while it was already held by the first process, a new process will be put to sleep on a waiting queue at the exact moment it tries to acquire the already locked mutex.

When finished, by using `mutex_unlock()`, we instead inform the kernel that the `mux` mutex has been released, and so, any awaiting (that is, sleeping) processes will be awakened; then, once finally rescheduled to run again, it could proceed and try, in turn, to grab the lock.

Please note that in *step 3*, in both functions, we grab the mutex when it's really useful to avoid race conditions and not at their beginning; in fact, we should try to keep the locking as small as possible in order to protect the shared data (in our example, the `ppos` pointer and the `buf` data buffer). By doing this, we are restricting the usage of our chosen mutual exclusion mechanism to the smallest possible section of code (the critical section), which accesses the shared data we want to protect from possible corruption introduced by a race condition happening under the previously specified conditions.

Also, note that we must be careful not to return before releasing the lock, otherwise new accessing processes will hang! That's why we removed all the `return` statements but the last one and we used the `goto` statement to skip to the `unlock` label.

See also

- For further information regarding the mutexes and locking a good document, see the kernel documentation directory at `linux/Documentation/locking/mutex-design.txt`.

Locking (and syncing) with the interrupt context

Now, let's see how we can avoid race conditions between the process context and the interrupt context. However, this time we must pay more attention than before because, this time, we must implement a locking mechanism to protect shared data between the process context and the interrupt context. However, we must also provide a syncing mechanism between the reading process and the driver too, to allow the reading process to proceed in its action if some data to be read is present within the driver's queues.

To explain this problem, it is better to do a practical example. Let's suppose we have a peripheral that generates data for reading processes. To signal that new data has arrived, the peripheral sends an interrupt to the CPU, so we can imagine implementing our driver by using a circular buffer where the interrupt handler will save data from the peripheral into, and where any reading processes may get data from.

Circular buffers (also known as ring buffers) are fixed-size buffers that work as if the memory is contiguous and all memory locations are handled in a circular manner. As the information is generated and consumed from the buffer, it does not need to be reshuffled; we simply adjust the head and tail pointers. When data is added, the head pointer advances, and while data is consumed, the tail pointer advances. If we reach the end of the buffer, then each pointer simply wraps around to pointing back to the beginning of the ring.

In this scenario, we must protect the circular buffer against race conditions from both process and interrupt contexts since both get access to it, but we must also provide a syncing mechanism to put to sleep any reading process when no data is available for reading!

In Chapter 5, *Managing Interrupts and Concurrency*, we presented spinlocks, which can be used to place a locking mechanism between the process and interrupt context; we also presented waitqueues, which can be used to sync the reading processes with the interrupt handler.

Getting ready

This time, we have to use a modified version of our chrdev driver. In the chapter_07/chrdev/ directory of the GitHub repository, we can find the chrdev_irq.c and chrdev_irq.h files, which implement our modified driver.

We can still use chrdev-req.ko to generate the chrdev devices within the system, but now the kernel module will be used chrdev_irq.ko instead of chrdev.ko.

Also, since we have a real peripheral, we can simulate the IRQ using a kernel timer (see Chapter 5, *Managing Interrupts and Concurrency*), which also triggers data generation using the following get_new_char() function:

```
/*
 * Dummy function to generate data
 */

static char get_new_char(void)
```

```
{
    static char d = 'A' - 1;

    if (++d == ('Z' + 1))
        d = 'A';

    return d;
}
```

This function simply generates a new character from A to Z each time it's called, restarting from character A after the generation of Z.

Just to focus our attention to the locking and syncing mechanisms of our driver, we present here, some useful functions to manage the circular buffer, which is self-explanatory. Here are two functions to check the buffer is empty or full:

```
/*
 * Circular buffer management functions
 */

static inline bool cbuf_is_empty(size_t head, size_t tail,
                                 size_t len)
{
    return head == tail;
}

static inline bool cbuf_is_full(size_t head, size_t tail,
                                size_t len)
{
    head = (head + 1) % len;
    return head == tail;
}
```

Then, there are two functions to check how much data or how many spaces are available until the end of the buffer's memory area. They are useful for when we have to use functions such as memmove():

```
static inline size_t cbuf_count_to_end(size_t head, size_t tail,
                                       size_t len)
{
    if (head >= tail)
        return head - tail;
    else
        return len - tail + head;
}

static inline size_t cbuf_space_to_end(size_t head, size_t tail,
```

```
                              size_t len)
{
    if (head >= tail)
        return len - head + tail - 1;
    else
        return tail - head - 1;
}
```

Finally, we can use function to properly move forward the head or tail pointer in such a way that it can restart from the beginning, whenever the end of the buffer is reached:

```
static inline void cbuf_pointer_move(size_t *ptr, size_t n,
                                 size_t len)
{
    *ptr = (*ptr + n) % len;
}
```

How to do it...

Let's see how to do it by following these steps:

1. The first step is to rewrite our driver's main structure by adding the mux mutex (as before), the lock spinlock, the kernel timer, and the waitqueue queue as follows:

```
/* Main struct */
struct chrdev_device {
    char label[NAME_LEN];
    unsigned int busy : 1;
    char *buf;
    size_t head, tail;
    int read_only;

    unsigned int id;
    struct module *owner;
    struct cdev cdev;
    struct device *dev;

    struct mutex mux;
    struct spinlock lock;
    struct wait_queue_head queue;
    struct hrtimer timer;
};
```

2. Then, we have to initialize them during device allocation in the `chrdev_device_register()` function, as shown here:

```
/* Init the chrdev data */
chrdev->id = id;
chrdev->read_only = read_only;
chrdev->busy = 1;
strncpy(chrdev->label, label, NAME_LEN);
mutex_init(&chrdev->mux);
spin_lock_init(&chrdev->lock);
init_waitqueue_head(&chrdev->queue);
chrdev->head = chrdev->tail = 0;

/* Setup and start the hires timer */
hrtimer_init(&chrdev->timer, CLOCK_MONOTONIC,
                    HRTIMER_MODE_REL | HRTIMER_MODE_SOFT);
chrdev->timer.function = chrdev_timer_handler;
hrtimer_start(&chrdev->timer, ns_to_ktime(delay_ns),
                    HRTIMER_MODE_REL | HRTIMER_MODE_SOFT);
```

3. Now, a possible implementation of the `read()` method is shown in the next snippet. We start by grabbing the mutex to do the first lock against other processes:

```
static ssize_t chrdev_read(struct file *filp,
                            char __user *buf, size_t count, loff_t
*ppos)
{
    struct chrdev_device *chrdev = filp->private_data;
    unsigned long flags;
    char tmp[256];
    size_t n;
    int ret;

    dev_info(chrdev->dev, "should read %ld bytes\n", count);

    /* Grab the mutex */
    mutex_lock(&chrdev->mux);
```

Now we are sure that no other process may go beyond this point, but some core running in the interrupt context can still do it!

4. That's why we need the following step to ensure that they are synced with the interrupt context:

```
/* Check for some data into read buffer */
if (filp->f_flags & O_NONBLOCK) {
```

```
        if (cbuf_is_empty(chrdev->head, chrdev->tail, BUF_LEN)) {
            ret = -EAGAIN;
            goto unlock;
        }
    } else if (wait_event_interruptible(chrdev->queue,
        !cbuf_is_empty(chrdev->head, chrdev->tail, BUF_LEN))) {
        count = -ERESTARTSYS;
        goto unlock;
    }

    /* Grab the lock */
    spin_lock_irqsave(&chrdev->lock, flags);
```

5. When we've grabbed the lock, we can be sure that we are the only reading process here and that we are protected from the interrupt context, too; therefore, we can safely proceed to read data from the circular buffer, and then release the lock as follows:

```
    /* Get data from the circular buffer */
    n = cbuf_count_to_end(chrdev->head, chrdev->tail, BUF_LEN);
    count = min(count, n);
    memcpy(tmp, &chrdev->buf[chrdev->tail], count);

    /* Release the lock */
    spin_unlock_irqrestore(&chrdev->lock, flags);
```

Note that we must copy data from the circular buffer to a local buffer and not directly into the user space buffer, `buf`, with the `copy_to_user()` function; this is because this function may go to sleep, and holding a spinlock while we are sleeping is evil!

6. Once the spinlock has been released, we can safely call `copy_to_user()` to send data to the user space:

```
    /* Return data to the user space */
    ret = copy_to_user(buf, tmp, count);
    if (ret < 0) {
        ret = -EFAULT;
        goto unlock;
    }
```

7. Finally, before releasing the mutex, we must update the circular buffer's `tail` pointer as follows:

```
        /* Now we can safely move the tail pointer */
        cbuf_pointer_move(&chrdev->tail, count, BUF_LEN);
        dev_info(chrdev->dev, "return %ld bytes\n", count);
```

```
unlock:
    /* Release the mutex */
    mutex_unlock(&chrdev->mux);

    return count;
}
```

Note that since there are only readers in the process context, which are the only ones that move the `tail` pointer (or the interrupt handler does it—see the following snippet), we can be sure that everything will work well.

8. In the end, the interrupt handler (in our case, it's simulated by a kernel timer handler) looks like the following:

```
static enum hrtimer_restart chrdev_timer_handler(struct hrtimer
*ptr)
{
    struct chrdev_device *chrdev = container_of(ptr,
                    struct chrdev_device, timer);

    spin_lock(&chrdev->lock);      /* grab the lock */

    /* Now we should check if we have some space to
     * save incoming data, otherwise they must be dropped...
     */
    if (!cbuf_is_full(chrdev->head, chrdev->tail, BUF_LEN)) {
        chrdev->buf[chrdev->head] = get_new_char();

        cbuf_pointer_move(&chrdev->head, 1, BUF_LEN);
    }
    spin_unlock(&chrdev->lock);    /* release the lock */

    /* Wake up any possible sleeping process */
    wake_up_interruptible(&chrdev->queue);

    /* Now forward the expiration time and ask to be rescheduled */
    hrtimer_forward_now(&chrdev->timer, ns_to_ktime(delay_ns));
    return HRTIMER_RESTART;
}
```

The handler's body is simple: it grabs the lock and then it adds a single character to the circular buffer.

 Note that, here, we simply drop data, due to the fact we have a real peripheral; in real cases, the driver developer may do whatever is needed to prevent data loss, for instance by stopping the peripheral and then signaling this error condition, in some way, to the user space!

Also, before exiting, it uses the `wake_up_interruptible()` function to awake possible sleeping processes on the waitqueue.

How it works...

The steps are quite self-explanatory. However, in *step 4*, we perform two important steps: the first one is to suspend the process if the circular buffer is empty and, if not, to grab the lock with the interrupt context since we're going to get access to the circular buffer.

The check against the O_NONBLOCK flag is just to respect the `read()` behavior, which says that if the O_NONBLOCK flag is used, then it should go ahead, and then returns the EAGAIN error if no data is available.

Note that the lock can be safely obtained before checking for buffer emptiness, due to the fact that if we decide that the buffer is empty, but some new data arrive in the meantime and O_NONBLOCK is active, we simply return EAGAIN (signaling to the reading process to redo the operation). If it is not, we go to sleep on the waitqueue and then we will be woken by the interrupt handler (see the following information). In both cases, our operations are correct.

There's more...

If you wish to test the code, compile the code and insert it in the ESPRESSObin:

```
# insmod chrdev_irq.ko
chrdev_irq:chrdev_init: got major 239
# insmod chrdev-req.ko
chrdev cdev-eeprom@2: chrdev cdev-eeprom with id 2 added
chrdev cdev-rom@4: chrdev cdev-rom with id 4 added
```

Now our peripheral is enabled (the kernel timer has been enabled in *step 2* in the `chrdev_device_register()` function) and some data should already be available to be read; in fact, if we do a `read()` on the driver by using the `cat` command we get the following:

```
# cat /dev/cdev-eeprom\@2
ACEGIKMOQSUWYACEGIKMOQSUWYACEGIKMOQSUWYACEGIKMOQSUWYACEGIKMOQSUWYACEGIKMOQS
UWYACEGIKMOQSUW
```

Here, we should notice that since we have defined two devices in the system (see the `chapter_04/chrdev/add_chrdev_devices.dts.patch` DTS file used at the beginning of this chapter) the `get_new_char()` function is executed twice per second, and that's why we get the sequence ACE... instead of ABC....

A good exercise here would be to modify the driver to start the kernel timer when the driver is opened the first time, and then stop it when it is released the last time. Also, you may try to provide a per device `get_new_char()` function to generate the right sequence (ABC...) for each device within the system.

The corresponding kernel messages are reported as follows:

```
chrdev cdev-eeprom@2: chrdev (id=2) opened
chrdev cdev-eeprom@2: should read 131072 bytes
chrdev cdev-eeprom@2: return 92 bytes
```

Here, thanks to *step 3* to *step 7*, the `read()` system call puts to sleep the calling process and then returns the new data as soon as it arrives.

In fact, if we wait a while, we see that we get a new character each second with the following kernel messages:

```
...
[ 227.675229] chrdev cdev-eeprom@2: should read 131072 bytes
[ 228.292171] chrdev cdev-eeprom@2: return 1 bytes
[ 228.294129] chrdev cdev-eeprom@2: should read 131072 bytes
[ 229.292156] chrdev cdev-eeprom@2: return 1 bytes
...
```

I left the timings to get an idea about the time when each message is generated.

This behavior is due to *step 8*, where the kernel timer generates new data.

See also

- For further information regarding spinlocks and locking a good document, see the kernel documentation directory at `linux/Documentation/locking/spinlocks.txt`.

Waiting for I/O operations with poll() and select()

In this recipe, we will find out how to ask to the kernel to check for us when our driver has new data to be read (or it's willing to accept new data to be written), and then to wake up the reading (or writing) process without the risk of being blocked on the I/O operation.

Getting ready

To test our implementation, we can still use the `chrdev_irq.c` driver as before; this is because we can use the *new data* event simulated by the kernel timer.

How to do it...

Let's see how to do it by following these steps:

1. First of all, we have to add our new `chrdev_poll()` method in the `struct file_operations` of our driver:

```
static const struct file_operations chrdev_fops = {
    .owner   = THIS_MODULE,
    .poll    = chrdev_poll,
    .llseek  = no_llseek,
    .read    = chrdev_read,
    .open    = chrdev_open,
    .release = chrdev_release
};
```

2. Then, the implementation is in the following. We start by passing to the
`poll_wait()` function, the which is waitqueue of the current device
`chrdev->queue`:

```
static __poll_t chrdev_poll(struct file *filp, poll_table *wait)
{
    struct chrdev_device *chrdev = filp->private_data;
    __poll_t mask = 0;

    poll_wait(filp, &chrdev->queue, wait);
```

3. Finally, before checking that the circular buffer isn't empty and we can proceed
to read data from it, we grab the mutex:

```
    /* Grab the mutex */
    mutex_lock(&chrdev->mux);

    if (!cbuf_is_empty(chrdev->head, chrdev->tail, BUF_LEN))
        mask |= EPOLLIN | EPOLLRDNORM;

    /* Release the mutex */
    mutex_unlock(&chrdev->mux);

    return mask;
}
```

Note that grabbing the spinlock, too, is not necessary. This is due to the fact that if the
buffer is empty we will be informed when new data has arrived by the interrupt (the kernel
timer in our simulation) handler. This will, in turn, call the
`wake_up_interruptible(&chrdev->queue)`, which acts on the waitqueue we supplied
earlier to the `poll_wait()` function. On the other hand, if the buffer is not empty, it cannot
become empty by the interrupt context and then we cannot have any race conditions at all.

There's more...

As before, if we wish to test the code, we need to realize a proper tool that executes our
new `poll()` method. When we add it within the driver, we get both the `poll()` and
`select()` system call support; an example of the `select()` usage is reported in
the `chrdev_select.c` file and, in the following, there is a snippet in which
the `select()` call is used:

```
while (1) {
    /* Set up reading file descriptors */
    FD_ZERO(&read_fds);
```

```
    FD_SET(STDIN_FILENO, &read_fds);
    FD_SET(fd, &read_fds);

    /* Wait for any data from our device or stdin */
    ret = select(FD_SETSIZE, &read_fds, NULL, NULL, NULL);
    if (ret < 0) {
        perror("select");
        exit(EXIT_FAILURE);
    }

    if (FD_ISSET(STDIN_FILENO, &read_fds)) {
        ret = read(STDIN_FILENO, &c, 1);
        if (ret < 0) {
            perror("read(STDIN, ...)");
            exit(EXIT_FAILURE);
        }
        printf("got '%c' from stdin!\n", c);
    }
  ...

    }
```

As we can see, this program will monitor the standard input channel (named stdin) of our process and the character device by using the select() system call, which, in turn, calls our new poll() method implemented in *step 2* and *step 3*.

Now, let's compile the chrdev_select.c program by using the next command line on our host PC:

```
$ make CFLAGS="-Wall -O2 -Ichrdev/" \
       CC=aarch64-linux-gnu-gcc \
           chrdev_select
aarch64-linux-gnu-gcc -Wall -O2 chrdev_ioctl.c -o chrdev_select
```

Note that this command can be executed in the ESPRESSObin by simply removing the CC=aarch64-linux-gnu-gcc setting.

Now, if we try to execute the command on a chrdev device, we should get this output:

```
# ./chrdev_select /dev/cdev-eeprom\@2
file /dev/cdev-eeprom@2 opened
got 'K' from device!
got 'M' from device!
got 'O' from device!
got 'Q' from device!
...
```

Of course, we'll have already loaded the `chrdev_irq` driver containing the `poll()` method.

If we try to insert some characters from the standard input, as shown in the following, we can see that when there is new data from the device, the process can safely do a read on it without blocking, while when there is new data from its standard input, the process can do the same, also without blocking:

```
...
got 'Y' from device!
got 'A' from device!
TEST
got 'T' from stdin!
got 'E' from stdin!
got 'S' from stdin!
got 'T' from stdin!
got '
' from stdin!
got 'C' from device!
got 'E' from device!
...
```

See also

- For further information regarding `poll()` or `select()`, a good starting point is their man pages (`man 2 poll` and `man 2 select`).

Managing asynchronous notifications with fasync()

In this recipe, we will see how we can generate asynchronous SIGIO signals whenever our driver has new data to be read (or it's willing to accept new data from the user space).

Getting ready

As done previously, we can still present our implementation using the chrdev_irq.c driver.

How to do it...

Let's see how to do it by following these steps:

1. First of all, we have to add our new chrdev_fasync() method in the struct file_operations of our driver:

```
static const struct file_operations chrdev_fops = {
    .owner   = THIS_MODULE,
    .fasync  = chrdev_fasync,
    .poll    = chrdev_poll,
    .llseek  = no_llseek,
    .read    = chrdev_read,
    .open    = chrdev_open,
    .release = chrdev_release
};
```

2. The implementation is as follows:

```
static int chrdev_fasync(int fd, struct file *filp, int on)
{
    struct chrdev_device *chrdev = filp->private_data;

    return fasync_helper(fd, filp, on, &chrdev->fasync_queue);
}
```

3. Finally, we have to add the `kill_fasync()` call into our (simulated) interrupt handler to signal that the signal `SIGIO` can be sent due to the fact that new data is ready to be read:

```
static enum hrtimer_restart chrdev_timer_handler(struct hrtimer
*ptr)
{
    struct chrdev_device *chrdev = container_of(ptr,
                                       struct chrdev_device, timer);

    ...

    /* Wake up any possible sleeping process */
    wake_up_interruptible(&chrdev->queue);
    kill_fasync(&chrdev->fasync_queue, SIGIO, POLL_IN);

    /* Now forward the expiration time and ask to be rescheduled */
    hrtimer_forward_now(&chrdev->timer, ns_to_ktime(delay_ns));
    return HRTIMER_RESTART;
}
```

There's more...

If you wish to test the code, you need to realize a proper tool that executes all of the steps presented to ask the kernel to receive the `SIGIO` signal. In the following, a snippet of the `chrdev_fasync.c` program is reported, which does what's needed:

```
/* Try to install the signal handler and the fasync stuff */
sigh = signal(SIGIO, sigio_handler);
if (sigh == SIG_ERR) {
        perror("signal");
        exit(EXIT_FAILURE);
}
ret = fcntl(fd, F_SETOWN, getpid());
if (ret < 0) {
        perror("fcntl(..., F_SETOWN, ...)");
        exit(EXIT_FAILURE);
}
flags = fcntl(fd, F_GETFL);
if (flags < 0) {
        perror("fcntl(..., F_GETFL)");
        exit(EXIT_FAILURE);
}
ret = fcntl(fd, F_SETFL, flags | FASYNC);
if (flags < 0) {
        perror("fcntl(..., F_SETFL, ...)");
```

```
        exit(EXIT_FAILURE);
    }
```

This code is needed to ask the kernel to invoke the `fasync()` method implemented in *step 2*. Then, whenever new data arrives, thanks to *step 3*, the `SIGIO` signal is sent to our process and the signal handler, `sigio_handler()`, is executed, even if the process is suspended, for example, on reading another file descriptor.

```
void sigio_handler(int unused) {
    char c;
    int ret;

    ret = read(fd, &c, 1);
    if (ret < 0) {
        perror("read");
        exit(EXIT_FAILURE);
    }
    ret = write(STDOUT_FILENO, &c, 1);
    if (ret < 0) {
        perror("write");
        exit(EXIT_FAILURE);
    }
}
```

Now, let's compile the `chrdev_fasync.c` program by using the next command line on our host PC:

```
$ make CFLAGS="-Wall -O2 -Ichrdev/" \
        CC=aarch64-linux-gnu-gcc \
            chrdev_fasync
aarch64-linux-gnu-gcc -Wall -O2 chrdev_ioctl.c -o chrdev_fasync
```

Note that this command can be executed in the ESPRESSObin by simply removing the `CC=aarch64-linux-gnu-gcc` setting.

Now, if we try to execute the command on a chrdev device, we should get the following output:

```
# ./chrdev_fasync /dev/cdev-eeprom\@2
file /dev/cdev-eeprom@2 opened
QSUWYACEGI
```

Of course, we'll have already loaded the `chrdev_irq` driver containing the `fasync()` method.

Here, the process is suspended on a `read()` on the stdin and whenever a signal arrives, the signal handler is executed and the new data is read. However, when we try to send some characters to the standard input, the process reads them as expected:

```
# ./chrdev_fasync /dev/cdev-eeprom\@2
file /dev/cdev-eeprom@2 opened
QSUWYACEGIKMOQS....
got '.' from stdin!
got '.' from stdin!
got '.' from stdin!
got '.' from stdin!
got '
' from stdin!
UWYACE
```

See also

- For further information regarding the `fasync()` method or the `fcntl()` system call, a good starting point is the `man 2 fcntl` man page.

Additional Information: Working with Char Drivers

Exchanging data with a char driver

Exchanging data with a peripheral means sending or receiving data to and from it, and, to do so, we have already seen that we have to use the `write()` and `read()` system calls, whose prototypes are defined in the kernel, as follows:

```
ssize_t write(struct file *filp,
              const char __user *buf, size_t count,
              loff_t *ppos);
ssize_t read(struct file *filp,
             char __user *buf, size_t count,
             loff_t *ppos);
```

On the other hand, their counterparts in user space look like the following:

```
ssize_t write(int fd, const void *buf, size_t count);
ssize_t read(int fd, void *buf, size_t count);
```

The preceding prototypes (both in the kernel or user space) look similar but, of course, they have different meanings and, as driver developers we must know perfectly what these meanings are to do our job accurately.

Let's start with `write()`; when we call the `write()` system call from our user space program, we must supply a file descriptor, `fd`; a buffer, `buf`, filled with data to write; and the buffer size, `count`. Then, the system call returns a value that can be negative (if there are errors), positive (which refers to how many bytes have actually been written), or zero (which means that nothing has been written).

Note that `count` does **not** represent how many bytes we wish to write, but just the buffer size! In fact, `write()` can return a positive value that is smaller than `count`. That's why I enclosed the `write()` system call of the `chrdev_test.c` program inside a `for()` loop! In fact, if I have to write a buffer that is 10 bytes long and `write()` returns, for instance, 4 bytes, I have to recall it until all the remaining 6 bytes have been written.

From the kernel space perspective, we see the file descriptor, fd, as `struct file *filp` (where kernel information about our file descriptor is stored), while the data buffer is specified by the `buf` pointer and the `count` variable (for the moment, do not consider the `ppos` pointer; it will be explained soon).

As we can see from the `write()` kernel prototype, the `buf` parameter is marked with the `__user` attribute, which points out the fact that this buffer comes from the user space, so we cannot read directly from it. In fact, this memory area is virtual and, as such, it cannot actually be mapped into real physical memory when our driver's `write()` method is executed! In order to address this situation, the kernel provides the `copy_from_user()` function, as follows:

```
unsigned long copy_from_user(void *to,
                const void __user *from, unsigned long n);
```

As we can see, this function takes data from the user space buffer, `from`, and then, after verifying that the memory area pointed by `from` is OK for reading, copies them to the buffer pointed by `to`. Once the data has been transferred to the kernel space (inside the buffer pointed by `to`), our driver can access it freely.

These same steps (even if in the opposite direction) are performed for the `read()` system call. We still have a file descriptor, fd; a buffer, `buf`, into which read data has to be placed, and its `count` size. Then, the system call returns a value that can be negative (if there are errors), positive (which means how many bytes have been actually read), or zero (which means we are at end-of-file).

Again, we should notice that `count` is **not** how many bytes we wish to read but just the buffer size. In fact, `read()` can return a positive value smaller than `count`, which is why I put it inside a `for()` loop in the `chrdev_test.c` program.
More significantly than in the preceding `write()` case, the `read()` system call can also return 0, which means **end-of-file**; that is, no more data is available from this file descriptor and we should stop reading.

As for the preceding `write()` case, we still have the `__user` attribute associated with the buffer pointed by `buf`, which means that to read data from it, we must use the `copy_to_user()` function, which is defined as follows:

```
unsigned long copy_to_user(void __user *to,
                const void *from, unsigned long n);
```

Both `copy_from_user()` and `copy_to_user()` are defined in the `linux/include/linux/uaccess.h` file.

Now, before the end of this section, we have to spend some time on the `ppos` pointer, which is present in both of the kernel prototypes.

When we wish to read some data stored in a file, we have to use the `read()` system call several times (especially if the file is quite big and our memory buffer is small). To do this, we'd like to simply call `read()` multiple times without bothering to keep track of where we arrived in each of the previous iterations; for example, if we have a file with a size of 16 KB and we wish to read it by using a 4 KB memory buffer, we simply call the `read()` system call four times, but how is each call supposed to know where the previous one finished its job? Well, this task is assigned to the `ppos` pointer: when the file is opened, it starts by pointing at the first byte of the file (at index 0) and then, each time `read()` is called, the system call itself moves it to the next position so that the following `read()` call knows exactly where it should start reading the next chunk of data.

Note that `ppos` is unique for both read and write operations, so if we perform `read()` first and then `write()`, the data will be written, not at beginning of the file, but exactly where the preceding `read()` call finished its operation!

Additional Information: Using the Device Tree

Device tree internals

A device tree is a tree data structure with nodes that tell you which devices are currently present in a system along with their configuration settings. Every node has property/value pairs that describe the attributes of the device being represented. Every node has exactly one parent but the root node has no parent.

The next code shows an example representation of a simple device tree that is nearly complete enough to boot a simple operating system, with the platform type, CPU, memory, and a single **universal synchronous and asynchronous receiver-transmitter** (**UART**) described with its clocks and interrupt lines. Device nodes are shown with properties and values inside each node.

The device tree syntax is quasi self-explanatory; however, we're going to explain it in detail in this paragraph by taking a look at the `simple_platform.dts` file from the GitHub repository related to Chapter 4. So, let's start by taking a look at the end of the file:

```
serial0: serial@11100 {
    compatible = "fsl,mpc5125-psc-uart", "fsl,mpc5125-psc";
    reg = <0x11100 0x100>;
    interrupt-parent = <&ipic>;
    interrupts = <40 0x8>;
    fsl,rx-fifo-size = <16>;
    fsl,tx-fifo-size = <16>;
    clocks = <&clks 47>, <&clks 34>;
    clock-names = "ipg", "mclk";
    };
  };
};
```

First of all, we should notice that property definitions are name/value pairs in the following form:

```
[label:] property-name = value;
```

This is true except for properties with an empty (zero length) value, which have the following form:

```
[label:] property-name;
```

For instance, in the preceeding example, we have
the `compatible` properties of `serial@11100` node (labeled as `serial0`) set to a list composed by two strings `"fsl,mpc5125-psc-uart"` and `"fsl,mpc5125-psc"`, while the `fsl,rx-fifo-size` property is set to the number `16`.

Property values may be defined as an array of 8, 16, 32, or 64-bit integer elements, as NULL-terminated strings, as byte strings, or a combination of these. The storage size of an element can be changed using the `/bits/` prefix as follows, which defines property `interrupts` as an array of bytes and `clock-frequency` as a 64-bit number:

```
interrupts = /bits/ 8 <17 0xc>;
clock-frequency = /bits/ 64 <0x0000000100000000>;
```

The `/bits/` prefix allows for the creation of 8, 16, 32, and 64-bit elements.

Each node in the device tree is named according to the following `node-name@unit-address` convention, where the `node-name` component specifies the name of the node (usually it describes the general class of device), while the `unit-address` component of the name is specific to the bus type on which the node sits. For instance, in the preceding example, we have `serial@11100`, which means we have a serial port at address with offset `0x11100` from the `soc` node's base address, which is `0x80000000`.

Looking at the preceding example, it is quite clear that each node is then defined by a node name and unit address, with braces marking the start and end of the node definition (they may be preceded by a label) as follows:

```
[label:] node-name[@unit-address] {
    [properties definitions]
    [child nodes]
};
```

Each node in the device tree has properties that describe the characteristics of the node; there exist standard properties that have a well-defined and standardized functionality, but we can also use our own properties to specify custom values. Properties consist of a name and a value, and for the example of our serial port, we set the `interrupts` property to the `<40 0x8>`array, while the `compatible` property is set to a list of strings and `fsl,rx-fifo-size` is set to a number.

A node in the device tree can be uniquely identified by clearly stating the full path from the root node, through all descendant nodes, to the desired node. The convention for specifying a device path is similar to the path names we usually use for a file in the filesystem; for example, in the preceding definition, the device path to our serial port is /soc@80000000/serial@11100, while the path to the root node is, obviously, /. This scenario is where labels come to play; in fact, they can be used in place of the full path to a node, that is, the clock used by serial port can be easily addressed using the clks labels as follows:

```
clks: clock@f00 {
    ...
};

serial0: serial@11100 {
    compatible = "fsl,mpc5125-psc-uart", "fsl,mpc5125-psc";
    ....
    clocks = <&clks 47>, <&clks 34>;
    clock-names = "ipg", "mclk";
};
```

We can also notice that serial0 is defined as an alias of tty0. This syntax gives the developer another way to reference a node using a label instead of using its full pathname:

```
aliases {
    tty0 = &serial0;
};
```

The preceding definition is equivalent to the following:

```
aliases {
    tty0 = "/soc@80000000/serial@11100";
}
```

It's quite clear now that a label can be used in a device tree source file as either a property handle (the label usually named as phandle) value or a path, depending on the context. In fact, the & character only refers to a phandle if it is inside an array; otherwise (if outside an array), it refers to a path!

Aliases are not used directly in the device tree source, but they are, instead, dereferenced by the Linux kernel. In fact, when we ask the kernel to find a node by its path (we will see soon, in this chapter, the usage of such functions such as of_find_node_by_path()) if the path does not begin with the / character then the first element of the path must be a property name in the /aliases node. That element is replaced with the full path from the alias.

Another device tree's important entity to understand among nodes, labels, and aliases are phandles. The official definition tells us that the phandle property specifies a numerical identifier for a node that is unique within the device tree. In fact, this property value is used by other nodes that need to refer to the node associated with the property, so it's really just a hack to get around the fact that a device tree does not have a pointer data type.

In the preceding example, the `serial@11100` node is a way to specify which node is the interrupt controller and which one is the node with clock definitions used by phandles. However, in that example, they are not explicitly defined because the `dtc` compiler kindly creates phandles from labels. So, in the preceding example, we have the following syntax (where information that is not needed has been removed for better readability):

```
ipic: interrupt-controller@c00 {
    compatible = "fsl,mpc5121-ipic", "fsl,ipic";
    ...
};

clks: clock@f00 {
    compatible = "fsl,mpc5121-clock";
    ...
};

serial0: serial@11100 {
    compatible = "fsl,mpc5125-psc-uart", "fsl,mpc5125-psc";
    ...
    interrupt-parent = <&ipic>;
    ...
    clocks = <&clks 47>, <&clks 34>;
    ...
};
```

 The `dtc` compiler is the device tree compiler, which will be introduced in Chapter 4, *Using the Device Tree*, using the device tree compiler and utilities.

This is equivalent to the next syntax in which phandles are made explicit:

```
interrupt-controller@c00 {
    compatible = "fsl,mpc5121-ipic", "fsl,ipic";
    ...
    phandle = <0x2>;
};

clock@f00 {
    compatible = "fsl,mpc5121-clock";
```

```
        ...
        phandle = <0x3>;
};

serial@11100 {
        compatible = "fsl,mpc5125-psc-uart", "fsl,mpc5125-psc";
        ...
        interrupt-parent = <0x2>;
        ...
        clocks = <0x3 0x2f 0x3 0x22>;
        ...
};
```

Simply speaking, the & character tells dtc that the following string is a phandle referencing the label matching the string; it will then create a unique u32 value for each label that is used for a phandle reference.

> Of course, you can define your own phandle property in one node and specify a label on a different node's name. Then, dtc will be aware of any phandle values explicitly stated and will not use those values when creating phandle values for labeled nodes.

There is a lot to say about device tree syntax. However, we've covered what is sufficient to understand how to use a device tree during the device drivers development.

> For complete documentation about this topic, you can read the device tree specifications at https://www.devicetree.org/specifications/.

Using the device tree compiler and utilities

Here are some notes about some interesting usages of the dtc and its utilities which can be really useful during device drivers development and kernel configuration.

Obtaining a source form of a running device tree

`dtc` can also be used to convert a running device tree into a human-readable form too! Let's suppose we wish to know how our ESPRESSObin has been configured; the first thing to do is to take a look at ESPRESSObin's DTS file in the kernel sources. However, suppose we don't have it. In this situation, we can ask `dtc` to revert to the corresponding DTB file, as seen in the preceding section, but suppose we still don't have it. What we can do? Well, `dtc` can help us again by reverting data stored in the `/proc/device-tree` directory, which holds a filesystem representation of the running device tree.

In fact, we can inspect the `/proc/device-tree` directory by using the `tree` command, as seen in the following (this output is just a snippet of the whole directory content):

```
# tree /proc/device-tree/proc/device-tree/
|-- #address-cells
|-- #size-cells
|-- aliases
|   |-- name
|   |-- serial0
|   `-- serial1
|-- chosen
|   |-- bootargs
|   |-- name
|   `-- stdout-path
|-- compatible
|-- cpus
|   |-- #address-cells
|   |-- #size-cells
|   |-- cpu@0
|   |   |-- clocks
|   |   |-- compatible
|   |   |-- device_type
|   |   |-- enable-method
|   |   |-- name
|   |   `-- reg
...
```

If not present, the `tree` command can be installed as usual with the `apt install tree` command.

Then we can read string data inside each file as follows:

```
# cat /proc/device-tree/compatible ; echo
globalscale,espressobinmarvell,armada3720marvell,armada3710
# cat /proc/device-tree/cpus/cpu\@0/compatible ; echo
arm,cortex-a53arm,armv8
```

The last `echo` commands have just been used to add a new line character after the `cat` output to have more readable output.

Numbers must be read as follows:

```
# cat /proc/device-tree/#size-cells | od -tx4
0000000 02000000
0000004
# cat /proc/device-tree/cpus/cpu\@1/reg | od -tx4
0000000 01000000
0000004
```

However, by using `dtc`, we can achieve better results. In fact, if we use the next command line, we ask `dtc` to convert all the DTB data into human-readable form:

```
# dtc -I fs -o espressobin-reverted.dts /proc/device-tree/
```

Of course, we must also install the `dtc` program into our ESPRESSObin with the `apt install device-tree-compiler` command.

Now, from the `espressobin-reverted.dts` file, we can easily read the device tree data:

```
# head -20 espressobin-reverted.dts
/dts-v1/;

/ {
    #address-cells = <0x2>;
    model = "Globalscale Marvell ESPRESSOBin Board";
    #size-cells = <0x2>;
    interrupt-parent = <0x1>;
    compatible = "globalscale,espressobin", "marvell,armada3720",
"marvell,armada3710";

    memory@0 {
        device_type = "memory";
        reg = <0x0 0x0 0x0 0x80000000 0x0 0x0 0x0 0x0 0x0 0x0 0x0 0x0 0x0
```

```
0x0 0x0 0x0>;
    };

    regulator {
        regulator-max-microvolt = <0x325aa0>;
        gpios-states = <0x0>;
        regulator-boot-on;
        enable-active-high;
        regulator-min-microvolt = <0x1b7740>;
    ..
```

Notes on the device tree utilities

If we take a look at programs in the `device-tree-compiler` package that we installed previously, we can see that there are more programs than `dtc`:

```
$ dpkg -L device-tree-compiler | grep '/usr/bin'
/usr/bin
/usr/bin/convert-dtsv0
/usr/bin/dtc
/usr/bin/dtdiff
/usr/bin/fdtdump
/usr/bin/fdtget
/usr/bin/fdtoverlay
/usr/bin/fdtput
```

These other programs are usually called **device tree utilities** and can be used to inspect or manipulate a device tree in its binary form (DTB).

For example, we can easily dump a DTB file using the `fdtdump` utility:

```
$ fdtdump simple_platform.dtb | head -23

**** fdtdump is a low-level debugging tool, not meant for general use.
**** If you want to decompile a dtb, you probably want
**** dtc -I dtb -O dts <filename>

/dts-v1/;
// magic: 0xd00dfeed
// totalsize: 0x642 (1602)
...

/ {
    model = "fsl,mpc8572ds";
    compatible = "fsl,mpc8572ds";
    #address-cells = <0x00000001>;
```

```
#size-cells = <0x00000001>;
interrupt-parent = <0x00000001>;
chosen {
    bootargs = "root=/dev/sda2";
};
aliases {
    tty0 = "/soc@80000000/serial@11100";
};
```

 A careful reader will notice that the fdtdump utility itself tells us that it's only a low-level debugging tool and then to use dtc instead of decompiling, (or revert to DTS) a DTB file!

Another two useful commands are fdtget and fdtput, which can be used to read and write data into our DTB file. The following are commands we can use to read the bootargs entry for the preceding DTB file:

```
$ fdtget simple_platform.dtb /chosen bootargs
root=/dev/sda2
```

Then, we can change it with the next command:

```
$ fdtput -ts simple_platform.dtb /chosen bootargs 'root=/dev/sda1 rw'
$ fdtget simple_platform.dtb /chosen bootargs
root=/dev/sda1 rw
```

 Note that we have had to use the -ts option argument to tell fdtput which type of data ours is, otherwise, the wrong values can be written!

Not only that, we can also ask fdtget to list all the subnodes for each supplied node:

```
$ fdtget -l simple_platform.dtb /cpus /soc@80000000
cpu@0
cpu@1
interrupt-controller@c00
clock@f00
serial@11100
```

Additionally, we can ask it to list all the properties for each node too:

```
$ fdtget -p simple_platform.dtb /cpus /soc@80000000
#address-cells
#size-cells
compatible
```

```
#address-cells
#size-cells
device_type
ranges
reg
bus-frequency
```

Getting application-specific data from a device tree

By using the functions from the `linux/drivers/of` directory, we'll be able to extract all the information we need for our driver from a device tree. For instance, by using the `of_find_node_by_path()` function, we can get a node pointer by its pathname:

```
struct device_node *of_find_node_by_path(const char *path);
```

Then, once we have a pointer to a device tree node, we can use it to extract the needed information by using the `of_property_read_*()` functions, as follows:

```
int of_property_read_u8(const struct device_node *np,
                        const char *propname,
                        u8 *out_value);
int of_property_read_u16(const struct device_node *np,
                        const char *propname,
                        u16 *out_value);
int of_property_read_u32(const struct device_node *np,
                        const char *propname,
                        u32 *out_value);
...
```

 Note that there are a lot of other functions we can use to extract information from a device tree, so you may take a look at the `linux/include/linux/of.h` file for a complete list.

In case we wish to parse each property of a node, we can iterate them using the `for_each_property_of_node()` macro, which is defined as follows:

```
#define for_each_property_of_node(dn, pp) \
        for (pp = dn->properties; pp != NULL; pp = pp->next)
```

Then, if our node has more than one child (or subnode), we can iterate them by using the `for_each_child_of_node()` macro, which is defined as follows:

```
#define for_each_child_of_node(parent, child) \
        for (child = of_get_next_child(parent, NULL); child != NULL; \
                child = of_get_next_child(parent, child))
```

Using a device tree to describe a character driver

We have seen that by using a device tree, we can specify different driver settings and then modify the driver's functionalities. However, our possibilities do not finish here! In fact, we can use the same code for different driver's releases or a different types of the same device.

How to manage different device types

Let's suppose our `chrdev` has two other implementations (plus the current one) in which the hardware is done in such a way that most parameters are fixed (and well known) and not selectable by the developer; in this case, we can still use node properties to specify them, but doing this is error prone and it forces the user to know these constraints. For example, if in these two implementations, the hardware can work in read-only or read/write modes only (that is, the user is not free to specify the `read-only` property), we can call these special cases `"chrdev-fixed"` for the read/write version and `"chrdev-fixed_read-only"` for the read-only one.

At this point, we can specify that the driver is now compatible with two other devices by modifying the `of_chrdev_req_match` array, as follows:

```
static const struct of_device_id of_chrdev_req_match[] = {
    {
        .compatible = "ldddc,chrdev",
    },
    {
        .compatible = "ldddc,chrdev-fixed",
        .data = &chrdev_fd,
    },
    {
        .compatible = "ldddc,chrdev-fixed_read-only",
        .data = &chrdev_fd_ro,
    },
    { /* sentinel */ }
```

```
    };
    MODULE_DEVICE_TABLE(of, of_chrdev_req_match);
```

We simply added two items with proper `compatible` strings and two special data entries, as defined in the following:

```
static const struct chrdev_fixed_data chrdev_fd = {
    .label = "cdev-fixed",
};

static const struct chrdev_fixed_data chrdev_fd_ro = {
    .label = "cdev-fixedro",
    .read_only = 1,
};
```

In this manner, we tell the driver that these devices can have one instance only and that they can work in read/write or read-only mode. By doing this, the user can use our devices by simply specifying a device tree as follows:

```
--- a/arch/arm64/boot/dts/marvell/armada-3720-espressobin.dts
+++ b/arch/arm64/boot/dts/marvell/armada-3720-espressobin.dts
@@ -41,6 +41,10 @@
            3300000 0x0>;
        enable-active-high;
    };
+
+    chrdev {
+        compatible = "ldddc,chrdev-fixed_read-only";
+    };
    };

    /* J9 */
```

Again, as before, you must modify the ESPRESSObin's DTS file and then recompile and reinstall the kernel.

By using this solution, the user doesn't need to know hardware internals since they are encapsulated into the driver by the driver developers (which are us, in this situation).

This compatible attribute can be evaluated for the driver by using `of_device_is_compatible()` function, as shown in the following example, where we've modified the `chrdev_req_probe()` function to support our `chrdev` special versions:

```
static int chrdev_req_probe(struct platform_device *pdev)
{
```

```
struct device *dev = &pdev->dev;
struct device_node *np = dev->of_node;
const struct chrdev_fixed_data *data = of_device_get_match_data(dev);
struct fwnode_handle *child;
struct module *owner = THIS_MODULE;
int count, ret;

/* Check the chrdev device type */
if (of_device_is_compatible(np, "ldddc,chrdev-fixed") ||
    of_device_is_compatible(np, "ldddc,chrdev-fixed_read-only")) {
    ret = chrdev_device_register(data->label, 0,
                     data->read_only, owner, dev);
    if (ret)
        dev_err(dev, "unable to register fixed");

    return ret;
}

/* If we are not registering a fixed chrdev device then get
 * the number of chrdev devices from DTS
 */
count = device_get_child_node_count(dev);
if (count == 0)
    return -ENODEV;
if (count > MAX_DEVICES)
    return -ENOMEM;

device_for_each_child_node(dev, child) {
    const char *label;
    unsigned int id, ro;
...
```

As we can see, before scanning the node's children, we simply verify which is the currently installed `chrdev` device version for our system; in this case, we have one of the two new devices so we register a new `chrdev` device accordingly.

 All these modifications can be done using the `add_fixed_chrdev_devices.patch` file with the following command line:

```
$ patch -p3 < add_fixed_chrdev_devices.patch
```

Now we can try the code by recompiling our `chrdev` driver and reinserting it (actually two modules) into ESPRESSObin as shown in the following:

```
# insmod chrdev.ko
chrdev:chrdev_init: got major 239
```

```
# insmod chrdev-req.ko
chrdev cdev-fixedro@0: chrdev cdev-fixedro with id 0 added
# ls -l /dev/cdev-fixedro\@0
crw------- 1 root root 239, 0 Feb 28 15:23 /dev/cdev-fixedro@0
```

As we can see, the driver has correctly recognized that a special version of the chrdev device (the read-only one) has been defined in the device tree.

How to add sysfs properties to devices

In a previous section, we briefly talked about the /sys/class/chrdev directory. We said that it's related to the device classes (which can be defined in the system) and to kernel devices. In fact, when we call the device_create() function, we must specify the first argument that the device class pointer we allocated for the chrdev_init(), function and this action creates the /sys/class/chrdev directory for which each chrdev device is reported as shown as follows:

```
# ls /sys/class/chrdev/
cdev-eeprom@2 cdev-rom@4
```

So, a device class groups all devices with common characteristics, but which characteristics are we talking about? Well, simply speaking, these characteristics or attributes (shortly we'll see what they are exactly called) are a set of common information regarding our devices.

Each time we add a new device to the system, the kernel creates default attributes that can be seen from the user space as files under the sysfs, as shown here:

```
# ls -l /sys/class/chrdev/cdev-eeprom\@2/
total 0
-r--r--r-- 1 root root 4096 Feb 28 10:51 dev
lrwxrwxrwx 1 root root 0 Feb 28 10:51 device -> ../../../chrdev
drwxr-xr-x 2 root root 0 Feb 28 10:51 power
lrwxrwxrwx 1 root root 0 Feb 27 19:53 subsystem ->
../../../../../class/chrdev
-rw-r--r-- 1 root root 4096 Feb 27 19:53 uevent
```

Well, in the preceding list, something is a file and something else is a directory or a symbolic link; however, here, the important thing is that, for each device, we have some attributes describing it. For instance, if we take a look at the dev attribute, we get the following:

```
# cat /sys/class/chrdev/cdev-eeprom\@2/dev
239:2
```

Which is exactly the major and minor number pair for our device? Now the question is, can we have more (and custom) attributes? Of course, the answer is yes, so let's see how to do this.

First, we have to modify the `chrdev.c` file, adding a line to `chrdev_init()` as follows:

```
--- a/chapter_4/chrdev/chrdev.c
+++ b/chapter_4/chrdev/chrdev.c
@@ -216,6 +288,7 @@ static int __init chrdev_init(void)
        pr_err("chrdev: failed to allocate class\n");
        return -ENOMEM;
    }
+   chrdev_class->dev_groups = chrdev_groups;

    /* Allocate a region for character devices */
    ret = alloc_chrdev_region(&chrdev_devt, 0, MAX_DEVICES, "chrdev");
```

This modification just set the `dev_groups` field of the struct pointed by `chrdev_class` equal to the `chrdev_groups` structure, as follows:

```
static struct attribute *chrdev_attrs[] = {
    &dev_attr_id.attr,
    &dev_attr_reset_to.attr,
    &dev_attr_read_only.attr,
    NULL,
};

static const struct attribute_group chrdev_group = {
    .attrs = chrdev_attrs,
};

static const struct attribute_group *chrdev_groups[] = {
    &chrdev_group,
    NULL,
};
```

All the modifications in this paragraph can be done by using patch file `add_sysfs_attrs_chrdev.patch`, with the following command line:
`$ patch -p3 < add_sysfs_attrs_chrdev.patch`

The preceding code is a complicated way of adding a group of attributes to our chrdev devices. To be more specific, the code just adds a single group of attributes named id, reset_to, and read_only. All of these attribute names are still defined in the modified chrdev.c file, as in the following snippet. Here is the read-only attribute:

```
static ssize_t id_show(struct device *dev,
            struct device_attribute *attr, char *buf)
{
    struct chrdev_device *chrdev = dev_get_drvdata(dev);

    return sprintf(buf, "%d\n", chrdev->id);
}
static DEVICE_ATTR_RO(id);
```

Then, the write-only attribute is as follows:

```
static ssize_t reset_to_store(struct device *dev,
            struct device_attribute *attr,
            const char *buf, size_t count)
{
    struct chrdev_device *chrdev = dev_get_drvdata(dev);

    if (count > BUF_LEN)
        count = BUF_LEN;
    memcpy(chrdev->buf, buf, count);

    return count;
}
static DEVICE_ATTR_WO(reset_to);
```

Finally, the read/write attribute is as follows:

```
static ssize_t read_only_show(struct device *dev,
            struct device_attribute *attr, char *buf)
{
    struct chrdev_device *chrdev = dev_get_drvdata(dev);

    return sprintf(buf, "%d\n", chrdev->read_only);
}

static ssize_t read_only_store(struct device *dev,
            struct device_attribute *attr,
            const char *buf, size_t count)
{
    struct chrdev_device *chrdev = dev_get_drvdata(dev);
    int data, ret;

    ret = sscanf(buf, "%d", &data);
```

```
    if (ret != 1)
        return -EINVAL;

    chrdev->read_only = !!data;

    return count;
}
static DEVICE_ATTR_RW(read_only);
```

By using DEVICE_ATTR_RW(), DEVICE_ATTR_WO(), and DEVICE_ATTR_RO(), we declare read/write, write-only, and read-only attributes, which are connected to entries in the array named chrdev_attrs, which is defined as the struct attribute type.

When we use DEVICE_ATTR_RW(read_only), then we must define two functions named read_only_show() and read_only_store() (the variable's name is read_only with the postfixes, _show and _store), so that the kernel invokes each time a user space process executes a read() or write() system call on the attribute file. Of course, the DEVICE_ATTR_RO() and DEVICE_ATTR_WO() variants require only the _show and _store functions, respectively.

To better understand how data is exchanged, let's take a closer look at these functions. By looking at the read_only_show() function, we can see that the data to be written is pointed by buf, while by using dev_get_drvdata(), we can obtain a pointer to our struct chrdev_device holding all the necessary information related to our custom implementation. For example, function read_only_show() function will return the value stored into the read_only variable, which states the read-only property of our device. Note that read_only_show() must return a positive value representing how many bytes are returned, or a negative value if there is any error.

In a similar manner, the read_only_store() function gives us data to be written into the buf buffer and count while we can use the same technique to get a pointer to the struct chrdev_device. The read_only_store() function reads a number in human-readable form (that is, ASCII representation) and then sets the read_only properties to 0 if we read value 0 or 1 otherwise.

Other attributes, id and reset_to, are used respectively to show the device's id or to force the internal buffer to the desired status independently of the fact the device itself was defined as read-only or not.

To test the code, we have to modify the `chrdev.c` file as described earlier, and then we have to recompile the code and move the resulting kernel modules to the ESPRESSObin. Now, if we insert the modules, we should get almost the same kernel messages as before, but now the content of the `/sys/class/chrdev` subdirectories should have changed. In fact, now we have the following:

```
# ls -l /sys/class/chrdev/cdev-eeprom\@2/
total 0
-r--r--r-- 1 root root 4096 Feb 28 13:45 dev
lrwxrwxrwx 1 root root 0 Feb 28 13:45 device -> ../../../chrdev
-r--r--r-- 1 root root 4096 Feb 28 13:45 id
drwxr-xr-x 2 root root 0 Feb 28 13:45 power
-rw-r--r-- 1 root root 4096 Feb 28 13:45 read_only
--w------- 1 root root 4096 Feb 28 13:45 reset_to
lrwxrwxrwx 1 root root 0 Feb 28 13:45 subsystem ->
../../../../../class/chrdev
-rw-r--r-- 1 root root 4096 Feb 28 13:45 uevent
```

As expected, we have three new attributes, as defined in our code. Then, we can try to read from them:

```
# cat /sys/class/chrdev/cdev-eeprom\@2/id
2
# cat /sys/class/chrdev/cdev-eeprom\@2/read_only
0
# cat /sys/class/chrdev/cdev-eeprom\@2/reset_to
cat: /sys/class/chrdev/cdev-eeprom@2/reset_to: Permission denied
```

All answers are as expected; in fact, the `cdev-eeprom` device has `id` equal to 2, and is not read-only, while the `reset_to` attributes are write-only, and not readable. A similar output can be obtained from `cdev-rom`, as follows:

```
# cat /sys/class/chrdev/cdev-rom\@4/id
4
# cat /sys/class/chrdev/cdev-rom\@4/read_only
1
```

These attributes are useful to inspect current device status but they can also be used to modify its behavior. In fact, we can set an initial value of the read-only `cdev-rom` device by using the `reset_to` attributes as follows:

```
# echo "THIS IS A READ ONLY DEVICE!" > /sys/class/chrdev/cdev-rom\@4/reset_to
```

Now the `/dev/cdev-rom@4` device is still read-only, but it's not filled by all zeros any more:

```
# cat /dev/cdev-rom\@4
THIS IS A READ ONLY DEVICE!
```

Or, we can remove the read-only property from the `/dev/cdev-rom@4` device:

```
# echo 0 > /sys/class/chrdev/cdev-rom\@4/read_only
```

Now, if we retry writing data into it, we succeed (the kernel messages below the `echo` command are reported from the serial console):

```
root@espressobin:~# echo "TEST STRING" > /dev/cdev-rom\@4
chrdev cdev-rom@4: chrdev (id=4) opened
chrdev cdev-rom@4: should write 12 bytes (*ppos=0)
chrdev cdev-rom@4: got 12 bytes (*ppos=12)
chrdev cdev-rom@4: chrdev (id=4) released
```

Note that this works, but with an unexpected side effect of reading; we can write into the device, but the new **TEST STRING** is overwritten onto the new (longer) `reset_to` string we just set up (that is, **THIS IS A READ-ONLY DEVICE**) so that a subsequent read will give:
```
# cat /dev/cdev-rom\@4
TEST STRING
AD ONLY DEVICE!
```
However, this is an example and we can safely accept this behavior.

Configuring the CPU pins for specific peripherals

Even if the ESPRESSObin is the reference platform of this book, in this paragraph, we'll explain how a kernel developer can modify the pins settings for different platforms due to the fact this task may vary across different implementations. In fact, even if all of these implementations are device tree-based, they have some differences among each other that must be outlined.

Current CPUs are very complex systems — so complex that most of them are given the acronym **SoC**, which means **System-On-Chip**; in fact, in a single chip, we may find not only the **Central Processing Unit (CPU)** but also a lot of peripherals, which the CPU can use to communicate with the external environment. So, we can have the display controller, the keyboard controller, a USB host or device controller, disks, and network controllers all together inside one chip. Not only that, but modern SoCs have several copies of them! All these peripherals have their own signals and each of them are routed over a dedicated physical line and each of these lines needs a pin to communicate with the external environment; however, it may happen that CPU pins are not enough to route all these lines to the outside, which is why most of them are multiplexed. This means that, for instance, a CPU may have six serial ports and two Ethernet ports but they cannot be used at the same time. Here is where the **pinctrl subsystem** comes into play.

Linux's pinctrl subsystem deals with enumerating, naming, and multiplexing controllable pins, such as software-controlled biasing and driving-mode-specific pins, such as pull-up/down, open-drain, load-capacitance, and more. All these settings can be done thanks to a **pin controller**, which is a piece of hardware (usually a set of registers) that can control CPU pins and it may be able to multiplex, bias, set load capacitance, or set drive strength for individual pins or groups of pins:

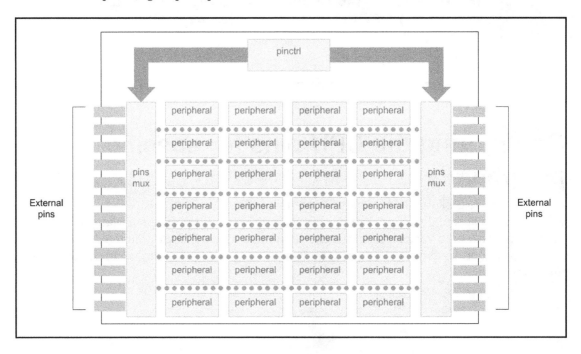

Unsigned integers ranging from 0 to maximum pin number are used to denote the packaging input or output lines we want to control.

This number space is local to each pin controller, so there may be several such number spaces in a system; each time a pin controller is instantiated it will register a descriptor containing an array of pin descriptors describing the pins handled by this specific pin controller.

In this book, we're not going to explain how we can define a pin controller within the kernel, since it's out of the scope of this book (and it's also quite a complex task), but we'll try to give to the reader the ability to configure each CPU pin in order for it to be used with the driver they are developing by using, for example, three of the most used CPUs in the industry of embedded systems.

The Armada 3720

ESPRESSObin's CPU is the Armada 3720 from Marvell and we can have an idea about its internal peripherals by taking a look at the `linux/arch/arm64/boot/dts/marvell/armada-37xx.dtsi` file. This file defines the memory map of internal peripherals (which is how and where each peripheral is mapped within the CPU's memory) and all the CPU pins grouped by pin controllers and pin functionalities.

For example, the following snippet defines a pin controller named `pinctrl@13800`:

```
pinctrl_nb: pinctrl@13800 {
    compatible = "marvell,armada3710-nb-pinctrl",
            "syscon", "simple-mfd";
    reg = <0x13800 0x100>, <0x13C00 0x20>;
    /* MPP1[19:0] */
    gpionb: gpio {
        #gpio-cells = <2>;
        gpio-ranges = <&pinctrl_nb 0 0 36>;
        gpio-controller;
        interrupt-controller;
        #interrupt-cells = <2>;
        interrupts =
        <GIC_SPI 51 IRQ_TYPE_LEVEL_HIGH>,
        <GIC_SPI 52 IRQ_TYPE_LEVEL_HIGH>,
        <GIC_SPI 53 IRQ_TYPE_LEVEL_HIGH>,
        <GIC_SPI 54 IRQ_TYPE_LEVEL_HIGH>,
        <GIC_SPI 55 IRQ_TYPE_LEVEL_HIGH>,
        <GIC_SPI 56 IRQ_TYPE_LEVEL_HIGH>,
        <GIC_SPI 57 IRQ_TYPE_LEVEL_HIGH>,
```

```
            <GIC_SPI 58 IRQ_TYPE_LEVEL_HIGH>,
            <GIC_SPI 152 IRQ_TYPE_LEVEL_HIGH>,
            <GIC_SPI 153 IRQ_TYPE_LEVEL_HIGH>,
            <GIC_SPI 154 IRQ_TYPE_LEVEL_HIGH>,
            <GIC_SPI 155 IRQ_TYPE_LEVEL_HIGH>;
    };

    xtalclk: xtal-clk {
        compatible = "marvell,armada-3700-xtal-clock";
        clock-output-names = "xtal";
        #clock-cells = <0>;
    };

    spi_quad_pins: spi-quad-pins {
        groups = "spi_quad";
        function = "spi";
    };

    ...
```

 We should remember that this notation means that it's mapped at offset `0x13800` from the beginning of the parent node named `internal-regs@d0000000` and mapped at `0xd0000000`.

Properties of the `compatible` states, which is the driver of this pin controller (stored into the `linux/drivers/pinctrl/mvebu/pinctrl-armada-37xx.c` file), while each sub-node describes the functionality of a pin. We can see a GPIO controller with a clock device and a set of pin definitions (starting from `spi_quad_pins`), which the pins controller are defined in the following reported code:

```
static struct armada_37xx_pin_group armada_37xx_nb_groups[] = {
    PIN_GRP_GPIO("jtag", 20, 5, BIT(0), "jtag"),
    PIN_GRP_GPIO("sdio0", 8, 3, BIT(1), "sdio"),
    PIN_GRP_GPIO("emmc_nb", 27, 9, BIT(2), "emmc"),
    PIN_GRP_GPIO("pwm0", 11, 1, BIT(3), "pwm"),
    PIN_GRP_GPIO("pwm1", 12, 1, BIT(4), "pwm"),
    PIN_GRP_GPIO("pwm2", 13, 1, BIT(5), "pwm"),
    PIN_GRP_GPIO("pwm3", 14, 1, BIT(6), "pwm"),
    PIN_GRP_GPIO("pmic1", 17, 1, BIT(7), "pmic"),
    PIN_GRP_GPIO("pmic0", 16, 1, BIT(8), "pmic"),
    PIN_GRP_GPIO("i2c2", 2, 2, BIT(9), "i2c"),
    PIN_GRP_GPIO("i2c1", 0, 2, BIT(10), "i2c"),
    PIN_GRP_GPIO("spi_cs1", 17, 1, BIT(12), "spi"),
    PIN_GRP_GPIO_2("spi_cs2", 18, 1, BIT(13) | BIT(19), 0, BIT(13), "spi"),
    PIN_GRP_GPIO_2("spi_cs3", 19, 1, BIT(14) | BIT(19), 0, BIT(14), "spi"),
    PIN_GRP_GPIO("onewire", 4, 1, BIT(16), "onewire"),
    PIN_GRP_GPIO("uart1", 25, 2, BIT(17), "uart"),
```

```
PIN_GRP_GPIO("spi_quad", 15, 2, BIT(18), "spi"),
PIN_GRP_EXTRA("uart2", 9, 2, BIT(1) | BIT(13) | BIT(14) | BIT(19),
        BIT(1) | BIT(13) | BIT(14), BIT(1) | BIT(19),
        18, 2, "gpio", "uart"),
PIN_GRP_GPIO("led0_od", 11, 1, BIT(20), "led"),
PIN_GRP_GPIO("led1_od", 12, 1, BIT(21), "led"),
PIN_GRP_GPIO("led2_od", 13, 1, BIT(22), "led"),
PIN_GRP_GPIO("led3_od", 14, 1, BIT(23), "led"),

};
```

The `PIN_GRP_GPIO()` and `PIN_GRP_GPIO_2()` macros are used to specify the fact that a pin's group can be used by an internal peripheral or just as normal GPIO lines. So, when we use the following code in the ESPRESSObin's DTS file (code from `linux/arch/arm64/boot/dts/marvell/armada-3720-espressobin.dts` file) we ask the pin's controller to reserve the `uart1_pins` group for the `uart0` device:

```
/* Exported on the micro USB connector J5 through an FTDI */
&uart0 {
    pinctrl-names = "default";
    pinctrl-0 = <&uart1_pins>;
    status = "okay";
};
```

Note that the line, `status = "okay"`, is needed because each device is normally disabled and if it is not specified, the device won't work.

Note that, this time, we have used the `pinctrl-0` property to declare peripheral's pins.

The usage of the `pinctrl-0` and `pinctrl-names` properties is strictly related to multiple pin's configuration states, which are not reported in this book due to limited space. However, curious readers can take a look at `https://www.kernel.org/doc/Documentation/devicetree/bindings/pinctrl/pinctrl-bindings.txt` for further information.

The i.MX7Dual

Another quite famous CPU is the **i.MX7Dual from Freescale**, which is described in the `linux/arch/arm/boot/dts/imx7s.dtsi` device tree file. Inside this file, we can see a definition of its two pin controllers as follows:

```
iomuxc_lpsr: iomuxc-lpsr@302c0000 {
    compatible = "fsl,imx7d-iomuxc-lpsr";
    reg = <0x302c0000 0x10000>;
    fsl,input-sel = <&iomuxc>;
};

iomuxc: iomuxc@30330000 {
    compatible = "fsl,imx7d-iomuxc";
    reg = <0x30330000 0x10000>;
};
```

By using the `compatiblle` properties, we can discover that the pin controller's driver is stored in the `linux/drivers/pinctrl/freescale/pinctrl-imx7d.c` file, where we can find the list of all CPU's pin pads as follows (for space reasons only pin pads of second pin;s controller have been reported):

```
enum imx7d_lpsr_pads {
    MX7D_PAD_GPIO1_IO00 = 0,
    MX7D_PAD_GPIO1_IO01 = 1,
    MX7D_PAD_GPIO1_IO02 = 2,
    MX7D_PAD_GPIO1_IO03 = 3,
    MX7D_PAD_GPIO1_IO04 = 4,
    MX7D_PAD_GPIO1_IO05 = 5,
    MX7D_PAD_GPIO1_IO06 = 6,
    MX7D_PAD_GPIO1_IO07 = 7,
};
```

Then, all peripherals that need pins just have to declare them, as in the following example below taken from the DTS file of the **i.MX 7Dual SABRE board** again from Freescale:

```
...
panel {
    compatible = "innolux,at043tn24";
    pinctrl-0 = <&pinctrl_backlight>;
    enable-gpios = <&gpio1 1 GPIO_ACTIVE_HIGH>;
    power-supply = <&reg_lcd_3v3>;

    port {
        panel_in: endpoint {
            remote-endpoint = <&display_out>;
        };
```

```
            };
        };
    };
    . . .
    &wdog1 {
        pinctrl-names = "default";
        pinctrl-0 = <&pinctrl_wdog>;
        fsl,ext-reset-output;
    };
    . . .
    &iomuxc_lpsr {
        pinctrl_wdog: wdoggrp {
            fsl,pins = <
                MX7D_PAD_LPSR_GPIO1_IO00__WDOG1_WDOG_B 0x74
            >;
        };

        pinctrl_backlight: backlightgrp {
            fsl,pins = <
                MX7D_PAD_LPSR_GPIO1_IO01__GPIO1_IO1 0x110b0
            >;
        };
    };
```

In the preceding example, the `panel` node asks for the `pinctrl_backlight` pins groups, while `wdog1` asks for the `pinctrl_wdog` pins group; all these groups require pins from the `lpsr` pad.

 Note that pins defines in the DTS can be found into file `linux/arch/arm/boot/dts/imx7d-pinfunc.h`. Also, the following numbers are specific pin settings, which are explained in the CPU's user manual, so refer to it for further information about these magic numbers.

Again, the `pinctrl-0` property has been used to address default pins configurations.

The SAMA5D3

The last example is about the CPU named SAMA5D3 from Microchip, which is described in the linux/arch/arm/boot/dts/sama5d3.dtsi file. The pins definitions schema is quite similar to the preceding one, in which we have a pins controller driver stored in the linux/drivers/pinctrl/pinctrl-at91.c file, and where all pins features are managed according to definitions in the device tree, as reported in the following example:

```
pinctrl@fffff200 {
    #address-cells = <1>;
    #size-cells = <1>;
    compatible = "atmel,sama5d3-pinctrl", "atmel,at91sam9x5-pinctrl",
"simple-bus";
    ranges = <0xfffff200 0xfffff200 0xa00>;
    atmel,mux-mask = <
        /* A B C */
        0xffffffff 0xc0fc0000 0xc0ff0000 /* pioA */
        0xffffffff 0x0ff8ffff 0x00000000 /* pioB */
        0xffffffff 0xbc00f1ff 0x7c00fc00 /* pioC */
        0xffffffff 0xc001c0e0 0x0001c1e0 /* pioD */
        0xffffffff 0xbf9f8000 0x18000000 /* pioE */
        >;

    /* shared pinctrl settings */
    adc0 {
        pinctrl_adc0_adtrg: adc0_adtrg {
            atmel,pins =
                <AT91_PIOD 19 AT91_PERIPH_A AT91_PINCTRL_NONE>; /* PD19
periph A ADTRG */
        };
        pinctrl_adc0_ad0: adc0_ad0 {
            atmel,pins =
                <AT91_PIOD 20 AT91_PERIPH_A AT91_PINCTRL_NONE>; /* PD20
periph A AD0 */
        };
...
        pinctrl_adc0_ad7: adc0_ad7 {
            atmel,pins =
                <AT91_PIOD 27 AT91_PERIPH_A AT91_PINCTRL_NONE>; /* PD27
periph A AD7 */
...
```

Again, when a peripheral needs one more group of pins, it simply declares them, as in the following code taken from the DTS file of the **SAMA5D3 Xplained board** from the Microchip Technology:

```
adc0: adc@f8018000 {
    atmel,adc-vref = <3300>;
    atmel,adc-channels-used = <0xfe>;
    pinctrl-0 = <
        &pinctrl_adc0_adtrg
        &pinctrl_adc0_ad1
        &pinctrl_adc0_ad2
        &pinctrl_adc0_ad3
        &pinctrl_adc0_ad4
        &pinctrl_adc0_ad5
        &pinctrl_adc0_ad6
        &pinctrl_adc0_ad7
        >;
    status = "okay";
};
```

In the preceding example, the adc0 node asks for several pins groups to be able to manage its internal ADC peripherals.

The DTS schema of SAMA5D3 CPU still uses the pinctrl-0 property to address the default pins configurations.

Using a device tree to describe a character driver

To test the code presented in the recipe in the chapter and to show how everything works, we have to compile it before any further steps are taken:

```
$ make KERNEL_DIR=../../../linux
make -C ../../../linux \
            ARCH=arm64 \
            CROSS_COMPILE=aarch64-linux-gnu- \
            SUBDIRS=/home/giometti/Projects/ldddc/github/chapter_4/chrdev
modules
make[1]: Entering directory '/home/giometti/Projects/ldddc/linux'
  CC [M] /home/giometti/Projects/ldddc/github/chapter_4/chrdev/chrdev.o
  CC [M] /home/giometti/Projects/ldddc/github/chapter_4/chrdev/chrdev-req.o
...
  LD [M] /home/giometti/Projects/ldddc/github/chapter_4/chrdev/chrdev.ko
make[1]: Leaving directory '/home/giometti/Projects/ldddc/linux'
```

Then, we have to move the `chrdev.ko` and `chrdev-req.ko` files to the ESPRESSObin. Now, if we insert the first module, we get exactly the same output we have seen before on the serial console (or in the kernel messages):

```
# insmod chrdev.ko
chrdev: loading out-of-tree module taints kernel.
chrdev:chrdev_init: got major 239
```

The differences will appear when we insert the second module:

```
# insmod chrdev-req.ko
chrdev cdev-eeprom@2: chrdev cdev-eeprom with id 2 added
chrdev cdev-rom@4: chrdev cdev-rom with id 4 added
```

Great! Now two new devices have been created. By doing this, the following two character files have been automatically created into the `/dev` directory:

```
# ls -l /dev/cdev*
crw------- 1 root root 239, 2 Feb 27 18:35 /dev/cdev-eeprom@2
crw------- 1 root root 239, 4 Feb 27 18:35 /dev/cdev-rom@4
```

In reality, there is nothing magic here, but it's the `udev` program that does it for us and this will be explained a bit more in depth in the next section.

The new devices have been named according to the labels specified in the device tree (as discussed previously) with minor numbers corresponding to the values used for each `reg` property.

Note that the `cdev-eeprom@2` and `cdev-rom@4` names are created by the `device_create()` function when we specified the printf-like format as in the following:

```
device_create(... , "%s@%d", label, id);
```

Now we can try to read and write data into our newly created devices. According to our definition in the device tree, the device labeled `cdev-eeprom` should be a read/write device, while the one labeled `cdev-rom` is a read-only device. So, let's try some simple read/write commands on the `/dev/cdev-eeprom@2` character device:

```
# echo "TEST STRING" > /dev/cdev-eeprom\@2
# cat /dev/cdev-eeprom\@2
TEST STRING
```

Note the backslash (\) character before @   otherwise, BASH will generate an error.

To verify that everything works as before, the related kernel messages are reported as follows:

```
chrdev cdev-eeprom@2: chrdev (id=2) opened
chrdev cdev-eeprom@2: should write 12 bytes (*ppos=0)
chrdev cdev-eeprom@2: got 12 bytes (*ppos=12)
chrdev cdev-eeprom@2: chrdev (id=2) released
chrdev cdev-eeprom@2: chrdev (id=2) opened
chrdev cdev-eeprom@2: should read 131072 bytes (*ppos=0)
chrdev cdev-eeprom@2: return 300 bytes (*ppos=300)
chrdev cdev-eeprom@2: should read 131072 bytes (*ppos=300)
chrdev cdev-eeprom@2: return 0 bytes (*ppos=300)
chrdev cdev-eeprom@2: chrdev (id=2) released
```

We can see that, by the first command, we call an `open()` system call and that the driver recognizes the device `id` equal to 2 then, we write 12 bytes (that is, the TEST STRING plus the termination character); after that, we close the device. Using the `cat` command instead, we still open the device, but after that, we do the first read of 131,072 bytes (and the driver correctly returns 300 bytes only) followed by another read of the same number of bytes, which achieves the answer 0, meaning an end-of-file condition; so, the `cat` command closes the device and prints the received data (or, at least, all the printable bytes) before exiting.

Now we can try the same commands on the other `/dev/cdev-rom@4` device. The output is as follows:

```
# echo "TEST STRING" > /dev/cdev-rom\@4
-bash: echo: write error: Invalid argument
# cat /dev/cdev-rom\@4
```

The first command failed as expected, while the second seemed to return nothing; however, this is because all the read data is 0 and to verify this, we can use the `od` command as follows:

```
# od -tx1 -N 16 /dev/cdev-rom\@4
0000000 00 00 00 00 00 00 00 00 00 00 00 00 00 00 00 00
0000020
```

This demonstrates that no data has been written into the `/dev/cdev-rom@4` device, which has been defined as read-only in the device tree.

As in the preceding code, we can take another look at the kernel messages to verify that everything works well (the following are reported kernel messages relative to the od command):

```
chrdev cdev-rom@4: chrdev (id=4) opened
chrdev cdev-rom@4: should write 12 bytes (*ppos=0)
chrdev cdev-rom@4: chrdev (id=4) released
chrdev cdev-rom@4: chrdev (id=4) opened
chrdev cdev-rom@4: should read 131072 bytes (*ppos=0)
chrdev cdev-rom@4: return 300 bytes (*ppos=300)
chrdev cdev-rom@4: should read 131072 bytes (*ppos=300)
chrdev cdev-rom@4: return 0 bytes (*ppos=300)
chrdev cdev-rom@4: chrdev (id=4) released
chrdev cdev-rom@4: chrdev (id=4) opened
chrdev cdev-rom@4: should read 16 bytes (*ppos=0)
chrdev cdev-rom@4: return 16 bytes (*ppos=16)
chrdev cdev-rom@4: chrdev (id=4) released
```

In the preceding output, we can see that we first open the device (this time, the device with id equal to four) and then we use the write() system call, which obviously fails so the device is simply closed. The two following readings then work in exactly the same way as the preceding ones.

Now we should try to modify the device tree to define different chrdev devices or, better still, should try to modify the driver to add more functionalities.

Additional Information: Managing Interrupts and Concurrency

Recalling what we did in Chapter 3, *Working with Char Drivers,* when we talked about the read() system call and how we can implement it for our char driver (see chapter_4/chrdev/chrdev.c file on GitHub), we noticed that our implementation was tricky because data was always available:

```
static ssize_t chrdev_read(struct file *filp,
              char __user *buf, size_t count, loff_t *ppos)
{
    struct chrdev_device *chrdev = filp->private_data;
    int ret;

    dev_info(chrdev->dev, "should read %ld bytes (*ppos=%lld)\n",
              count, *ppos);

    /* Check for end-of-buffer */
    if (*ppos + count >= BUF_LEN)
        count = BUF_LEN - *ppos;

    /* Return data to the user space */
    ret = copy_to_user(buf, chrdev->buf + *ppos, count);
    if (ret < 0)
        return ret;

    *ppos += count;
    dev_info(chrdev->dev, "return %ld bytes (*ppos=%lld)\n", count, *ppos);

    return count;
}
```

In the preceding example, the data inside `chrdev->buf` is always there, but in a real peripheral, this is very often not true; we must usually wait for new data and then the current process should be suspended (that is, *put to sleep*). That is why our `chrdev_read()` should be something like this:

```
static ssize_t chrdev_read(struct file *filp,
                char __user *buf, size_t count, loff_t *ppos)
{
    struct chrdev_device *chrdev = filp->private_data;
    int ret;

    /* Wait for available data */
    wait_for_event(chrdev->available > 0);

    /* Check for end-of-buffer */
    if (count > chrdev->available)
        count = chrdev->available;

    /* Return data to the user space */
    ret = copy_to_user(buf, ..., count);
    if (ret < 0)
        return ret;

    *ppos += count;

    return count;
}
```

 Please note that this example is deliberately not complete, due to the fact that a real (and complete) `read()` system call implementation will be presented in Chapter 7, *Advanced Char Driver Operations*. In this chapter, we simply introduce mechanisms and not how we can use them in a device driver.

By using the `wait_for_event()` function, we are asking the kernel to test whether there is some available data and, if so, to permit process execution, otherwise, the current process will be put to sleep and then woken up again once the condition, `chrdev->available > 0` is true.

Peripherals usually use interrupts to notify the CPU that some new data is available (or that some important activity must be done with them), and then it's quite obvious that it's there, inside the interrupt handler, where we, as device driver developers, have to inform the kernel that the sleeping process, waiting for that data, should be awakened. In the following sections, we'll see, by using very simple examples, which mechanisms are available in the kernel and how they can be used to suspend a process, and we'll also see when we can do it safely! In fact, if we ask the scheduler to revoke the CPU to the current process to give it to another process within an interrupt handler, we're simply trying to carry out a nonsense operation. When we are in an interrupt context, we are not executing process code, so what process can we revoke the CPU? Simply speaking, the executing process can *go to sleep* when the CPU is in the process context, while, when we are in interrupt context we can't because no process is currently, officially, holding the CPU!

This last concept is very important and it must be well understood by device driver developers; in fact, if we try to go to sleep when the CPU is in the interrupt context, then a severe exception will be generated and, most probably, the complete system will hang.

Another important concept to be really clear about is **atomic operations.** A device driver is not a normal program with a regular beginning and end; instead, a device driver is a collection of methods and asynchronous interrupt handlers that can run simultaneously. That's why we'll most probably have to protect our data from race conditions that may corrupt them.

For instance, if we use a buffer to save just the received data from a peripheral, we must be sure that the data is correctly queued so that the reading process can read valid data and no information is lost. Then, in these cases, we should use some mutual exclusion mechanisms that Linux offers to us to do our job. However, we must pay attention to what we do since some of these mechanisms can be safely used in both processes or interrupt contexts, while others can't; some of them can be used only in the process context and they can damage our system if we use them in the interrupt context.

Moreover, we should take into account that modern CPUs have more than one core, so using the trick to disable a CPU's interrupts to get atomic code doesn't work at all, and a specific mutual exclusion mechanism must be used instead. In Linux, this mechanism is called **spinlocks** and it can be used in both the interrupt or process context, but for very short periods of time, since they are implemented using a busy-waiting approach. This means that, in order to perform an atomic operation, while one core is operating in the critical section of the code belonging to such an atomic operation, all the other cores in the CPU are kept out of the same critical section, making them wait by actively spinning in a tight loop, which, in turn, signifies that you are effectively throwing away the CPU's cycles, which are doing nothing useful.

In the next sections, we're going to see, in detail, all these aspects and we'll try to explain their usage with very simple examples; in `Chapter 7`, *Advanced Char Driver Operations*, we'll see how we can use these mechanisms in a device driver.

Deferring work

A long time ago, there were the **bottom halves**, that is, a hardware event was split into two halves: the top half (the hardware interrupt handler) and the bottom half (the software interrupt handler). This is because an interrupt handler must execute as quickly as possible to be ready to serve the next incoming interrupts, so, for instance, the CPU cannot stay for a long time in the interrupt handler's body waiting for the slow peripheral sending or receiving of its data. That's why we used bottom halves; interrupts were split into two parts: the top one, the real hardware interrupt handler, which executes quickly and with disabled interrupts that simply acknowledges the peripheral and then starts a bottom half, executed with enabled interrupts, which can safely complete the sending/receiving job by taking its time.

However, bottom halves were very limiting, so kernel developers introduced **tasklets** in Linux 2.4 series. Tasklets allowed the dynamic creation of deferrable functions in a very simple manner; they were executed in the software interrupt context and were suitable for fast execution as they couldn't sleep. However, if we need to sleep, we must use another mechanism. In the Linux 2.6 series, **workqueues** were introduced as a replacement for a similar construct called taskqueue, which was already present in the Linux 2.4 series; they allow kernel functions to be activated (or deferred) for later execution as tasklets do, but in comparison tasklets (which are executed within software interrupts), they are executed in special kernel threads called **worker threads**. This implies that both can be used to defer jobs, but workqueue handlers can sleep. This handler, of course, has higher latency but, in comparison, workqueues include a richer API for work deferral.

There are two other important concepts to talk about before ending this recipe: the shared work queue and the `container_of()` macro.

The shared work queue

The preceding example in the recipe can be simplified by using the **shared work queue**. This is a special work queue defined by the kernel itself that can be used by device drivers (and other kernel entities) if they *promise* not to monopolize the queue for long periods of time (that is no long periods of sleep and no long-running tasks), if they accept the fact that their handlers may take longer to get their fair share of CPU. If both conditions are met, we can avoid creating a custom work queue with `create_singlethread_workqueue()` and we can schedule work by simply using `schedule_work()` and `schedule_delayed_work()` as follows. Here are the handlers:

```
--- a/drivers/misc/irqtest.c
+++ b/drivers/misc/irqtest.c
...
+static void irqtest_work_handler(struct work_struct *ptr)
+{
+       struct irqtest_data *info = container_of(ptr, struct irqtest_data,
+                                                               work);
+       struct device *dev = info->dev;
+
+       dev_info(dev, "work executed after IRQ %d", info->irq);
+
+       /* Schedule the delayed work after 2 seconds */
+       schedule_delayed_work(&info->dwork, 2*HZ);
+}
+
 static irqreturn_t irqtest_interrupt(int irq, void *dev_id)
 {
        struct irqtest_data *info = dev_id;
@@ -36,6 +60,8 @@ static irqreturn_t irqtest_interrupt(int irq, void
*dev_id)

        dev_info(dev, "interrupt occurred on IRQ %d\n", irq);

+       schedule_work(&info->work);
+
        return IRQ_HANDLED;
 }
```

Then, the modifications for the initialization and removal:

```
@@ -80,6 +106,10 @@ static int irqtest_probe(struct platform_device *pdev)
        dev_info(dev, "GPIO %u correspond to IRQ %d\n",
                                irqinfo.pin, irqinfo.irq);

+       /* Init works */
+       INIT_WORK(&irqinfo.work, irqtest_work_handler);
```

```
+        INIT_DELAYED_WORK(&irqinfo.dwork, irqtest_dwork_handler);
+
         /* Request IRQ line and setup corresponding handler */
         irqinfo.dev = dev;
         ret = request_irq(irqinfo.irq, irqtest_interrupt, 0,
@@ -98,6 +128,8 @@ static int irqtest_remove(struct platform_device *pdev)
 {
         struct device *dev = &pdev->dev;

+        cancel_work_sync(&irqinfo.work);
+        cancel_delayed_work_sync(&irqinfo.dwork);
         free_irq(irqinfo.irq, &irqinfo);
         dev_info(dev, "IRQ %d is now unmanaged!\n", irqinfo.irq);
```

The preceding patch can be found in the GitHub repository in the `add_workqueue_2_to_irqtest_module.patch` file and it can be applied as usual with the following command:

```
$ patch -p1 < add_workqueue_2_to_irqtest_module.patch
```

The container_of() macro

As a final note, we should utilize some words to explain a bit about the `container_of()` macro. This macro is defined in `linux/include/linux/kernel.h` as follows:

```
/**
 * container_of - cast a member of a structure out to the containing
structure
 * @ptr: the pointer to the member.
 * @type: the type of the container struct this is embedded in.
 * @member: the name of the member within the struct.
 *
 */
#define container_of(ptr, type, member) ({ \
    void *__mptr = (void *)(ptr); \
    BUILD_BUG_ON_MSG(!__same_type(*(ptr), ((type *)0)->member) && \
                     !__same_type(*(ptr), void), \
                     "pointer type mismatch in container_of()"); \
    ((type *)(__mptr - offsetof(type, member))); })
```

The `container_of()` function takes three arguments: a pointer `ptr`, the `type` of the container, and the name of the `member` the pointer refers to within the container. By using this information, the macro can expand to a new address pointing to the containing structure, which accommodates the respective member.

So, in our example, in `irqtest_work_handler()`, we can get a `struct irqtest_data` pointer to tell `container_of()` which is the address of its member named `work`.

 For further information regarding `container_of()` function, the internet is your friend; however, a good starting point is in kernel sources within the `linux/Documentation/driver-model/design-patterns.txt` file, which describes a few common design patterns found in device drivers using this macro.

It could be interesting to take a look at **Notifier Chains**, simply called **notifiers**, which are a general mechanism provided by the kernel and designed to provide a way for kernel elements to express interest in being informed about the occurrence of general **asynchronous events**.

Notifiers

The basic building block of the notifiers' mechanism is the `struct notifier_block` defined in the `linux/include/linux/notifier.h` header file, as follows:

```
typedef int (*notifier_fn_t)(struct notifier_block *nb,
                        unsigned long action, void *data);

struct notifier_block {
    notifier_fn_t notifier_call;
    struct notifier_block __rcu *next;
    int priority;
};
```

The structure contains the pointer `notifier_call` to the function to be called when the event occurs. The parameters passed to the notifier function when it's called, include an `nb` pointer to the notifier block itself, an event `action` code, which depends on the particular used chain, and a `data` pointer to an unspecified private data type, which can be used in a similar manner as tasklets or waitqueues.

The next field is managed by notifier internals, while the priority field defines the priority of the function pointed by notifier_call within the notifier chain. First the functions having higher priority are executed. In reality, priority is left by nearly all registrations out of the notifier block definition, which means it gets 0 as the default value and execution order ends up depending only on the registration order (that is a semi-random order).

Device driver developers shouldn't need to create their own notifiers, and very often it happens that they need to use an existing one. Linux defines several notifiers, as follows:

- Netdevice notifier (see linux/include/linux/netdevice.h)—reports networking device's events
- Backlight notifier (see linux/include/linux/backlight.h)—reports LCD backlight events
- Suspend notifier (see linux/include/linux/suspend.h)—reports power to suspend and resume related events
- Reboot notifier (see linux/include/linux/reboot.h)—reports rebooting requests
- Power supply notifier (see linux/include/linux/power_supply.h)—reports power supply activities

Each notifier has a register function that can be used to ask the system to be informed whenever a particular event happens. For example, the following code is reported as a useful example to request networking device and rebooting events:

```
static int __init notifier_init(void)
{
    int ret;

    ninfo.netdevice_nb.notifier_call = netdevice_notifier;
    ninfo.netdevice_nb.priority = 10;

    ret = register_netdevice_notifier(&ninfo.netdevice_nb);
    if (ret) {
        pr_err("unable to register netdevice notifier\n");
        return ret;
    }

    ninfo.reboot_nb.notifier_call = reboot_notifier;
    ninfo.reboot_nb.priority = 10;

    ret = register_reboot_notifier(&ninfo.reboot_nb);
    if (ret) {
        pr_err("unable to register reboot notifier\n");
```

```
        goto unregister_netdevice;
    }

    pr_info("notifier module loaded\n");

    return 0;

unregister_netdevice:
    unregister_netdevice_notifier(&ninfo.netdevice_nb);
    return ret;
}

static void __exit notifier_exit(void)
{
    unregister_netdevice_notifier(&ninfo.netdevice_nb);
    unregister_reboot_notifier(&ninfo.reboot_nb);

    pr_info("notifier module unloaded\n");
}
```

 All code presented here is in the `notifier.c` file from GitHub repository regarding this chapter.

Both the `register_netdevice_notifier()` and `register_reboot_notifier()` functions work on two struct notifier_block defined as follows:

```
static struct notifier_data {
    struct notifier_block netdevice_nb;
    struct notifier_block reboot_nb;
    unsigned int data;
} ninfo;
```

Notifier functions are defined like this:

```
static int netdevice_notifier(struct notifier_block *nb,
                                unsigned long code, void *unused)
{
    struct notifier_data *ninfo = container_of(nb, struct notifier_data,
                                               netdevice_nb);

    pr_info("netdevice: event #%d with code 0x%lx caught!\n",
                ninfo->data++, code);

    return NOTIFY_DONE;
}
static int reboot_notifier(struct notifier_block *nb,
```

```
                           unsigned long code, void *unused)
    {
        struct notifier_data *ninfo = container_of(nb, struct notifier_data,
                                                   reboot_nb);
        pr_info("reboot: event #%d with code 0x%lx caught!\n",
                    ninfo->data++, code);

        return NOTIFY_DONE;
    }
```

By using `container_of()`, as usual, we can get a pointer to our data structure, `struct notifier_data`; then, once our job is done, we have to return a well-fixed value defined in the `linux/include/linux/notifier.h` header:

```
#define NOTIFY_DONE         0x0000                  /* Don't care */
#define NOTIFY_OK           0x0001                  /* Suits me */
#define NOTIFY_STOP_MASK    0x8000                  /* Don't call further
*/
#define NOTIFY_BAD          (NOTIFY_STOP_MASK|0x0002)  /* Bad/Veto action */
```

Their meanings are as follows:

- `NOTIFY_DONE`: Not interested in this notification.
- `NOTIFY_OK`: Notification was correctly processed.
- `NOTIFY_BAD`: Something went wrong with this notification, so stop calling callback functions for this event!

`NOTIFY_STOP_MASK` can be used to encapsulate (negative) `errno` values as follows:

```
/* Encapsulate (negative) errno value (in particular, NOTIFY_BAD <=>
EPERM). */
static inline int notifier_from_errno(int err)
{
    if (err)
        return NOTIFY_STOP_MASK | (NOTIFY_OK - err);

    return NOTIFY_OK;
}
```

The `errno` value can then be retrieved with `notifier_to_errno()`, as follows:

```
/* Restore (negative) errno value from notify return value. */
static inline int notifier_to_errno(int ret)
{
    ret &= ~NOTIFY_STOP_MASK;
    return ret > NOTIFY_OK ? NOTIFY_OK - ret : 0;
}
```

To test our simple example, we have to compile the `notifier.c` kernel module and then move the `notifier.ko` module to the ESPRESSObin, where it can be inserted into the kernel as follows:

```
# insmod notifier.ko
notifier:netdevice_notifier: netdevice: event #0 with code 0x5 caught!
notifier:netdevice_notifier: netdevice: event #1 with code 0x1 caught!
notifier:netdevice_notifier: netdevice: event #2 with code 0x5 caught!
notifier:netdevice_notifier: netdevice: event #3 with code 0x5 caught!
notifier:netdevice_notifier: netdevice: event #4 with code 0x5 caught!
notifier:netdevice_notifier: netdevice: event #5 with code 0x5 caught!
notifier:notifier_init: notifier module loaded
```

Just after insertion, some events are already notified; however, to generate new events, we can try, for instance, to disable or enable a network device using the following `ip` command:

```
# ip link set lan0 up
notifier:netdevice_notifier: netdevice: event #6 with code 0xd caught!
RTNETLINK answers: Network is down
```

Code `0xd` corresponds to the `NETDEV_PRE_UP` event as defined in `linux/include/linux/netdevice.h`:

```
/* netdevice notifier chain. Please remember to update netdev_cmd_to_name()
 * and the rtnetlink notification exclusion list in rtnetlink_event() when
 * adding new types.
 */
enum netdev_cmd {
    NETDEV_UP = 1, /* For now you can't veto a device up/down */
    NETDEV_DOWN,
    NETDEV_REBOOT, /* Tell a protocol stack a network interface
                      detected a hardware crash and restarted
                      - we can use this eg to kick tcp sessions
                      once done */
    NETDEV_CHANGE, /* Notify device state change */
    NETDEV_REGISTER,
    NETDEV_UNREGISTER,
    NETDEV_CHANGEMTU, /* notify after mtu change happened */
    NETDEV_CHANGEADDR,
    NETDEV_GOING_DOWN,
    NETDEV_CHANGENAME,
    NETDEV_FEAT_CHANGE,
    NETDEV_BONDING_FAILOVER,
    NETDEV_PRE_UP,
    ...
```

If we reboot the system, we should see the following message within the kernel messages:

```
# reboot
...
[ 2804.502671] notifier:reboot_notifier: reboot: event #7 with code 1
caught!
```

Kernel timers

A **kernel timer** is an easy way to ask the kernel to execute a specific function after a well-defined amount of time. Linux implements two different types of kernel timers: old but still valid kernel timers defined in the `linux/include/linux/timer.h` header file and new **high-resolution** kernel timers defined in the `linux/include/linux/hrtimer.h` header file. Even if they are implemented differently, both mechanisms work in a very similar manner: we have to declare a structure holding timer's data, which can be initialized by proper functions, and then the timer can be started using the proper function. Once expired, the timer calls a handler to execute the desired actions and, eventually, we have the possibility of stopping or restarting the timer.

Legacy kernel timers are only supported at a resolution of 1 jiffy. The length of a jiffy is dependent on the value of the defined HZ in the Linux kernel (see the `linux/include/asm-generic/param.h` file); usually, it's 1 millisecond on PCs and some other platforms, while it's set to 10 milliseconds on most embedded platforms. Having a resolution of 1 millisecond resolved most problems for device drivers developers in the past, but nowadays, most peripherals need higher resolution to be correctly managed. This is why higher resolution timers come into play, allowing the system to wake up and process data quickly at more accurate time intervals. Currently, kernel timers have been obsoleted by high-resolution timers (even if they are still used around the kernel sources), which have the target to implement the POSIX 1003.1b Section 14 (Clocks and Timers) API in Linux, that is, timers with accuracy better than 1 jiffy.

 Note that we just saw that, to delay a job, we can also use delayed workqueues.

Additional Information: Miscellaneous Kernel Internals

Here's some general information on dynamic memory allocation and I/O memory access methods.

While talking about dynamic memory allocation, we should keep in mind that we're programming in the C language inside the kernel, so it's really important to remember that each allocated memory chunk must be freed up when not used anymore. This is very important because in userspace, when a process ends its execution, the kernel (which actually knows all about memory chunks owned by the process) can easily get back all process-allocated memory; but this does not hold true for the kernel. In fact, a driver (or other kernel entity) that asks for a memory chunk must be sure to free it, otherwise, nobody will ask for it back and the memory chunk will be lost until the machine is restarted.

Regarding access to I/O memory, which is that area composed by the memory cells underlying peripheral registers, we must consider that we can't access them using their physical memory address; instead, we'll have to use the corresponding virtual one. In fact, Linux is an operating system that uses a **Memory Management Unit** (**MMU**) to virtualize and protect memory accesses, so we'll have to remap each peripheral's physical memory area to its corresponding virtual memory area to be able to read from and write to them.

This operation can be easily done by using the kernel functions presented in the code snippet in Chapter , but it is of paramount importance to point out that it must be done before any I/O memory access is attempted, or a segmentation fault will be triggered. This can terminate the process in user space, or possibly terminate the kernel itself for a bug in a device driver.

Dynamic memory allocation

The most straightforward way to allocate memory is to use the `kmalloc()` function, and, to be on the safe side, it's best to use routines that clear the allocated memory to zero, such as the `kzalloc()` function. On the other hand, if we need to allocate memory for an array, there are `kmalloc_array()` and `kcalloc()` dedicated functions.

Here are some snippets containing memory allocation kernel functions (and the relative kernel memory deallocation functions) as reported in the header file, `linux/include/linux/slab.h`:

```
/**
 * kmalloc - allocate memory
 * @size: how many bytes of memory are required.
 * @flags: the type of memory to allocate.
...
*/
static __always_inline void *kmalloc(size_t size, gfp_t flags);

/**
 * kzalloc - allocate memory. The memory is set to zero.
 * @size: how many bytes of memory are required.
 * @flags: the type of memory to allocate (see kmalloc).
 */
static inline void *kzalloc(size_t size, gfp_t flags)
{
    return kmalloc(size, flags | __GFP_ZERO);
}

/**
 * kmalloc_array - allocate memory for an array.
 * @n: number of elements.
 * @size: element size.
 * @flags: the type of memory to allocate (see kmalloc).
 */
static inline void *kmalloc_array(size_t n, size_t size, gfp_t flags);

/**
 * kcalloc - allocate memory for an array. The memory is set to zero.
 * @n: number of elements.
 * @size: element size.
 * @flags: the type of memory to allocate (see kmalloc).
 */
static inline void *kcalloc(size_t n, size_t size, gfp_t flags)
{
    return kmalloc_array(n, size, flags | __GFP_ZERO);
}

void kfree(const void *);
```

All the preceding functions expose two main differences between the userspace counterpart `malloc()` and other memory allocation functions:

1. The maximum size of a chunk that can be allocated with `kmalloc()` and friends is limited. The actual limit depends on the hardware and the kernel configuration, but it is a good practice to use `kmalloc()` and other kernel helpers for objects smaller than a page size.

   The number of bytes that make a page size is stated by defined `PAGE_SIZE` info kernel sources in the `linux/include/asm-generic/page.h` file; usually, it's 4096 bytes for 32-bit systems and 8192 bytes for 64-bit systems. It can be explicitly chosen by the user via the usual kernel configuration mechanism.

2. Kernel functions for dynamic memory allocation, such as `kmalloc()` and similar functions take an extra argument; the allocation flags are used to specify the behavior of `kmalloc()` in a number of ways, as reported in the snippet below from the `linux/include/linux/slab.h` file of kernel sources:

```
/**
 * kmalloc - allocate memory
 * @size: how many bytes of memory are required.
 * @flags: the type of memory to allocate.
 *
 * kmalloc is the normal method of allocating memory
 * for objects smaller than page size in the kernel.
 *
 * The @flags argument may be one of:
 *
 * %GFP_USER - Allocate memory on behalf of user. May sleep.
 *
 * %GFP_KERNEL - Allocate normal kernel ram. May sleep.
 *
 * %GFP_ATOMIC - Allocation will not sleep. May use emergency
pools.
 * For example, use this inside interrupt handlers.
 *
 * %GFP_HIGHUSER - Allocate pages from high memory.
 *
 * %GFP_NOIO - Do not do any I/O at all while trying to get memory.
 *
 * %GFP_NOFS - Do not make any fs calls while trying to get memory.
 *
 * %GFP_NOWAIT - Allocation will not sleep.
 ...
```

As we can see, there exist a lot of flags; however, a device driver developer will be interested mainly in GFP_KERNEL and GFP_ATOMIC.

It is clear that the main difference between the two flags is that the former can allocate normal kernel RAM and it may sleep, while the latter does the same without allowing the caller to sleep. This is a big difference between the two functions because it tells us which flag we have to use when we are in interrupt context or process context.

As seen in Chapter 5, *Managing Interrupts and Concurrency*, when we are in interrupt context we cannot sleep (as reported in the code above), in these situations, we must call kmalloc() and friends by specifying the GFP_ATOMIC flag, while the GFP_KERNEL flag can be used elsewhere, keeping in account that it can lead the caller to sleep and then the CPU may leave us to execute something else; therefore, we should avoid doing the following:

```
spin_lock(...);
ptr = kmalloc(..., GFP_KERNEL);
spin_unlock(...);
```

In fact, even if we're executing in the process context, executing a sleeping kmalloc() while holding a spinlock is considered evil! So, we must use the GFP_ATOMIC flag anyway in this case. Moreover, be aware that the maximum size for a successful GFP_ATOMIC allocation request tends to be smaller than a GFP_KERNEL request for the same reasons mentioned here clearly, related to physically-contiguous memory allocation and that the kernel keeps a limited pool of memory readily available for atomic allocation.

Regarding the first point above, on the limited size of an allocable memory chunk, for large allocations, we can alternatively consider using another class of functions: vmalloc() and vzalloc(), even if we have to underline the fact that memory allocated by vmalloc() and related functions are not physically contiguous and can't be used for **Direct Memory Access** (**DMA**) activities (while kmalloc() and friends, as stated previously, allocate contiguous memory areas in both virtual and physical addressing spaces).

 Allocating memory for DMA activities is currently not addressed in this book; however, you may get further information regarding this issue in kernel sources within the linux/Documentation/DMA-API.txt and linux/Documentation/DMA-API-HOWTO.txt files.

In the following, there is the prototype of the `vmalloc()` function and friends definitions as reported in the `linux/include/linux/vmalloc.h` header file:

```
extern void *vmalloc(unsigned long size);
extern void *vzalloc(unsigned long size);
```

If we are not sure whether the allocation size is too large for `kmalloc()`, we can use `kvmalloc()` and its derivatives. This function will try to allocate memory with `kmalloc()`, and if the allocation fails it will fall back to `vmalloc()`.

 Note that `kvmalloc()` may return memory that is not physically contiguous.

There are also restrictions on which `GFP_*` flags can be used with `kvmalloc()`, as reported in `kvmalloc_node()` documentation at `https://www.kernel.org/doc/html/latest/core-api/mm-api.html#c.kvmalloc_node`.

Here are code snippets about `kvmalloc()`, `kvzalloc()`, `kvmalloc_array()`, `kvcalloc()`, and `kvfree()` as reported in the `linux/include/linux/mm.h` header file:

```
static inline void *kvmalloc(size_t size, gfp_t flags)
{
    return kvmalloc_node(size, flags, NUMA_NO_NODE);
}

static inline void *kvzalloc(size_t size, gfp_t flags)
{
    return kvmalloc(size, flags | __GFP_ZERO);
}

static inline void *kvmalloc_array(size_t n, size_t size, gfp_t flags)
{
    size_t bytes;

    if (unlikely(check_mul_overflow(n, size, &bytes)))
        return NULL;

    return kvmalloc(bytes, flags);
}

static inline void *kvcalloc(size_t n, size_t size, gfp_t flags)
{
    return kvmalloc_array(n, size, flags | __GFP_ZERO);
```

```
}
extern void kvfree(const void *addr);
```

Kernel doubly linked lists

When working with the Linux's **doubly linked list** interface, we should always bear in mind that these list functions perform no locking, so there is a possibility that our device driver (or other kernel entities) could attempt to perform concurrent operations on the same list. That's why we must be sure to implement a good locking scheme to protect our data against race conditions.

To use the list mechanism, our driver must include the header file `linux/include/linux/list.h`; this file includes the header, `linux/include/linux/types.h`, where a simple structure of the `struct list_head` type is defined as follows:

```
struct list_head {
    struct list_head *next, *prev;
};
```

As we can see, this structure contains two pointers (`prev` and `next`) to a `list_head` structure; these two pointers implement the doubly linked list functionality. However, the interesting thing is that `struct list_head` has no dedicated data field as it would in a canonical list implementation. In fact, in the Linux kernel list implementation, the data field is not embedded in the list element itself; rather it's the list structure that is meant to be enclosed in the related data structure. This may be confusing but, in reality, it is not; in fact, to use the Linux list facility in our code, we just need to embed a `struct list_head` inside the structure that makes use of the list.

A simple example of how we can declare our object structure into our device driver is as follows:

```
struct l_struct {
    int data;
    ...
    /* other driver specific fields */
    ...
    struct list_head list;
};
```

By doing this, we create a doubly linked list with custom data. Then, to effectively create our list, we just need to declare and initialize the list head using the following code:

```
struct list_head data_list;
INIT_LIST_HEAD(&data_list);
```

 As per other kernel structures, we have the compile time counterpart macro `LIST_HEAD()`, which can be used to do the same in case of non-dynamic list allocation. In our example, we can do as follows:
`LIST_HEAD(data_list);`

Once the list head has been declared and properly initialized, we can use several functions, still from the `linux/include/linux/list.h` file, to add, remove, or do other list entry manipulation.

If we take a look at the header file, we can see the following functions to add or remove an element from the list:

```
/**
 * list_add - add a new entry
 * @new: new entry to be added
 * @head: list head to add it after
 *
 * Insert a new entry after the specified head.
 * This is good for implementing stacks.
 */
static inline void list_add(struct list_head *new, struct list_head *head);

 * list_del - deletes entry from list.
 * @entry: the element to delete from the list.
 * Note: list_empty() on entry does not return true after this, the entry is
 * in an undefined state.
 */
static inline void list_del(struct list_head *entry);
```

The following function to replace an old entry by a new one are also visible:

```
/**
 * list_replace - replace old entry by new one
 * @old : the element to be replaced
 * @new : the new element to insert
 *
 * If @old was empty, it will be overwritten.
 */
static inline void list_replace(struct list_head *old,
```

```
                                    struct list_head *new);
...
```

This is just a subset of all available functions. You are encouraged to take a look at the `linux/include/linux/list.h` file to discover more.

However, apart from the preceding functions, which can be used to add or remove an entry from the list, it is more interesting to see the macros used to create loops that iterate through lists. For example, if we wish to add a new entry in an ordered manner, we can do something like this:

```
void add_ordered_entry(struct l_struct *new)
{
    struct list_head *ptr;
    struct my_struct *entry;

    list_for_each(ptr, &data_list) {
        entry = list_entry(ptr, struct l_struct, list);
        if (entry->data < new->data) {
            list_add_tail(&new->list, ptr);
            return;
        }
    }
    list_add_tail(&new->list, &data_list)
}
```

By using the `list_for_each()` macro, we iterate the list and by using `list_entry()`, we obtain a pointer to our enclosing data. Note that we must pass to `list_entry()` the pointer to the current element `ptr`, our struct type, and then the name of the list entry within our struct (which is `list` in the preceding example).

Finally, we can add our new element at the right position using the `list_add_tail()` function.

Note that `list_entry()` simply uses the `container_of()` macro to do its job. The macro is explained in Chapter 5, *Managing Interrupts and Concurrency*, The container_of() macro section.

If we take a look again at the `linux/include/linux/list.h` file, we can see more functions that we can use to get an entry from the list or to iterate all list elements in a different manner:

```
/**
 * list_entry - get the struct for this entry
 * @ptr:    the &struct list_head pointer.
 * @type:   the type of the struct this is embedded in.
 * @member: the name of the list_head within the struct.
 */
#define list_entry(ptr, type, member) \
    container_of(ptr, type, member)

/**
 * list_first_entry - get the first element from a list
 * @ptr:    the list head to take the element from.
 * @type:   the type of the struct this is embedded in.
 * @member: the name of the list_head within the struct.
 *
 * Note, that list is expected to be not empty.
 */
#define list_first_entry(ptr, type, member) \
        list_entry((ptr)->next, type, member)

/**
 * list_last_entry - get the last element from a list
 * @ptr:    the list head to take the element from.
 * @type:   the type of the struct this is embedded in.
 * @member: the name of the list_head within the struct.
 *
 * Note, that list is expected to be not empty.
 */
#define list_last_entry(ptr, type, member) \
        list_entry((ptr)->prev, type, member)
...
```

Some macros are also useful to iterate over the elements of each list:

```
/**
 * list_for_each - iterate over a list
 * @pos:  the &struct list_head to use as a loop cursor.
 * @head: the head for your list.
 */
#define list_for_each(pos, head) \
        for (pos = (head)->next; pos != (head); pos = pos->next)

/**
 * list_for_each_prev - iterate over a list backwards
```

```
 * @pos: the &struct list_head to use as a loop cursor.
 * @head: the head for your list.
 */
#define list_for_each_prev(pos, head) \
        for (pos = (head)->prev; pos != (head); pos = pos->prev)
...
```

Again you should note that this is just a subset of all available functions, so you are encouraged to take a look at the `linux/include/linux/list.h` file to discover more.

Kernel hash tables

As stated previously, for linked lists, when working with the Linux's **hash table** interface, we should always bear in mind that these hashing functions perform no locking, so it is possible that our device driver (or other kernel entities) could attempt to perform concurrent operations on the same hash table. This is why we must be sure to also implement a good locking scheme to protect our data against race conditions.

As with kernel lists, we can declare and then initialize a hash table with a size of power-of-2 bits, using the following code:

```
DECLARE_HASHTABLE(data_hash, bits)
hash_init(data_hash);
```

As per lists, we have the compile time counterpart macro `DEFINE_HASHTABLE()`, which can be used to do the same in case of a non-dynamic hash table allocation. In our example, we can use `DEFINE_HASHTABLE(data_hash, bits)`;

This creates and initializes a table named `data_hash` and a power-of-2 size based on bits. As just said, the table is implemented using buckets containing a kernel `struct hlist_head` type; this is due to the fact that kernel hash tables are implemented using a hash chain, whereas hash collisions are simply added to the head of the list. To better see this, we can refer to the `DECLARE_HASHTABLE()` macro definition:

```
#define DECLARE_HASHTABLE(name, bits) \
    struct hlist_head name[1 << (bits)]
```

Once that's done, a structure containing a `struct hlist_node` pointer can be constructed to hold the data to be inserted, as we did before for lists:

```
struct h_struct {
    int key;
    int data;
    ...
    /* other driver specific fields */
    ...
    struct hlist_node node;
};
```

The `struct hlist_node` and its head, `struct hlist_head`, are defined in the `linux/include/linux/types.h` header file as follows:

```
struct hlist_head {
    struct hlist_node *first;
};

struct hlist_node {
    struct hlist_node *next, **pprev;
};
```

A new node can then be added into the hash table using the `hash_add()` function as follows, where `&entry.node` is a pointer to `struct hlist_node` within the data structure, and `key` is the hashed key:

```
hash_add(data_hash, &entry.node, key);
```

The key can be whatever; however, usually it's computed by using a special hash function applied to the data to be stored. For instance, having a hash table of 256 buckets, the key can be computed with the following `hash_func()`:

```
u8 hash_func(u8 *buf, size_t len)
{
    u8 key = 0;

    for (i = 0; i < len; i++)
        key += data[i];

    return key;
}
```

The opposite operation, which is deletion, can be done by using the `hash_del()` function as follows:

```
hash_del(&entry.node);
```

However, as for lists, the most interesting macros are the ones used to iterate the table. There exist two mechanisms; one iterates through the entire hash table, returning the entries in each bucket:

```
hash_for_each(name, bkt, node, obj, member)
```

The other returns only the entries that correspond to the key's hash bucket:

```
hash_for_each_possible(name, obj, member, key)
```

By using this last macro, a procedure to delete a node from the hash table looks like this:

```
void del_node(int data)
{
    int key = hash_func(data);
    struct h_struct *entry;

    hash_for_each_possible(data_hash, entry, node, key) {
        if (entry->data == data) {
            hash_del(&entry->node);
            return;
        }
    }
}
```

 Note that this implementation just deletes the first matching entry.

By using `hash_for_each_possible()`, we can iterate the list into the bucket related to a key.

In the following, there are definitions of `hash_add()`, `hash_del()`, and `hash_for_each_possible()` as reported in the `linux/include/linux/hashtable.h` file:

```
/**
 * hash_add - add an object to a hashtable
 * @hashtable: hashtable to add to
 * @node: the &struct hlist_node of the object to be added
 * @key: the key of the object to be added
```

```
 */
#define hash_add(hashtable, node, key) \
        hlist_add_head(node, &hashtable[hash_min(key,
HASH_BITS(hashtable))])

/**
 * hash_del - remove an object from a hashtable
 * @node: &struct hlist_node of the object to remove
 */
static inline void hash_del(struct hlist_node *node);

/**
 * hash_for_each_possible - iterate over all possible objects hashing to
the
 * same bucket
 * @name: hashtable to iterate
 * @obj: the type * to use as a loop cursor for each entry
 * @member: the name of the hlist_node within the struct
 * @key: the key of the objects to iterate over
 */
#define hash_for_each_possible(name, obj, member, key) \
        hlist_for_each_entry(obj, &name[hash_min(key, HASH_BITS(name))],
member)
```

These are just a subset of all available functions to manage hash tables. You are encouraged to take a look at the `linux/include/linux/hashtable.h` file to see more.

Getting access to I/O memory

To be able to effectively talk with a peripheral, we need to have a way to read and write within its registers and, to do that, we have two ways: by using **I/O ports** or by using **I/O memory**. The former mechanism is not covered in this book because it is not used so much in modern platforms (apart form x86 and x86_64 ones), while the latter just uses normal memory areas to map each peripheral register and is the one that is commonly used in modern CPUs. In fact, I/O memory mapping is really common in **System-on-Chip** (**SoC**) systems, where the CPU can talk to its internal peripherals just by reading and writing into well-known physical addresses; in this scenario, each peripheral has its own reserved address and each one is connected to a register.

To see a simple example of what I'm talking about, you can get the SAMA5D3 CPU's datasheet from `http://ww1.microchip.com/downloads/en/DeviceDoc/Atmel-11121-32-bit-Cortex-A5-Microcontroller-SAMA5D3_Datasheet_B.pdf`; look up page 30, where a complete memory mapping of the whole CPU is reported.

This I/O memory mapping is then reported in the device tree files related to a platform. Just as an example, if we take a look at the definition of the UART controller of our ESPRESSObin's CPU in the `linux/arch/arm64/boot/dts/marvell/armada-37xx.dtsi` file of the kernel sources, we can see the following settings:

```
soc {
    compatible = "simple-bus";
    #address-cells = <2>;
    #size-cells = <2>;
    ranges;

    internal-regs@d0000000 {
        #address-cells = <1>;
        #size-cells = <1>;
        compatible = "simple-bus";
        /* 32M internal register @ 0xd000_0000 */
        ranges = <0x0 0x0 0xd0000000 0x2000000>;

...

        uart0: serial@12000 {
            compatible = "marvell,armada-3700-uart";
            reg = <0x12000 0x200>;
            clocks = <&xtalclk>;
            interrupts =
            <GIC_SPI 11 IRQ_TYPE_LEVEL_HIGH>,
            <GIC_SPI 12 IRQ_TYPE_LEVEL_HIGH>,
            <GIC_SPI 13 IRQ_TYPE_LEVEL_HIGH>;
            interrupt-names = "uart-sum", "uart-tx", "uart-rx";
            status = "disabled";
        };
```

As explained in `Chapter 4`, *Using the Device Tree,* we can deduce that the UART0 controller is mapped at a physical address `0xd0012000`. This is also confirmed by the following kernel message we can see at boot:

```
d0012000.serial: ttyMV0 at MMIO 0xd0012000 (irq = 0, base_baud =
1562500) is a mvebu-uart
```

OK, now we have to keep in mind that `0xd0012000` is the **physical address** of the UART controller, but our CPU knows **virtual addresses** because it uses its MMU to get access to RAM! So, how can we do the translation between the physical address `0xd0012000` and its virtual counterpart? The answer is: by memory remapping. This operation must be done in the kernel before every read or write operation on the UART controller's registers, otherwise, a segmentation fault will be raised.

Just to have an idea about the difference between physical and virtual addresses and about how the remap operation behaves, we can have a look at the utility program named `devmem2`, which is downloadable within the ESPRESSObin via the `wget` program from `http://free-electrons.com/pub/mirror/devmem2.c`:

```
# wget http://free-electrons.com/pub/mirror/devmem2.c
```

If we take a look at the code, we see the following operations:

```
if((fd = open("/dev/mem", O_RDWR | O_SYNC)) == -1) FATAL;
printf("/dev/mem opened.\n");
fflush(stdout);
/* Map one page */
map_base = mmap(0, MAP_SIZE,
                PROT_READ | PROT_WRITE,
                MAP_SHARED, fd, target & ~MAP_MASK);
if(map_base == (void *) -1) FATAL;
printf("Memory mapped at address %p.\n", map_base);
fflush(stdout);
```

So the `devmem2` program just opens the `/dev/mem` device and then it calls the `mmap()` system call. This operation will cause the execution of the `mmap_mem()` method in the `linux/ drivers/char/mem.c` file , in kernel sources, where the `/dev/mem` char device is implemented:

```
static int mmap_mem(struct file *file, struct vm_area_struct *vma)
{
    size_t size = vma->vm_end - vma->vm_start;
    phys_addr_t offset = (phys_addr_t)vma->vm_pgoff << PAGE_SHIFT;

    ...

    /* Remap-pfn-range will mark the range VM_IO */
    if (remap_pfn_range(vma,
                    vma->vm_start, vma->vm_pgoff,
                    size,
                    vma->vm_page_prot)) {
        return -EAGAIN;
    }
```

```
    return 0;
}
```

 Further information regarding these memory-remap operations and usage of the `remap_pfn_range()` functions and similar functions will be more clear in `Chapter 7`, *Advanced Char Driver Operations*.

Well, the `mmap_mem()` method conducts the memory remapping operation of the physical address `0xd0012000` into a virtual one suitable to be used by the CPU to access the UART controller's registers.

If we try to compile the code with the following command on the ESPRESSObin, we get an executable suitable access from the user space to the UART controller's registers:

```
# make CFLAGS="-Wall -O" devmem2
cc -Wall -O devmem2.c -o devmem2
```

You can safely ignore possible warning messages shown below:

```
devmem2.c:104:33: warning: format '%X' expects argument
of type 'unsigned int',
but argument 2 has type 'off_t {aka long int}' [-
Wformat=]
printf("Value at address 0x%X (%p): 0x%X\n", target,
virt_addr, read_result
);
devmem2.c:104:44: warning: format '%X' expects argument
of type 'unsigned int',
but argument 4 has type 'long unsigned int' [-Wformat=]
printf("Value at address 0x%X (%p): 0x%X\n", target,
virt_addr, read_result
);
devmem2.c:123:22: warning: format '%X' expects argument
of type 'unsigned int',
but argument 2 has type 'long unsigned int' [-Wformat=]
printf("Written 0x%X; readback 0x%X\n", writeval,
read_result);
devmem2.c:123:37: warning: format '%X' expects argument
of type 'unsigned int',
but argument 3 has type 'long unsigned int' [-Wformat=]
printf("Written 0x%X; readback 0x%X\n", writeval,
read_result);
```

Then, if we execute the program, we should get the following output:

```
# ./devmem2 0xd0012000
/dev/mem opened.
Memory mapped at address 0xffffbd41d000.
Value at address 0xD0012000 (0xffffbd41d000): 0xD
```

As we can see, the devmem2 programs prints the remapping result as expected and the actual read is done using the virtual address, which, in turn, the MMU translates into the desired physical one at 0xd0012000.

OK, now that it's clear that a memory remap is needed to access the peripheral's registers, we may suppose that once we have a virtual address physically mapped to a register, we can simply reference it to actually read or write data. Well this is wrong! In fact, despite the strong similarity between hardware registers mapped in memory and the usual RAM memory, when we get access to I/O registers, we must be careful to avoid being tricked by the CPU or compiler optimizations that can modify the expected I/O behavior.

The main difference between I/O registers and RAM is that I/O operations have side effects, while memory operations do not; in fact, when we write a value into RAM, we expect it to be unchanged by someone else, but for I/O memory, this is not true due to the fact that our peripheral may change some data in registers, even if we wrote a specific value into them. This is a really important fact to keep in mind, because, to attain good performance, RAM content can be cached and read/write instructions can be reordered by the CPU instruction pipeline; moreover, the compiler can autonomously decide to put data values in CPU registers without writing them to memory, and even if it finally stores them to memory, both write and read operations can operate on cache memory without ever reaching physical RAM. Even if it finally stores them to memory, both optimizations are not acceptable on I/O memory. In fact, these optimizations are transparent and benign when applied to conventional memory, but they can be fatal on I/O operations because a peripheral has a well-defined way of being programmed, and read and write operations on its registers can't be reordered or cached without causing malfunctions.

These are the main reasons we can't simply reference a virtual memory address to read and write data from a memory mapped peripheral. And a driver must, therefore, ensure that no caching is performed and no read or write reordering takes place when accessing registers; the solution is to use special functions that actually do read and write operations. In the linux/include/asm-generic/io.h header file, we can find these functions, as in the following example:

```
static inline void writeb(u8 value, volatile void __iomem *addr)
{
    __io_bw();
    __raw_writeb(value, addr);
```

```
        __io_aw();
}

static inline void writew(u16 value, volatile void __iomem *addr)
{
        __io_bw();
        __raw_writew(cpu_to_le16(value), addr);
        __io_aw();
}

static inline void writel(u32 value, volatile void __iomem *addr)
{
        __io_bw();
        __raw_writel(__cpu_to_le32(value), addr);
        __io_aw();
}

#ifdef CONFIG_64BIT
static inline void writeq(u64 value, volatile void __iomem *addr)
{
        __io_bw();
        __raw_writeq(__cpu_to_le64(value), addr);
        __io_aw();
}
#endif /* CONFIG_64BIT */
```

The preceding functions are to write data only; you are encouraged to take a look at the header file to see definitions of reading functions, such as `readb()`, `readw()`, `readl()`, and `readq()`.

Each function is defined to be used with a well-defined data type according to the size of the register to be operated on; also, each of them uses memory barriers to instruct the CPU to execute read and write operations in a well-defined order.

I'm not going to explain what memory barriers are in this book; if you're curious, you can always read more about it in the kernel documentation directory in the `linux/Documentation/memory-barriers.txt` file

As a simple example of the preceding functions, we can take a look at the `sunxi_wdt_start()` function within the `linux/drivers/watchdog/sunxi_wdt.c` file of Linux sources:

```
static int sunxi_wdt_start(struct watchdog_device *wdt_dev)
{
```

```
...
    void __iomem *wdt_base = sunxi_wdt->wdt_base;
    const struct sunxi_wdt_reg *regs = sunxi_wdt->wdt_regs;

...

    /* Set system reset function */
    reg = readl(wdt_base + regs->wdt_cfg);
    reg &= ~(regs->wdt_reset_mask);
    reg |= regs->wdt_reset_val;
    writel(reg, wdt_base + regs->wdt_cfg);

    /* Enable watchdog */
    reg = readl(wdt_base + regs->wdt_mode);
    reg |= WDT_MODE_EN;
    writel(reg, wdt_base + regs->wdt_mode);

    return 0;
}
```

Once the register's base address, `wdt_base`, and the register's mapping `regs` have been obtained, we can simply perform our read and write operations by using `readl()` and `writel()`, as shown in the preceding section, and we can rest assured that they will be executed properly.

Spending time in the kernel

In `Chapter 5`, *Managing Interrupts and Concurrency*, we saw how we can defer action at a later time; however, it may happen that we still have to wait some time between two operations on a peripheral, as follows:

```
writeb(0x12, ctrl_reg);
wait_us(100);
writeb(0x00, ctrl_reg);
```

That is, if we have to write a value into a register, then wait for 100 microseconds, then write another value, these operations can be done by simply using functions defined in the `linux/include/linux/delay.h` header file (and other ones) instead of using techniques presented before (kernel timers and workqueues, and so on):

```
void ndelay(unsigned long nsecs);
void udelay(unsigned long usecs);
void mdelay(unsigned long msecs);

void usleep_range(unsigned long min, unsigned long max);
```

```
void msleep(unsigned int msecs);
unsigned long msleep_interruptible(unsigned int msecs);
void ssleep(unsigned int seconds);
```

All these functions are just used to delay for a specific amount of time expressed in nano, micro, or milliseconds (or just in seconds, as for `ssleep()`).

The first functions set (that is, the `*delay()` functions) can be used everywhere in both interrupt or process context, while the second set of functions must be used in the process context only due to the fact they may implicitly go to sleep.

Moreover, we see that, for instance, the `usleep_range()` function takes minimal and maximal sleep time to reduce power usage by allowing high-resolution timers to take advantage of an already scheduled interrupt, rather than scheduling a new one just for this sleep. The following is the function description in the `linux/kernel/time/timer.c` file:

```
/**
 * usleep_range - Sleep for an approximate time
 * @min: Minimum time in usecs to sleep
 * @max: Maximum time in usecs to sleep
 *
 * In non-atomic context where the exact wakeup time is flexible, use
 * usleep_range() instead of udelay(). The sleep improves responsiveness
 * by avoiding the CPU-hogging busy-wait of udelay(), and the range reduces
 * power usage by allowing hrtimers to take advantage of an already-
 * scheduled interrupt instead of scheduling a new one just for this sleep.
 */
void __sched usleep_range(unsigned long min, unsigned long max);
```

Also, in the same file we see that the `msleep_interruptible()` is a variant of `msleep()`, which can be interrupted by a signal (in *Waiting for an event* recipe, in Chapter 5, *Managing Interrupts and Concurrency*, we talked about this possibility) and the return value is simply the time in milliseconds not slept due to the interruption:

```
/**
 * msleep_interruptible - sleep waiting for signals
 * @msecs: Time in milliseconds to sleep for
 */
unsigned long msleep_interruptible(unsigned int msecs);
```

Finally, we should also notice the following:

- `*delay()` functions use the jiffy estimation of clock speed (`loops_per_jiffy` value) and will busy wait for enough loop cycles to achieve the desired delay.
- `*delay()` functions may return early in case of too low computed `loops_per_jiffy` (due to the time taken to execute the timer interrupt), or cache behavior affecting the time it takes to execute the loop function, or due to CPU clock rate changes.
- `udelay()` is the generally preferred API, and `ndelay()`'s level precision may not actually exist on many non-PC devices.
- `mdelay()` is a macro wrapper around `udelay()`, to account for possible overflow when passing large arguments to `udelay()`. That's why the usage of `mdelay()` is discouraged and the code should be refactored to allow for the use of `msleep()`.

Additional Information: Advanced Char Driver Operations

Technical requirements

When we have to manage a peripheral, it's quite common to need to modify its internal configuration settings, or it may be useful to map it from the user space as if it was a memory buffer in which we can modify internal data just by referencing a pointer.

For example, frame buffers or frame grabbers are good candidates to be mapped as a big chunk of memory from the user space point of view.

In this case, having the support of the `lseek()`, `ioctl()`, and `mmap()` system calls is fundamental. If, from the user space, the usage of these system calls is not tricky, within the kernel they require some attention by the driver developer, especially the `mmap()` system call, which involves the kernel **Memory Management Unit** (**MMU**).

Not only that one of the principal tasks a driver developer must pay attention to is the data exchanging mechanism with the user space; in fact, realizing a good implementation of this mechanism may simplify a lot of the peripheral's management. Using read and write memory buffers, for example, may increase the system performance when one or more processes get access to the peripheral, giving to the userspace developer a good range of setup and management mechanisms to allow them to get the maximum from our hardware.

Going up and down within a file with lseek()

Here we should remember that the prototypes of the `read()` and `write()` system calls were the following:

```
ssize_t (*read) (struct file *filp,
                 char __user *buf, size_t len, loff_t *ppos);
ssize_t (*write) (struct file *filp,
                  const char __user *buff, size_t len, loff_t *ppos);
```

When we tested our char driver using the program in the `chapter_03/chrdev_test.c` file, we noticed that we weren't able to reread written data unless we patched our file as follows:

```
--- a/chapter_03/chrdev_test.c
+++ b/chapter_03/chrdev_test.c
@@ -55,6 +55,16 @@ int main(int argc, char *argv[])
        dump("data written are: ", buf, n);
    }

+   close(fd);
+
+   ret = open(argv[1], O_RDWR);
+   if (ret < 0) {
+       perror("open");
+       exit(EXIT_FAILURE);
+   }
+   printf("file %s reopened\n", argv[1]);
+   fd = ret;
+
    for (c = 0; c < sizeof(buf); c += n) {
        ret = read(fd, buf, sizeof(buf));
        if (ret == 0) {
```

That was without closing and then reopening the file connected with our driver (in this manner, the kernel automatically resets the value pointed by `ppos` to 0).

However, this is not the only way to modify the value pointed by `ppos`; in fact, we can also use the `lseek()` system call to do it. The prototype of the system call, as reported by its man page (`man 2 lseek`), is as follows:

```
off_t lseek(int fd, off_t offset, int whence);
```

Here, the `whence` parameter can assume the following values (represented by definitions in the following code):

```
SEEK_SET
    The file offset is set to offset bytes.

SEEK_CUR
    The file offset is set to its current location plus offset
    bytes.

SEEK_END
    The file offset is set to the size of the file plus offset
    bytes.
```

So, for instance, if we wish to move `ppos` to point to the beginning of our device's data buffer as we did in `Chapter 3`, *Working with Char Drivers*, but without closing and the reopening the device file, we can do so as follows:

```
--- a/chapter_03/chrdev_test.c
+++ b/chapter_03/chrdev_test.c
@@ -55,6 +55,13 @@ int main(int argc, char *argv[])
        dump("data written are: ", buf + c, n);
    }

+   ret = lseek(fd, SEEK_SET, 0);
+   if (ret < 0) {
+       perror("lseek");
+       exit(EXIT_FAILURE);
+   }
+   printf("*ppos moved to 0\n");
+
    for (c = 0; c < sizeof(buf); c += n) {
        ret = read(fd, buf, sizeof(buf));
        if (ret == 0) {
```

 Note that all these modifications are stored in `modify_lseek_to_chrdev_test.patch` file from GitHub repository and they can be applied by using the next command within the `chapter_03` directory, where the file `chrdev_test.c` is located:
`$ patch -p2 < ../../chapter_07/modify_lseek_to_chrdev_test.patch`

If we take a look at the `linux/include/uapi/linux/fs.h` header file, we can see how these definitions are declared:

```
#define SEEK_SET    0 /* seek relative to beginning of file */
#define SEEK_CUR    1 /* seek relative to current file position */
#define SEEK_END    2 /* seek relative to end of file */
```

The `lseek()` implementation is so trivial that in the `linux/fs/read_write.c` file we can find a default implementation of this method named `default_llseek()`. Its prototype is reported as follows:

```
loff_t default_llseek(struct file *file,
                      loff_t offset, int whence);
```

This is because if we don't specify our own implementation, then the kernel will automatically use the one in the preceding code block. However, if we take a quick look at the `default_llseek( )` function, we notice that it's not suitable for our device because it's too *file-oriented* (that is, it works well when the file against which the `lseek()` operates on is a real file and not a peripheral), so we can instead use one of the two next alternative implementations for `lseek()` to perform no operations, by using the `noop_llseek()` function:

```
/**
 * noop_llseek - No Operation Performed llseek implementation
 * @file: file structure to seek on
 * @offset: file offset to seek to
 * @whence: type of seek
 *
 * This is an implementation of ->llseek useable for the rare special case
when
 * userspace expects the seek to succeed but the (device) file is actually
not
 * able to perform the seek. In this case you use noop_llseek() instead of
 * falling back to the default implementation of ->llseek.
 */
loff_t noop_llseek(struct file *file, loff_t offset, int whence)
{
    return file->f_pos;
}
```

Or we can just return an error, and then signal the user space that our device is not suitable to be sought by using the `no_llseek()` function:

```
loff_t no_llseek(struct file *file, loff_t offset, int whence)
{
    return -ESPIPE;
}
```

 The two preceding functions are located in the `linux/fs/read_write.c` file of the kernel sources.

The different usage of these two functions is well described by the comment above regarding `noop_llseek()`; while `default_llseek()` is not usually suitable for a char device, we can simply use `no_llseek()` or, in those rare special cases when the user space expects the seek to succeed, but the (device) file is actually unable to perform the seek, we can use `no_llseek()` as follows:

```
static const struct file_operations chrdev_fops = {
    .owner   = THIS_MODULE,
    .llseek  = no_llseek,
    .read    = chrdev_read,
    .write   = chrdev_write,
    .open    = chrdev_open,
    .release = chrdev_release
};
```

 This piece of code is referred to by the chrdev character driver as discussed in `Chapter 4`, *Using the Device Tree*, within the `chapter_04/chrdev/chrdev.c` file on GitHub.

Using ioctl() for custom commands

In `Chapter 3`, *Working with Char Drivers*, we discussed the file abstraction and mentioned that a char driver is very similar to a usual file, from the user space point of view. However, it's not a file at all; it is used as a file but it belongs to a peripheral, and, usually, peripherals need to be configured to work correctly, due to the fact they may support different methods of operation.

Let's consider, for instance, a serial port; it looks like a file where we can (forever) read or write using both the `read()` and `write()` system calls, but to do so, in most cases, we must also set some communication parameters such as the baud rate, parity bit, and so on. Of course, these parameters can't be set with `read()` or `write()`, nor by using the `open()` system call (even if it can set some accessing modes as read or write only), so the kernel offers us a dedicated system call that we can use to set such serial communication parameters. This system call is the `ioctl()`.

From the userspace point of view, it looks like its man page (available by using the `man 2 ioctl` command):

```
SYNOPSIS
    #include <sys/ioctl.h>

    int ioctl(int fd, unsigned long request, ...);

DESCRIPTION
    The ioctl() system call manipulates the underlying device parameters of
    special files. In particular, many operating characteristics of character
    special files (e.g., terminals) may be controlled with ioctl() requests.
```

As stated in the preceding paragraph, the `ioctl()` system call manipulates the underlying device parameters of special files (as with our char devices, but not only this in fact, it can be used on net or block devices too) by taking, as the first argument, the file descriptor (obtained by opening our device), and as the second argument, a device-dependent request code. Finally, as the third and optional argument, an untyped pointer to memory that userspace programmers can use to exchange data with the driver.

So, thanks to this general definition, a driver developer can implement their custom commands to manage the underlying device. Even if not strictly required, an `ioctl()` command has encoded in it whether the argument is an in parameter or out parameter, and the size of the third argument in bytes. Macros and definitions used to specify an `ioctl()` request are located in the `linux/include/uapi/asm-generic/ioctl.h` file, as reported in the following:

```
/*
 * Used to create numbers.
 *
 * NOTE: _IOW means userland is writing and kernel is reading. _IOR
 * means userland is reading and kernel is writing.
 */
#define _IO(type,nr)            _IOC(_IOC_NONE,(type),(nr),0)
#define _IOR(type,nr,size)
_IOC(_IOC_READ,(type),(nr),(_IOC_TYPECHECK(size)))
#define _IOW(type,nr,size)
```

```
_IOC(_IOC_WRITE,(type),(nr),(_IOC_TYPECHECK(size)))
#define _IOWR(type,nr,size)
_IOC(_IOC_READ|_IOC_WRITE,(type),(nr),(_IOC_TYPECHECK(size)))
```

As we can also read in the preceding comment, the `read()` and `write()` operations are from the user space point of view, so when we mark a command as *writing* we mean that the userspace is writing and the kernel is reading, while when we mark a command as *reading* we mean exactly the inverse.

As a really simple example about how to use these macros, we can take a look at an implementation regarding watchdogs within the file `linux/include/uapi/linux/watchdog.h`:

```
#include <linux/ioctl.h>
#include <linux/types.h>

#define WATCHDOG_IOCTL_BASE 'W'

struct watchdog_info {
    __u32 options;          /* Options the card/driver supports */
    __u32 firmware_version; /* Firmware version of the card */
    __u8 identity[32];      /* Identity of the board */
};

#define WDIOC_GETSUPPORT    _IOR(WATCHDOG_IOCTL_BASE, 0, struct
watchdog_info)
#define WDIOC_GETSTATUS     _IOR(WATCHDOG_IOCTL_BASE, 1, int)
#define WDIOC_GETBOOTSTATUS _IOR(WATCHDOG_IOCTL_BASE, 2, int)
#define WDIOC_GETTEMP       _IOR(WATCHDOG_IOCTL_BASE, 3, int)
#define WDIOC_SETOPTIONS    _IOR(WATCHDOG_IOCTL_BASE, 4, int)
#define WDIOC_KEEPALIVE     _IOR(WATCHDOG_IOCTL_BASE, 5, int)
#define WDIOC_SETTIMEOUT    _IOWR(WATCHDOG_IOCTL_BASE, 6, int)
#define WDIOC_GETTIMEOUT    _IOR(WATCHDOG_IOCTL_BASE, 7, int)
#define WDIOC_SETPRETIMEOUT _IOWR(WATCHDOG_IOCTL_BASE, 8, int)
#define WDIOC_GETPRETIMEOUT _IOR(WATCHDOG_IOCTL_BASE, 9, int)
#define WDIOC_GETTIMELEFT   _IOR(WATCHDOG_IOCTL_BASE, 10, int)
```

A watchdog (or watchdog timer) is usually used in automated systems. It is an electronic timer that is used to detect and recover from computer malfunctions. In fact, during its normal operation, a process in the system should regularly reset the watchdog timer to prevent it from timing out so, if due to a hardware fault or program error, the system fails to reset the watchdog, the timer will elapse, and the system automatically restarts.

Here we have the definition of some commands to manage watchdog peripherals, each of them defined using the `_IOR()` macro (used to specify a reading command) or the `_IOWR` macro (used to specify a read/write command). Each command has a progressive number followed by the type of data pointed to by the third argument, which can be a simple type (as with the preceding `int` type) or a more complex one (as with the preceding `struct watchdog_info`). Finally, the `WATCHDOG_IOCTL_BASE` common parameter is simply used to add a random value to avoid command duplication.

 Usage of the `type` parameter (`WATCHDOG_IOCTL_BASE` in the preceding example) in these macros will be more clear later when we're going to explain our example.

Of course this is a pure convention, we can simply use progressive integer numbers to define our `ioctl()` commands and it will work perfectly anyway; however, by acting this way, we will embed into the command code a lot of useful information.

Once all commands are defined, we need to add our custom `ioctl()` implementation, and by taking a look at the `struct file_operations` in the `linux/include/linux/fs.h`, file we see that there exist two of them:

```
struct file_operations {
...
    long (*unlocked_ioctl) (struct file *, unsigned int, unsigned long);
    long (*compat_ioctl) (struct file *, unsigned int, unsigned long);
```

In kernels older than 2.6.36, there was only one `ioctl()` method that acquired the **Big Kernel Lock (BKL)**, so nothing else could execute at the same time. This led to very bad performance on a multiprocessor machine, so there was a big effort to get rid of it, which is why `unlocked_ioctl()` was introduced. By using it, each driver developer can choose which lock to use instead.

On the other side, `compat_ioctl()`, even though it was added at the same time, is actually unrelated to `unlocked_ioctl()`. Its purpose is to allow 32-bit userspace programs to make `ioctl()` calls on a 64-bit kernel.

Finally, we should first note that the commands and structure definitions must be used in both user and kernel spaces, so when we define the exchanged data types, we must use those data types available to both spaces (that's why the `__u32` type has been used instead of `u32`, which actually only lives inside the kernel).

Moreover, when we wish to use custom `ioctl()` commands, we must define them into a separate header file, which must be shared with the user space; in this manner, we can keep kernel codes separate from the userspace. However, just in case it was difficult to separate all userspace codes from the kernel space, we can use the `__KERNEL__`definition as in the following snippet to instruct the preprocessor to exclude some code according to the space we are compiling into:

```
#ifdef __KERNEL__
  /* This is code for kernel space */
  ...
#else
  /* This is code for user space */
  ...
#endif
```

That's why, usually, header files holding `ioctl()` commands are usually located under the `linux/include/uapi` directory, which holds all header files needed by userspace programs for compilation.

Accessing I/O memory with mmap()

In the *Getting access to I/O memory* recipe in `Chapter 6`, *Miscellaneous Kernel Internals*, we saw how the MMU works and how we can get access to a memory-mapped peripheral. Within the kernel space, we must instruct the MMU in order to correctly translate a virtual address into a proper one, which must point to a well-defined physical address to which our peripheral belongs, otherwise, we can't control it!

On the other hand, in that section, we also used a userspace tool named `devmem2`, which can be used to get access to a physical address from the user space, using the `mmap()` system call. This system call is really interesting, because it allows us to do a lot of useful things, so let's start by taking a look at its man page (`man 2 mmap`):

```
NAME
    mmap, munmap - map or unmap files or devices into memory

SYNOPSIS
    #include <sys/mman.h>

    void *mmap(void *addr, size_t length, int prot, int flags,
                int fd, off_t offset);
    int munmap(void *addr, size_t length);
```

```
DESCRIPTION
    mmap() creates a new mapping in the virtual address space of the call-
    ing process. The starting address for the new mapping is specified in
    addr. The length argument specifies the length of the mapping (which
    must be greater than 0).
```

As we can see from the preceding snippet, by using `mmap()` we can create a new mapping in the virtual address space of the calling process, which can be related to the file descriptor, `fd`, passed as a parameter.

Usually, this system call is used to map a normal file within the system memory in such a way that it can be then addressed using a normal pointer and not by the usual `read()` and `write()` system calls.

Just as a simple example, let's consider a usual file as follows:

```
$ cat textfile.txt
This is a test file

This is line 3.

End of the file
```

This is a normal text file holding three lines of text. We can read and write it on our Terminal just using the `cat` command as stated previously; of course, we now know that the `cat` command runs an `open()` and then one or more `read()` operation on the file, followed by one or more `write()` operation on the standard output (which, in turn, is a file abstraction connected to our terminal). However, this file can also be read as it was a memory buffer of chars, using the `mmap()` system call, and this can be done through the following steps:

```
ret = open(argv[1], O_RDWR);
if (ret < 0) {
    perror("open");
    exit(EXIT_FAILURE);
}
printf("file %s opened\n", argv[1]);
fd = ret;

/* Try to remap file into memory */
addr = mmap(NULL, len, PROT_READ | PROT_WRITE,
            MAP_FILE | MAP_SHARED, fd, 0);
if (addr == MAP_FAILED) {
    perror("mmap");
    exit(EXIT_FAILURE);
}
```

```
ptr = (char *) addr;
for (i = 0; i < len; i++)
    printf("%c", ptr[i]);
```

 A complete code implementation of the preceding example will be presented in the following snippet. This is a snippet of the chrdev_mmap.c file.

So, as we can see, we first opened the file as usual, but then, instead of using the read() system call, we did a mmap() and, finally, we used the returned memory address as a char pointer to print out the memory buffer. Note that after the mmap() we'll have something like an image of the file within the memory.

If we try to execute the preceding code on the textfile.txt file, we get what we expected:

```
# ls -l textfile.txt
-rw-r--r-- 1 root root 54 May 11 16:41 textfile.txt
# ./chrdev_mmap textfile.txt 54
file textfile.txt opened
got address=0xffff8357b000 and len=54
---
This is a test file

This is line 3.

End of the file
```

 Note that I used the ls command to get the file length needed by the chrdev_mmap program.

Now we should ask ourselves whether there is a way to map a character device (which looks very similar to a file from the user space point of view) as we did for the text file above; obviously, the answer is yes! We have to use the mmap() method defined in struct file_operations as follows:

```
struct file_operations {
...
        int (*mmap) (struct file *, struct vm_area_struct *);
```

Besides the usual `struct file` pointer that we already perfectly know, this function requires the `vma` argument (which is a pointer to `struct vm_area_struct`) used to indicate a virtual address space, in which the memory should be mapped by the driver.

A struct `vm_area_struct` holds information about a contiguous virtual memory area, which is characterized by a start address, a stop address, length, and permissions.

Each process owns more virtual memory areas, which can be inspected by looking at the relative procfs file named `/proc/<PID>/maps` (where `<PID>` is the PID number of the process).

The virtual memory areas are a really complex part of Linux memory manager, which is not covered in this book. Curious readers can take a look at `https://www.kernel.org/doc/html/latest/admin-guide/mm/index.html` for further information.

The mapping of a physical address to the user address space, as indicated by the `vma` parameter, can be easily done using helper functions such as `remap_pfn_range()`, defined in the header file `linux/include/linux/mm.h` as follows:

```
int remap_pfn_range(structure vm_area_struct *vma,
                    unsigned long addr,
                    unsigned long pfn, unsigned long size,
                    pgprot_t prot);
```

It will map a contiguous physical address space addressed by `pfn` into the virtual space represented by the `vma` pointer. In particular, the parameters are:

- `vma` - The virtual memory space in which mapping is made
- `addr` - The virtual address space from where remapping begins
- `pfn` - The physical address (expressed in terms of page frame number) to which the virtual address should be mapped
- `size` - The size in bytes of the memory to be mapped
- `prot` - Protection flags for this mapping

So, a really simple `mmap()` implementation, considering a peripheral as having a memory area at physical address `base_addr` and size of `area_len`, can be done as follows:

```
static int my_mmap(struct file *filp, struct vm_area_struct *vma)
{
    struct my_device *my_ptr = filp->private_data;
    size_t size = vma->vm_end - vma->vm_start;
    phys_addr_t offset = (phys_addr_t) vma->vm_pgoff << PAGE_SHIFT;
```

```
    unsigned long pfn;

    /* Does it even fit in phys_addr_t? */
    if (offset >> PAGE_SHIFT != vma->vm_pgoff)
        return -EINVAL;

    /* We cannot mmap too big areas */
    if ((offset > my_ptr->area_len) ||
        (size > my_ptr->area_len - offset))
        return -EINVAL;

    /* Remap-pfn-range will mark the range VM_IO */
    if (remap_pfn_range(vma, vma->vm_start,
                        my_ptr->base_addr, size,
                        vma->vm_page_prot))
        return -EAGAIN;

    return 0;
}
```

As a final note, we have to keep in mind that remap_pfn_range() works with a physical address, while memory allocated using kmalloc() or vmalloc() functions and friends (see Chapter 6, *Miscellaneous Kernel Internals*) must be managed using a different approach. For kmalloc(), we can use something like the following to get the pfn parameter:

```
    unsigned long pfn = virt_to_phys(kvirt) >> PAGE_SHIFT;
```

Where kvirt is the kernel virtual address to be remapped returned by kmalloc(), for vmalloc() we can do as follows:

```
    unsigned long pfn = vmalloc_to_pfn(vvirt);
```

Here, vvirt is the kernel's virtual address to be remapped returned by vmalloc().

Note that the memory allocated with vmalloc() is not physically contiguous, so if we want to map a range allocated with it we have to map each page individually and compute the physical address for each page. This is a more complicated action, which is not explained in this book due to the fact that it's not device-driver related (real peripherals only use physical addresses).

Locking with the process context

It's good to understand how to avoid race conditions in case more than one process tries to get access to our driver, or how to put to sleep a reading process (we talk about reading here, but the same thing also holds true for writing) in case our driver has no data to supply. The former case will be presented here, while the latter will be presented in the next section.

If we take a look at how read() and write() system calls have been implemented in our chrdev driver, we can easily notice that, if more than one process tries to do a read() call or even if one process attempts a read() call and another tries a write() call, a race condition will occur. This is because the ESPRESSObin's CPU is a multiprocessor composed of two cores and so it can effectively execute two processes at the same time.

However, even if our system had just one core, it still may happen that read() or write() code inside these methods' critical sections is executed in an interleaved (that is non-atomic) manner due to the fact that, for instance, functions copy_to_user() and copy_from_user() may put to sleep the calling process and so the scheduler may revoke the CPU to one of them in favor of another process, which, in turn, calls again into the same driver's read() or write() methods.

To avoid possible race conditions in these situations, a really reliable solution is using a mutex as presented in Chapter 5, *Managing Interrupts and Concurrency*.

We simply need a mutex for each chrdev device to protect multiple access to the driver's methods.

Waiting for I/O operations with poll() and select()

In a complex system such as a modern computer, it's quite common to have several useful peripherals to acquire information about the external environment and/or the system's status. Sometimes, we may use different processes to manage them but we may need to manage more than one peripheral at a time, but with just a single process.

In this scenario, we can imagine doing several `read()` system calls on each peripheral to acquire its data, but what happens if one peripheral is quite slow and it takes a lot of time to return its data? If we do the following, we may slow down all data acquisition (or even lock it if one peripheral doesn't receive new data):

```
fd1 = open("/dev/device1", ...);
fd2 = open("/dev/device2", ...);
fd3 = open("/dev/device3", ...);

while (1) {
    read(fd1, buf1, size1);
    read(fd2, buf2, size2);
    read(fd3, buf3, size3);

    /* Now use data from peripherals */
    ...
}
```

In fact, if one peripheral is slow, or if it takes a long time to return its data, our loop will be stopped to wait for it and our program may not work correctly.

One possible solution may be to use the `O_NONBLOCK` flag on the offending peripheral, or even on all peripherals, but doing this we may overload the CPU with unnecessary system calls. It could be more elegant (and efficient) to ask the kernel to tell us which file descriptor belongs to peripheral holding data ready to be read (or free to be used for a write).

To do so, we can use the `poll()` or `select()` system calls. The `poll()` man page states the following:

```
NAME
    poll, ppoll - wait for some event on a file descriptor

SYNOPSIS
    #include <poll.h>

    int poll(struct pollfd *fds, nfds_t nfds, int timeout);

    #define _GNU_SOURCE /* See feature_test_macros(7) */
    #include <signal.h>
    #include <poll.h>

    int ppoll(struct pollfd *fds, nfds_t nfds,
            const struct timespec *tmo_p, const sigset_t *sigmask);
```

The `select()` man page, on the other hand, is as follows:

```
NAME
   select, pselect, FD_CLR, FD_ISSET, FD_SET, FD_ZERO - synchronous I/O
   multiplexing

SYNOPSIS
   /* According to POSIX.1-2001, POSIX.1-2008 */
   #include <sys/select.h>

   /* According to earlier standards */
   #include <sys/time.h>
   #include <sys/types.h>
   #include <unistd.h>

   int select(int nfds, fd_set *readfds, fd_set *writefds,
              fd_set *exceptfds, struct timeval *timeout);

   void FD_CLR(int fd, fd_set *set);
   int FD_ISSET(int fd, fd_set *set);
   void FD_SET(int fd, fd_set *set);
   void FD_ZERO(fd_set *set);
```

Even if they look quite different, they do almost the same things; in fact, inside the kernel, they are implemented by using the same `poll()` method, which is defined inside the well-known `struct file_operations` as follows (see the `linux/include/linux/fs.h` file):

```
struct file_operations {
...
    __poll_t (*poll) (struct file *, struct poll_table_struct *);
```

From the kernel's point of view, the implementation of the `poll()` method is really simple; we just need the waitqueue we used above and then we have to verify whether our device has some data to return. Simply speaking, a generic `poll()` method is like the following:

```
static __poll_t simple_poll(struct file *filp, poll_table *wait)
{
    struct simple_device *chrdev = filp->private_data;
    __poll_t mask = 0;

    poll_wait(filp, &simple_device->queue, wait);

    if (has_data_to_read(simple_device))
        mask |= EPOLLIN | EPOLLRDNORM;

    if (has_space_to_write(simple_device))
        mask |= EPOLLOUT | EPOLLWRNORM;
```

```
    return mask;
}
```

We simply have to use the `poll_wait()` function to tell the kernel which waitqueue the driver uses to put reading or writing processes to sleep, and then we return the variable `mask` equal to 0; if no data is ready to be read or we cannot accept new data to write, we return the `EPOLLIN | EPOLLRDNORM` value if there is something to read bitwise and if we're willing to accept that data, too.

 All of the available `poll()` events are defined in the header file `linux/include/uapi/linux/eventpoll.h`.

Once the `poll()` method has been implemented, we can use it, for instance, with `select()` as shown in the following:

```
fd_set read_fds;

fd1 = open("/dev/device1", ...);
fd2 = open("/dev/device2", ...);
fd3 = open("/dev/device3", ...);

while (1) {
    FD_ZERO(&read_fds);
    FD_SET(fd1, &read_fds);
    FD_SET(fd2, &read_fds);
    FD_SET(fd2, &read_fds);

    select(FD_SETSIZE, &read_fds, NULL, NULL, NULL);

    if (FD_ISSET(fd1, &read_fds))
        read(fd1, buf1, size1);
    if (FD_ISSET(fd2, &read_fds))
        read(fd2, buf2, size2);
    if (FD_ISSET(fd3, &read_fds))
        read(fd3, buf3, size3);

    /* Now use data from peripherals */
    ...
}
```

After opening all of the needed file descriptors, we have to use the FD_ZERO() macro to clean the read_fds variable and then we use the FD_SET() macro to add each file descriptor to the set of the reading process represented by read_fds. When done we can pass read_fds to select() to point out to the kernel which file descriptors are to be observed.

> Note that, usually, we should pass, as the first parameter of the select() system call, the highest number plus 1 of the file descriptors within the observed set; however, we can also pass the FD_SETSIZE value, which is the maximum allowed value permitted by the system. This can be a very large value, so programming this way leads to inefficiency in scanning the whole file descriptor bitmap; good programmers should use the maximum value plus 1 instead.
> Note, also, that our example is valid for reading, but exactly the same can be used for writing!

Managing asynchronous notifications with fasync()

In the previous section, we considered the special case in which we can have a process that must manage more than one peripheral. In this situation, we can ask the kernel, which is the ready file descriptor, where to get data from or where to write data to using the poll() or select() system call. However, this is not the only solution. Another possibility is to use the fasync() method.

By using this method, we can ask the kernel to send a signal (usually SIGIO) whenever a new event has occurred on a file descriptor; the event, of course, is a ready-to-read or read-to-write event and the file descriptor is the one connected with our peripheral.

The fasync() method does not have a userspace counterpart due to the already presented methods in this book; there is no fasync() system call at all. We can use it indirectly by utilizing the fcntl() system call. If we take a look at its man pages, we see the following:

```
NAME
    fcntl - manipulate file descriptor

SYNOPSIS
    #include <unistd.h>
    #include <fcntl.h>

    int fcntl(int fd, int cmd, ... /* arg */ );
```

```
...

    F_SETOWN (int)
            Set the process ID or process group ID that will receive SIGIO
            and SIGURG signals for events on the file descriptor fd. The
            target process or process group ID is specified in arg. A
            process ID is specified as a positive value; a process group ID
            is specified as a negative value. Most commonly, the calling
            process specifies itself as the owner (that is, arg is specified
            as getpid(2)).
```

Now, let's do one step at a time. From the kernel point of view, we have to implement the `fasync()` method, which is defined, as usual, within `struct file_operations` as below (see the `linux/include/linux/fs.h` file):

```
struct file_operations {
...
    int (*fsync) (struct file *, loff_t, loff_t, int datasync);
```

Its implementation is really trivial because by using the `fasync_helper()` helper function, the only steps we need are reported for a generic driver in the following:

```
static int simple_fasync(int fd, struct file *filp, int on)
{
    struct simple_device *simple = filp->private_data;

    return fasync_helper(fd, filp, on, &simple->fasync_queue);
}
```

Where `fasync_queue` is a pointer of a `struct fasync_struct` that the kernel uses to enqueue all processes interested in receiving the `SIGIO` signal whenever the driver is ready for reading or writing operations. These events are notified using the `kill_fasync()` function, usually within an interrupt handler or whenever we know that new data has arrived or we are ready to write:

```
kill_fasync(&simple->fasync_queue, SIGIO, POLL_IN);
```

Note that we have to use `POLL_IN` when data is available to read, while we should use `POLL_OUT` when our peripheral is ready to accept new data.

 Please see the `linux/include/uapi/asm-generic/siginfo.h` file for all available `POLL_*` definitions.

From the userspace point of view, we need to take some steps to achieve the SIGIO signal:

1. First, we have to install a proper signal handler.
2. Then we have to call fcntl() with the F_SETOWN command to set the process ID (usually called a PID) that will receive the SIGIO related to our device (addressed by the file descriptor fd).
3. Then we have to alter the flags describing the file access mode by setting the FASYNC bit.

A possible implementation is as follows:

```
long flags;

fd = open("/dev/device", ...);

signal(SIGIO, sigio_handler);

fcntl(fd, F_SETOWN, getpid());

flags = fcntl(fd, F_GETFL);

fcntl(fd, F_SETFL, flags | FASYNC);
```

Other Books You May Enjoy

If you enjoyed this book, you may be interested in these other books by Packt:

Mastering Embedded Linux Programming - Third Edition
Chris Simmonds

ISBN: 978-1-78953-038-4

- Evaluate the board support packages offered by most manufacturers of a system.
- Explore Buildroot and the Yocto project to create embedded Linux systems.
- Update IoT devices in the field without compromising security
- Install Buildroot and use it to build images for the QEMU and BeagleBone Black targets
- Learn to install Yocto Project and build basic images for QEMU and BeagleBone Black.
- Reduce the power budget of devices to make batteries last longer
- Interact with the hardware without having to write kernel device drivers

Embedded Linux Development Using Yocto Project Cookbook - Second Edition
Alex González

ISBN: 978-1-78839-921-0

- Optimize your Yocto Project setup to speed up development and debug build issues
- Use Docker containers to build Yocto Project-based systems
- Take advantage of the user-friendly Toaster web interface to the Yocto Project build system
- Build and debug the Linux kernel and its device trees
- Customize your root filesystem with already-supported and new Yocto packages
- Optimize your production systems by reducing the size of both the Linux kernel and root filesystems
- Explore the mechanisms to increase the root filesystem security
- Understand the open source licensing requirements and how to comply with them when cohabiting with proprietary programs
- Create recipes, and build and run applications in C, C++, Python, Node.js, and Java

Leave a review - let other readers know what you think

Please share your thoughts on this book with others by leaving a review on the site that you bought it from. If you purchased the book from Amazon, please leave us an honest review on this book's Amazon page. This is vital so that other potential readers can see and use your unbiased opinion to make purchasing decisions, we can understand what our customers think about our products, and our authors can see your feedback on the title that they have worked with Packt to create. It will only take a few minutes of your time, but is valuable to other potential customers, our authors, and Packt. Thank you!

Index

example 146, 147, 149
reference 153
testing 152
time
   managing, with kernel timers 154, 156, 158, 159

U

U-Boot
   reference 37
udev rules
   reference 115
uevents 115
Universal Asynchronous Receiver/Transmitter (UART) 203

V

v7, EXPRESSObin
   reference 15

W

waiting queues 163
waitqueues
   reference 172
   testing 171, 172
   used, to wait for event 164, 166
   working with 168, 169
workqueues
   example 149, 150, 151
   reference 153
   testing 153